T4-AJW-645

WITHDRAWN

BENTHAMITE REVIEWING

The First Twelve Years of
The Westminster Review

1824-1836

BENTHAMITE REVIEWING

The First Twelve Years of
The Westminster Review

1824-1836

BY
GEORGE L. Lyman NESBITT

AMS Press, Inc.
New York
1966

PREFACE

John Morley suggests in his *Reminiscences* that the center "for the best observation of fresh flowing currents of thought, interest, and debate" in the nineteenth century is to be found in the reviews. In this suggestion there may be some degree of overstatement. Yet unquestionably an understanding of the work of the journalists of that period, who both reflected and influenced the thought of their time, is necessary for a correct interpretation of the society for which they wrote. Accordingly I have chosen in this study to examine the propaganda of one particularly earnest group of reformers, the followers of Jeremy Bentham.

The Westminster Review, which continued under various auspices from 1824 to 1914, was for its first twelve years the official organ of this radical party. During those years, the reviewers described in its pages the social and political organization of a Benthamite Utopia, and endeavored to define the place of literature, education, and religion in that ideal state. Since these writers were largely interested in founding a civilization adapted to and directed by the middle class, which was gradually to become dominant in English life following the Reform Bill of 1832, their opinions are of particular importance as part of the complex background of the Victorian era.

I have endeavored to summarize the content of the review during its strictly Benthamite period, limiting myself principally to those first twelve years because during that time alone it was the official literary organ of a definite party with clear objectives. Wherever possible, I have used the reviewers' own words. The *Westminister* being an adventure in journalism as well as an organ of opinion, I have tried to make clear its place in the realm of early nineteenth-century periodicals and to trace its history as one of the three great reviews of the period.

Two men who died before the completion of my work contributed more than any others to its development. The study was planned with the generous and kindly assistance of the late Ashley

H. Thorndike, who read in manuscript all but the last chapter, and for whose wise suggestions I am deeply grateful. In London, the late Graham Wallas aided me not only in my search for materials, but also in my understanding of the aims and purposes of the Benthamite party. I am also particularly indebted to Professor Emery Neff, of Columbia University, who along with Professor Thorndike assisted in the development of the work throughout, and who made many helpful suggestions concerning its style and content.

To many other members of the Columbia University faculty, especially Dr. C. W. Everett and Professors Jefferson B. Fletcher, H. N. Fairchild, and W. W. Lawrence, and to Dean Frank H. Ristine of Hamilton College, I wish to express my thanks for valuable advice, particularly on matters of style. I am indebted also to Professor Berrian R. Shute of Hamilton College, with whose assistance I arrived at my interpretation of the *Westminster's* articles on music, and to Mr. T. Rowland Hughes, of Colleg Harlech, Wales, who generously supplied me with helpful information.

I am glad also to acknowledge the courtesy of the officials and staff of the British Museum, of the Bodleian Library, of Dr. Williams' Library, London, and of the libraries of Columbia University, Cornell University, Hamilton College, and University College, London.

G. L. N.

HAMILTON COLLEGE
March 30, 1934

CONTENTS

BENTHAMITE REVIEWING

*The First Twelve Years of
the Westminster Review*

1824-1836

I

AN AGE OF JOURNALISM

We should not have condescended to notice this strange farrago of *diablerie*, dullness, and absurdity, had we not been informed that its unfortunate author, whom we would recommend as a fit object of commiseration to the patrons of St. Luke's, was admired by some people as a respectable playwright.

Thus a parodist of 1811, writing in a would-be humorous monthly called *The Scourge*, begins his review of "Macbeth, a tragedy, by William Shakespeare." The review carries the subtitle, "A critique after the most approved models."

Meanly as we think, however, of the taste of the present age [continues the anonymous parodist], we cannot persuade ourselves that this performance can be seen or read with complacency by any persons but a few lunatics as distorted in their intellects as Mr. Shakespeare himself, or by one or two of those bottle companions who were whilome his associates in the noble profession of deer-stealing, and now besiege him in the character of parasites. Had this been a first production, indeed, there might have been some hopes of his improvement. . .

It is excellent parody, quite typical of the tone and method of the best reviewing of its time. The author declares the whole play absurd nonsense, and exhibits his samples, plucked by main force from their context. He is particularly concerned about the witches, because they seem to consider it a remarkable discovery that three times three "make up nine." He also dislikes the "ghost of a dagger" which appears to Macbeth, its handle toward his hand. Throughout there is an undercurrent of suggestion that this Mr. Shakespeare is a low fellow, anyhow.

He is a low fellow. He has bottle companions and a deer-stealing record. He probably has revolutionary tendencies. Perhaps he is as low as Leigh Hunt, whose *Rimini*, the *Quarterly Review* pointed out, was partly composed during its author's term in jail.

Perhaps he is as low as the Lake poets, whom the *Edinburgh Review* accused in its first number of "a splenetic and idle discontent for the existing institutions of society." Such persons could not hope to write good poetry; no wonder *Rimini* and *Thalaba* were bad. And how could a play by the deer-stealing Mr. Shakespeare be anything but "this strange farrago of *diablerie,* dullness and absurdity"?

The story of the genesis and development of this characteristic early nineteenth-century reviewing is well known. The *Edinburgh Review,* oldest of the English quarterlies, was founded in 1802. At the time of its birth there was no critical journal worth reading, though the *Monthly* and the *Critical* still survived; and it occurred to certain literary men of Edinburgh that something should be done. So the review was established, under the editorship of Francis Jeffrey, a barrister then in his thirtieth year. It was not intended originally as a party organ, but, since Jeffrey and most of his contributors were Whigs, it naturally became Whiggish. Consequently Walter Scott, a contributor to the early issues of the review and a thoroughly good Tory, withdrew, and, with the Tory leaders in London, sponsored the *Quarterly,* established in 1809 with William Gifford as editor. This review was frankly intended as a party organ, and succeeded admirably in living up to intentions.

To a reader of our own book notices, an article from the early nineteenth-century reviews appears a strange thing. It was usually at least fifteen pages in length. It always made some allusion to the book supposedly being reviewed, but generally did not confine itself to the book; the reviewer expressed, in detail, his own opinions on the subject of which the book treated. Macaulay's famous essay on Milton is a book review, published in the *Edinburgh,* but no one would suspect it of being such. Carlyle reviewed Lockhart's *Life of Burns,* and we think of the article as Carlyle on Burns, not as Carlyle on Lockhart. Thus an issue of the *Edinburgh* or the *Quarterly,* though ostensibly devoted exclusively to book reviews, affords more variety of content than one might expect.

Moreover, all reviews were unsigned. The principle of anonymous reviewing was religiously adhered to by both the reviews.

It is generally agreed that in unsigned articles the reviewers often ventured utterances which they might have hesitated to include if the work had been signed. Furthermore, an article was supposed to represent not the opinion of an individual reviewer, but the infallible judgment of the *Edinburgh* or the *Quarterly*. This assumption of infallibility added much to the vigor and incisiveness of the articles. Apparently it awed the reading public. There must have been, as Copleston pointed out, "a mysterious authority in the plural *we*, which no single name, whatever may be its reputation, can acquire"; and his contention that anonymous reviews were received "as the judgments of a tribunal who decide only on mature deliberation, and who protect the interests of literature with unceasing vigilance"[1] must be at least partly true. For both reviews prospered exceedingly. At six shillings a number, in a country where the mere ability to read was none too general, and where shillings were by no means plentiful in every pocket, the *Edinburgh* in 1814 circulated thirteen thousand a number,[2] and the *Quarterly* in 1816 sold only four thousand less.

So it came about that a review carried with it a prestige that nothing calling itself a magazine or a newspaper could hope to equal, and exercised tremendous power over public opinion. Never before had English periodicals possessed such authority. With its huge circulation, a review could ruin the sale of a volume of poetry, or insure its success. For the review-buying public of the early 1800's was also the book-buying public, the aristocracy and the well-to-do of the middle class.

The reviews were probably more important as organs of political opinion than as judges of literature. Fully half of a typical number of the *Edinburgh* or the *Quarterly* of about 1810 consists of articles on affairs of the day. Such a number also contains reviews of books of travel, of sermons, of mathematical treatises. Perhaps not more than one or two articles are concerned with strictly literary productions, and even these articles are more likely than not to be colored by the politics of the review.

This state of affairs, fatal as it was to the potential development of careful and unbiased book reviewing, resulted inevitably from the spirit of the times. Politics was the subject of greatest interest and importance to the reading public. "The condition-of-England question" has at all times been uppermost in the minds of Englishmen; and at this time a more than usual degree of fear and uncertainty characterized the thinking of all lovers of law and order, the readers of reviews. Memories of the French Revolution were painfully vivid, and it was well known that the revolutionists had had many English sympathizers. It was well known, too, that the nation was by no means unanimously in favor of participating in the Napoleonic Wars in the first place, and did not enjoy paying for them in the second place. High taxes, both direct and indirect, affected aristocratic landowner and starved factory laborer, and everyone between these two extremes. High taxes are never conducive to political peace and quiet: everyone was dissatisfied. These matters could have been adjusted in the old England, but now things were different, and different in an unprecedented way. Factories were springing up, hundreds of them, supplanting the stable rural population of a century ago with an urban population of employers and employees. The employers and employees included many agitators, who thought that the landed aristocracy had things too much their own way. The journalists could not be depended upon—Leigh Hunt, for one, evidently did not have his price. Too many people in England were clamoring for reform—the House of Commons should be elected not by a mere handful under safe aristocratic control, but by all the people; the House of Lords served no useful purpose; the Established Church had too many privileges; the Corn Laws, tariffs on grain, ought to be repealed so that the price of bread would be lower. People were starving, the agitators maintained.

This agitation was not pleasant for the agricultural aristocracy, or for anyone who was really prospering under the existing system. The noble Whigs and Tories did not want the tariffs on grain reduced, because that would lower the price of what they had to sell. The House of Lords was part of the constitutional government of England, and had existed for centuries. It, with the Established Church, stood for order, for the continuance of what had proved pleasant and profitable. Most alarming of all was the demand for the extension of the franchise. Give all these people the vote, and who could tell how it would end? England might follow France. One hardly blames respectable and substantial citizens for being afraid.

One hardly blames the erstwhile radical Wordsworth, even, for his advocacy of the organization of a huge citizen militia.

If the whole island was covered with a force of this kind [he wrote to Lord Lonsdale in 1814], the Press properly curbed, the Poor Laws gradually reformed, provision made for new churches to keep pace with the population . . . order may yet be preserved among us, and the people remain free and happy.³

This proposal is typical of the Tory approach. They proposed meeting the situation by thoroughly safeguarding the old institutions. There must be no concessions to the popular demands; once inroads on the Matchless Constitution had begun, there would be no stopping them. The Whigs, on the other hand, wanted to save the country by a program of moderate reform—some education for the lower classes, a few concessions to dissenters from the Established Church, a few reforms in the methods of electing members to the House of Commons. They also wanted to be in office, though they were out most of the time. It is not surprising, then, considering the gravity of the situation, that Whigs and Tories should be violently opposed not only to radicals but to each other as well; that they should view with alarm anyone outside their party who could use a pen, and bear down upon him with a violence that today appears incredible. *Edinburgh* reviewers venomously accused radical poets of revolutionary tendencies and Tory poets of loose thinking; while the *Quarterly* accused all liberals of revolutionary tendencies and loose thinking—and bad morals, always on the assumption that if one's morals were bad, so were his writings. The *Edinburgh* sometimes accused its opponents of bad morals, but not so often as the *Quarterly*.

The continued opposition of the *Edinburgh* to the work of the Lake school, particularly to that of Southey and Wordsworth, is well known. This opposition is partly accounted for by the fact that Jeffrey was an honest admirer of the classicism of Pope, and, though he favored moderate reform in politics, could not tolerate any reform, however moderate, in literature. Besides, no one would have called Wordsworth's literary theories moderate.

But it must also be remembered that the Lake poets suffered politically on two counts—what they had been, and what they became. Southey as Pantisocratic idealist was little more in favor with the Whigs than Southey as Tory laureate. Reviewing *Thalaba* in the first number of the *Edinburgh*, October, 1802, Jeffrey points out that the Lake school productions are based on "the anti-social principles and distempered sensibility of Rousseau"—a statement to strike terror to the heart of any good Englishman. While the poetry of *Thalaba* is revolutionary and bad, Jeffrey maintains, the ideas are worse. He finds the whole school at this time guilty of

a splenetic and idle discontent for the existing institutions of society. . . . Instead of contemplating the wonders and pleasures which civilization has created for mankind, they are perpetually brooding over the disorders by which the progress has been attended.

For the existence of evil in the world, in their opinion, "the present vicious constitution of society alone is responsible."[4] This verdict, even more than the charge of unconventionality brought against the work itself, would do serious injury to the sale of the volume among conservative readers, concerned as they were about the Jacobin Menace.

Jeffrey found good in Southey, and said so. He made efforts to reform him. But Southey went from one enemy camp to another, and his *Carmen Triumphale* of 1814 offered occasion for giving him up entirely. He had become a Tory, and laureate, and written a worse poem than ever.

This marvellous falling off of Mr. Southey [was the *Edinburgh* comment], we are most willing to attribute to the benumbing influence of that chaplet of Bays, with which the favour of the Prince Regent has recently adorned his brows.[5]

From this time on the *Edinburgh* reviewers are sworn enemies of Southey as poet, thinker, and reviewer for the *Quarterly,* and their delight in his embarrassment at the publication in 1817 of the revolutionary *Wat Tyler,* written years earlier, manifested itself in twenty-three pages of jeering dissection.[6]

For similar reasons the Whig reviewers were equally unfriendly to Wordsworth. In 1807, Jeffrey declared that his literary enmity toward the poet sprang from "a sense of public duty";[7] whether the sense of duty directed the reviewers to warn the public against literary or political anarchy, or both, is not made clear. Even Lamb, for his connection with the Lakist revolutionaries, fell under the axe. He was charged with crudeness and indelicacy—a curious charge to be made against Lamb, hardly to be accounted for in any other way than by his association with the Lake school. It seems that in his play of *John Woodvil*, which the *Edinburgh* reviewed unfavorably,[8] he had written a line referring to "a rape on fortune." This the reviewer pointed out as a sample of the indelicacy to which he was objecting.

The strange history of the *Edinburgh's* reviewing of Tom Moore sheds further light on the extent of the disinterestedness and justice of the criticism of the time. The young Irish bard had come to seek his fortune in London, and had placed himself under the protecting wing of Lord Moira, who secured for him the favor of the Prince Regent. In 1800, Moore dedicated his translation of Anacreon to the Prince, with His Royal Highness's gracious consent, and was in high hopes of a good sinecure appointment almost immediately. Time passed, and with it the hopes. In *Corruption and Intolerance* (1809) and *The Sceptic* (1810), he began attacking the government, though he still held to his Tory connections. In 1813, however, he thoroughly confirmed his already incipient Whiggism by *Intercepted Letters, or the Twopenny Post Bag*, personal satire directed against the Prince. And soon he became a reviewer for the *Edinburgh*—the same journal which had treated him most unkindly in his old Tory days, under the editor with whom he had almost fought a duel.

The translation of Anacreon, under the pseudonym of Thomas Little, had received a rather unfavorable notice in the *Edinburgh*.[9] It was pointed out that Moore had translated the work in an unduly ornate fashion, and that the tone of the production accomplished nothing toward making better citizens of its readers. As well, perhaps, that Anacreon should remain untranslated. This article is mild, however, compared with the review of Thomas

Little's *Epistles, Odes, and Other Poems,* three years later. The reviewer, stating that he has "reasons to suppose that it was abetted by patrons," declares the book "a public nuisance" and its author "the most licentious of modern versifiers."[10] Moore, it is claimed, is attempting "to impose corruption upon his readers by concealing it under the mask of refinement"—all, it is assumed, at the instigation of those unnamed patrons who are well known to be Tories. For this review Moore challenged Jeffrey to a duel, and they met at Chalk Farm. The affair proved a fiasco, and supplied Byron with material for several couplets of *English Bards and Scotch Reviewers:*

> Can none remember that eventful day,
> That ever-glorious, almost fatal fray,
> When Little's leadless pistols met the eye,
> And Bow Street's myrmidons stood laughing by?

The myrmidons appeared suddenly from behind bushes and placed the would-be duelists under arrest. Ten years later, Moore was one of Jeffrey's best paid reviewers; he had transferred his political allegiance in the meantime. The Whig journal tactfully neglected to notice his books for a few years. In 1817, Jeffrey in a judicious review of *Lallah Rookh*[11] declared it "the finest orientalism we have had yet," and in 1826 we find the *Edinburgh* praising the *Life of Sheridan* for "dignified impartiality and practical wisdom, for which a poet and a satirist is so little apt to get credit."[12] The other reviews declared the book considerably biased in favor of the Whigs, though Lord Lansdowne, Whig leader, objected to it as being too conciliatory to the Tories. No one appears to have been particularly concerned about the real truth.

There is, then, clear evidence of political bias in the *Edinburgh's* reviewing of literature. The *Quarterly* became even more notorious for the same crime during its early years.* It excelled particularly in searching out and hunting down radicalism. Leigh Hunt, editor of the *Examiner* weekly newspaper, annoyed Gifford and his reviewers most; and everyone whom Hunt touched shared the Tory animosity. Shelley, a thoroughgoing revolutionary, and Keats,

---

* For a complete discussion see Graham: *Tory Criticism in the Quarterly Review.*

quite innocent of political agitation, were treated with equal harshness. *Quarterly* reviewers thought that they were low fellows, and said so. Shelley had been expelled from Oxford, and later had been guilty of domestic irregularities. Keats was a protegé of Hunt's, and Hunt in 1813 was imprisoned for libel on the Prince Regent, whom he accused of being a fat Adonis. In Newgate he continued to edit the *Examiner* while being fed and housed by the state, pointing out the corruption of the Regent and the ministry, though keeping discreetly silent about the Prince's personal shortcomings. By this ungracious behavior he aggravated the already bitter hostility of the government and the government's *Quarterly Review*, as he was to discover on the publication of his *The Story of Rimini* in 1816.[13] The *Edinburgh*, probably somewhat impressed with the relative merits of the protagonists, and probably more afraid that the Tories would remain in office than that the radicals would precipitate a revolution, followed up the *Quarterly's* violent attack by a favorable review.[14] The *Edinburgh* also defended Keats[15] against the *Quarterly*. Jeffrey in 1820 praised his work highly, warning him at the same time against over-luxuriance. Pointing out that his search for striking images and expressions had often led the poet astray, he declared, with evident intent to kill, "There is no work, accordingly, from which a malicious critic could cull more matter for ridicule."

This culling of individual lines and isolated passages for ridicule was only part of the machinery which the *Quarterly* brought into action against Hunt and his associates. Charges, sometimes justified, sometimes not, against the literary value of their work, always made up part of the review. But the government organ usually placed the greater emphasis upon the fact that these writers were not gentlemen, not "regulars" at all.

The opening and closing sentences of the review of Hunt's *Rimini* indicate clearly that the attack is primarily on Hunt rather than on the poem. "A considerable portion of this poem was written in Newgate," the reviewer begins. For this the *Quarterly* was taken to task in the *Edinburgh* some years later, in Hazlitt's article on the periodical press.[16] The review of *Rimini* closes with a reference to Hunt's dedicating the poem to Byron—

the clear work of the vulgar impatience of a low man, conscious and ashamed of his wretched vanity, and laboring, with coarse flippancy, to scramble over the bounds of birth and education, and fidget himself into the stout-heardedness of being familiar with a LORD.

So much for Hunt.

In this first onslaught of the *Quarterly,* the method to be employed throughout their reviewing of Hunt, Keats, and Shelley is already apparent. For Keats and Shelley, the charge of unintelligibility was added, that of a prison record omitted. Shelley, too, was dangerous. His Utopia, it was stated in the review of *Laon and Cyntha* and *The Revolt of Islam,*[17] required a civilization in which it would be man's business to "enjoy himself, to abstain from no gratification, to repent of no sin, hate no crime, but be wise, happy, and free, with plenty of 'lawless love'." In the same article the reviewer takes occasion to state that "his residence at Oxford was indeed a short one, and, if we mistake not, rather abruptly terminated." The conclusion of this review is very typical of the brand of literary criticism indulged in by the *Quarterly* during the campaign of radical-extermination.

He has indeed [mourns the reviewer] wounded us in the tenderest part. As far as in him lay, he has loosened the hold of our protecting laws, and sapped the principles of our venerable polity; he has invaded the purity and chilled the unsuspecting ardour of our fireside intimacies; he has slandered, blasphemed, and ridiculed our holy religion.

His poetry is growing steadily worse—"so it is and ever must be in the downward course of infidelity and immorality." Surely such disturbers of the established order could not be expected to write good poetry.

Here it seems pertinent to inquire if any favorable reviews were written during the first twenty years of the nineteenth century. The answer is a distinct affirmative. The *Quarterly* regularly praised the work of Tory men of letters, except Coleridge, whom no one defended with any consistency. Wordsworth and Southey, however, became *Quarterly* favorites. Gifford assigned the reviewing of *The Excursion* to Lamb, one of Wordsworth's best friends, after consultation with the author himself; and the review, which appeared in October, 1814, was highly laudatory. It became the practice for the *Quarterly* to congratulate Southey, its own star reviewer, on each successive work. The same periodical optimistically promised *The Fall of Jerusalem*, a poem by another of its contributors, Dean Milman of St. Paul's, "without extravagant encomium . . . whatever immortality the English language can bestow." The *Edinburgh's* defense of Hunt and Keats has already been noted. Both the reviews, the *Edinburgh* as well as the *Quarterly*, were always at least moderately kind to Scott, though the *Edinburgh* was not so kind as Scott wished. The *Quarterly* made a practice of attempting judiciousness, and regularly pointed out some few flaws in the Waverly Novels, never doubting, however, that they were all unquestionably works of genius. Scott's own *Quarterly* article on his *Tales of my Landlord*,[18] which the practice of anonymous reviewing enabled him to undertake, is not the least judicious criticism of the Great Unknown, nor is it the least laudatory.

Both reviews up to 1820 were likewise kind to Byron. He was a lord, and Murray was his publisher, so the *Quarterly*, likewise one of Murray's enterprises, could endure him; and he had somewhat liberal principles, so, except for his début with *Hours of Idleness*, he was also admired by the *Edinburgh*. The chief objection to *Hours of Idleness* had been that Byron in his preface had used his noble birth to bolster up the volume of poetry. This offense he did not repeat. He was less heterodox in his verse form than the other romantics. Furthermore, and perhaps most important of all, he was for a time so popular that a review attacking him would have injured itself instead. He did, however, finally become unpopular, and consorted too freely with Hunt and Shelley and the radical politician Hobhouse. For this he had to suffer. Instead of pleading with him to repent and be saved, as both reviews had frequently done in the past, they finally gave him up for lost, and rushed to the attack. In 1822, Milman reviewed him for the *Quarterly*[19]—Murray no longer being his publisher— as "the professed and systematic poet of seduction, adultery, and incest, the contemner of patriotism," and, of course, as the arch-atheist. Worse, however, to condone seduction and contemn patriotism than to be arch-atheist, says Dean Milman. He does, however, defend God at length against the implications of *Cain*, and put in a word or two, all that appears necessary, in defense of Mr. Southey against Byron's continual unpleasantness. Jeffrey in the *Edinburgh Review* launched a less bitter attack on Byron[20] somewhat earlier in the same year.

It should be noted, in passing, that both reviews were consistently courteous to ladies, and always found some word of praise for the works of "female genius."

No account of political partisanship in reviewing can omit some notice of the magazines, though they were generally less biased, as they were less powerful, than the reviews. Their inferior political importance is probably due largely to the fact that in the nineteenth century the great reviews were founded earlier than the great magazines; for the difference between a review and a magazine is not particularly marked. The leading magazines: *Blackwood's*, the *London*, and the *New Monthly*, were published monthly rather than quarterly, and were smaller than the reviews. They differed from the reviews in theory in that their articles did not all pretend to be book notices, and in practice in that they contained along with their heavier articles miscellaneous light essays and verse, and cost 2s. 6d. In general they were less ponderous and dignified, and so probably less impressive to their readers, than the reviews.

Blackwood's Edinburgh Magazine, commonly known as *Blackwood's*, was established by William Blackwood in 1817, and conducted after the early numbers by two youths of promise, J. G. Lockhart, afterwards editor of the *Quarterly*, and John Wilson, more famous as Christopher North. They were clever Tories, who decided that a dash of the sensational would be of service both to the party and to the Blackwood coffers. Besides, they found it extremely amusing. So they set about annihilating whatever was low and vulgar, principally Leigh Hunt and his circle, on whom they conferred the title of the Cockney School. "Back to the shop, Mr. John, back to the plasters, pills, and ointment boxes,"[21] they advised Keats. For he was one of this detestable London group of "uneducated and flimsy striplings" and had received favorable though judicious reviews in Hunt's *Examiner*. No more violent than the *Quarterly* on the same theme, *Blackwood's* showed much greater impudence—and much more humor.

As a matter of fact, their impudence outran their Toryism. During their first ten years they managed, at one time or another, to find something wrong with all their contemporaries, even Scott and Wordsworth. They were sometimes cruel even to Coleridge, though he was an occasional contributor to the magazine. *Blackwood's* was the most devastating and the most amusing periodical of its day.

The *London Magazine,* famous for Elia and the Opium Eater, was established in 1820. Most of its contributors being Londoners of the liberal group, its editor, John Scott, championed the Cockneys against the Blackwood onslaughts, and for that championship lost his life in 1821 in a duel with Lockhart's representative. Surprisingly enough, this was the only fatality occasioned by the brutal reviewing of the period. Outraged authors and outrageous editors frequently talked of duels, and a few meetings actually took place, but Scott was the only actual victim.

The *New Monthly,* under the editorship of Thomas Campbell, took its place in the 1820's with the liberal press, clamoring for popular education and electoral reform. Its prosperity in this decade was due in part to the decline of the *London* after the death of John Scott, for it was a journal in many respects similar to the *London,* and attracted many of that journal's luminaries as contributors. However, as we shall see, it gradually acquired a bad reputation among those who knew, and its influence suffered accordingly.

In 1824 these five—the *Edinburgh* and *Quarterly,* reviews; *Blackwood's,* the *New Monthly,* and the *London,* monthly magazines—were the most important periodicals. Though the *London* was steadily growing weaker, and the *Quarterly* just at that time was seeing bad days, this group of journals would appear to offer formidable competition to any new enterprise in magazine publishing. But this competition did not daunt publishers. New periodicals were constantly being born, some to live for two months, some for two years, some few to reach maturity. "By and by it will be found that all Literature has become one boundless self-

devouring Review," wrote Carlyle in 1831;[22] and his fears were
not unjustified. The French Institute's *Revue encyclopédique*
lists,[23] in 1826, twenty-seven weeklies, eighty-eight monthlies, and
twenty-six quarterlies for London alone, and this list is not complete. Titles for the decade 1818-28 number well over two hundred, ranging from the venerable and respectable *Gentleman's
Magazine*, one of the few survivors from the previous century,
to *The Terrific Register, or record of crimes, judgments, and
calamities.* There were periodicals appealing to all interests, to
all conceivable shades of opinion. For scurrilous ultra-liberals
there was *The Black Dwarf* or *The Theological Comet*, the latter
in its brief career quoting "Beauties of Tom Paine" and commenting on the private lives of Old Testament heroes. Perhaps a step
higher on the ladder leading to respectability were the publications
of William Hone and Richard Carlile. Cobbett's *Political Register*
and Leigh Hunt's *Examiner* were much more nearly respectable
than any of these. For scurrilous ultra-conservatives one would
recommend Theodore Hook's *John Bull*, or perhaps the short-lived
Gridiron, which announced that for its meat it would broil "Old
Cobbett" and the wicked Byron. Somewhat obscure but thoroughly respectable, Byron's "grandmother's review, the *British*" did
its small bit for the Tories, and the *Monthly Magazine*, with an
honorable history of liberalism behind it, did well by a small following of Whiggish non-partisans.

Periodicals under theological auspices flourished in abundance,
fifty-nine being included in the *Revue encyclopédique* list. Most
of these were monthlies. *The Methodist Magazine*, which sold
for sixpence, was said to have an enormous circulation, something over twenty thousand, and *The Baptist Magazine*, at the
same price, was not far behind. An intellectual would not read
either consistently. He might, however, like the Unitarian *Monthly
Repository*, edited by Robert Aspland and W. J. Fox, always very
alert, intelligent, and well written. The Unitarians had another
magazine, *The Christian Reformer*, also edited by Aspland, generally inferior to *The Monthly Repository*. Members of the Established Church could choose from a number of titles—*The
Eclectic Review* for conservative and intelligent orthodoxy; *The*

Christian Observer, Zachary Macaulay's at one time, for evangelical enthusiasm; *The Quarterly Theological Review* for dogmatic rant; *The Christian Remembrancer* for cheap sentimentalism. No phase of theological opinion went unrepresented. There were *The Christian Moderator, The Christian Monitor, The New Jerusalem Magazine, The Congregational Magazine,* and many others of miscellaneous sectarian affiliations, all short lived.*

There were magazines expressly for "the people." Such were *The Cottager's Monthly Visitor* (1821-56) and *The Mirror of Literature, Amusement, and Instruction.* The latter was a slender and diminutive weekly, selling at twopence. It lived from 1823 to 1846, and contained digests of books and of articles from contemporary magazines. It ran a synopsis of Scott's *Redgauntlet* in installments, and extracted Fletcher's account of Byron's last days from the *Westminster Review,* devoting an entire supplement to the noble lord's death and funeral. Each number was adorned with an engraving—the palace of the King of the Sandwich Islands—the Guillotine—Bethlehem, the birthplace of Christ. Its circulation appears to have been enormous; the preface to Volume Five (1825) states that "it has reached a circulation far surpassing every other periodical of the day," and refers to Brougham's statement, in his *Observation on the Education of the Lower Classes,* "that of some numbers of the Mirror eighty thousand copies have been sold."

A host of other tiny sheets, such as Jerdan's *Literary Gazette* and Alaric Watts's *Literary Souvenir,* catered to the desire for getting literature in tabloid form. There were a few magazines for children, most of them endeavoring primarily to inculcate good moral principles. There were magazines for music-lovers, for amateur botanists, for theater enthusiasts, for journeymen and artisans. The list of the *Revue encyclopédique* includes forty-nine periodicals devoted to natural science. John Silk Buckingham's *Calcutta Journal* and his *Oriental Herald* specialized in the affairs of India. The Owenites had a magazine, the *Coöperative,* which ran for three years. And it was during this decade that Christmas

---

* *Monthly Repository,* XV, 540ff, "Monthly Religious Magazines," contains many important notes.

was first gladdened by the annuals—*The Amulet, The Gem, Keep-sake, Friendship's Offering,* and *Forget-Me-Not.* These sold by the thousands at around twelve shillings to a guinea each.*

With this output of periodical literature, it is not surprising that there were many failures. Of the non-specialized magazines, most of which sold at 2*s.* 6*d.* or 3*s.*, only the *New Monthly* and *Black-wood's* really prospered for any considerable period of time. Not more than half the journals of the 1820's were in existence in 1830. The career of John Silk Buckingham, under whose owner-ship died *The Calcutta Journal, The Sphinx,* and *The Oriental Herald,* and who had to sell *The Athenaeum,* must be typical. The overwhelming success of the greater journals, the cheapness of steam printing, and the clearly increasing demand for reading matter led to the founding of many periodicals which could not hope to survive.

Thus the activity of the journalists was unprecedentedly great; but what of its value? A retrospect is disheartening. One does not suspect the annuals, the music magazines, or the tabloid literary journals of political bias. But we have seen the extent to which politics colored reviewing down to 1820, and this condition con-tinued to prevail, though more feebly, through the '20's. No sooner did it show signs of weakening than another source of cor-ruption made itself felt. Publishers began advertising in periodi-cals that carried book reviews. One notorious firm, Colburn and Bentley, actually owned three magazines, one of them the *New Monthly,* in which books published by the house were enthusiasti-cally praised. Not all publishing houses controlled magazines by ownership, but they all advertised more and more in them. We begin to hear of threatened withdrawal of advertising unless book notices become more favorable. Diaries and memoirs are replete with allusions to the scandalous practice of puffing.† Henry Brougham wrote of Macaulay's *Edinburgh Review* article on this practice[24] that "it is required by the follies of the puffing press,"[25]

---

* Ackerman, advertising his *Forget-Me-Not,* stated that his orders for the 1826 number totalled over ten thousand (*Westminster Review* ad-vertisements, July, 1826, p. 6).

† For a full account see Emery Neff, *Carlyle,* 127ff.

citing the Colburn firm as the most pernicious practitioners of the art, an art which man was destined not to lose.

It is uncertain to what extent the reading public was aware of the vitiating influence of political and commercial forces on reviewing, though both were attacked by the press itself. Macaulay's article to which we have alluded was only one of several to expose the evil practice of puffers. On the effect of political bias Sir Richard Phillips's *Monthly Magazine* in 1823 commented thus:

Honest country readers, who are little acquainted with the world of literature, are accustomed to take the character of a book which they have never seen from the opinion of the review which they chance to read. We, however, of the metropolis, are much better informed with regard to the manufacture of criticism. The several benches of our literary tribunals have each its set of judges that are nominated by a party; and should an author happen to write anything that is reckoned heterodox by one or other of these parties—that is, should he write anything at all worthy of mankind—he is sure to be condemned by one set, at least, of these impartial judges.[26]

The comment of Thomas Love Peacock, who had no personal grudges against reviewers, is equally bitter.

If periodical criticism were honestly and conscientiously conducted [he wrote in his *Essay on Fashionable Literature*], it might be a question how far it has been beneficial or injurious to literature; but being as it is merely a fundamental and exclusive tool of party, that it is highly detrimental to it none but a trading critic will deny. . . Personal or political bias being the only passport to critical notice, the independence and high thinking that keeps an individual aloof from all filthy subdivisions of faction makes every several gang his foe.[27]

Yet the fact remains that the reviews were purchased and presumably read. Perhaps most buyers did not know what unreliable criticism they were obtaining, and possibly many did not much care. They had to accept someone's opinion; why not follow a journal which shared their political beliefs? So by 1820 the review was an institution.

II

BENTHAMITE RADICALS

For the members of the rapidly growing public who did not sympathize with either of the great political parties, who never became one united third party, but who did agree in demanding governmental reform, appropriate periodicals were soon available. As time passed, the number of these radical publications increased rapidly, particularly during the second and third decades of the century. Hence political bias in reviewing was not confined to Whig and Tory journals.

The career of Leigh Hunt in radical journalism is well known. In 1808 he founded his weekly, *The Examiner,* in which he, and later his successor, Albany Fonblanque, continued to urge electoral reform and annual parliaments, to condemn the existing government, and to object to most measures sponsored by it. His two short-lived quarterlies, *The Reflector* (1810) and the distinguished *Liberal* (1822), have a similar discontented and carping tone politically. William Cobbett, proprietor of the *Political Register* (1802-38), was equally dissatisfied with things as they were, but he, unlike Hunt, would have preferred a benevolent and humanitarian Toryism. However, finding the Toryism of the day quite devoid of benevolence and humanitarianism, he proceeded to champion manhood suffrage in the hope that the people, once given the vote, would somehow restore the quiet agricultural society of olden times. His *Register,* the best written of the radical journals, had great vigor and sincerity, and represents in this early period the longing for the repeal of machinery that later appeared in the writings of Ruskin and William Morris.

Cobbett was much more sensational than Hunt. In 1810, he was jailed for his utterances, and in 1817, when a cheap edition of the *Register* was circulating forty to fifty thousand copies a week, he left England for two years, fearing the suspension of habeas corpus. In comparison with the howling revolutionaries who swarmed after Waterloo, however, he was distinctly mild. Richard Carlile, who, in his numerous short-lived publications, *The Moralist* (1823), *The Lion* (1825), and *The Prompter* (1830), and in his more successful *Republican* (founded 1819), attempted to save England on the principles of Tom Paine, indulged in what we today would regard as real radical journalism. "Liberty is the Property of Man. Only a Republic can protect it," was the slogan of the *Republican*. Carlile, who appears to have found it particularly amusing to write leading articles in the form of impudent letters to the Prince Regent, kept hammering away, with the help of his wife, even during his six years' imprisonment. William Hone, the parodist pamphleteer, was a radical of the same stamp, and he, too, was forever being prosecuted.

Another propaganda sheet, T. J. Wooler's *The Black. Dwarf* (1817-24), a weekly selling at fourpence, was devoted to the cause of reform in the electoral system and to the repeal of the Corn Laws. Its appearance was regularly heralded by flaming posters, and it utilized all the apparatus of the radical journalist, including scare headlines. Wade's *The Gorgon* (1818-19) was very similar to *The Black Dwarf*. Another similar weekly, called *The People,* published in 1817 by William Butler, like Cobbett's *Register* emphasized the miserable condition of the factory laborer. "Universal suffrage and Annual Parliaments, with the Abolition of the Borough System, are now the only adequate remedies to infuse new life into the Constitution," declared this pamphlet. *The People's* short-lived fight for reform was waged with many capitals and exclamation points, and it made abundant use of gruesome details. The editor, describing a destitute creature whom he met in a park, wrote:

It was a tall, middle-aged woman. She was not disgustingly squalid, but she was frightfully worn away to emaciation. Her bones almost pierced through. Wretchedness embodied fixed on her, and stared on every feature. Famine spoke in every look of hers. The day was cold, and she was naked; for though she wore and had on her a kind of cloak and petticoat, there was scarcely an inch of her shrivelled skin that was not open to the view and to the wind. She was bare-footed, bare-legged, bare-headed, and bare-necked. . .[1]

The combined circulation of radical sheets presenting this sort of material must have been very large.

We are to be concerned with something different in almost all respects from such propaganda. Far removed from the type of radical journalism represented in *The Black Dwarf*, *The People*, and others of that breed, was *The Westminster Review*, the official organ of the most important group of reformers, those who came to be known as Benthamites, Philosophic Radicals, or Utilitarians. They alone achieved the dignity of controlling a periodical boasting the authoritative name of review; and indeed, though it never made money, their *Westminster*, launched in 1824 during a decade of intense competition in the periodical field, soon became known as the third of the great reviews.

The Benthamites were as far removed personally as journalistically from Wooler, Carlile, Hone, or even Cobbett. None of them were poor, most of them were thoroughly respectable gentlemen. At their head was Jeremy Bentham, who had reached the age of seventy-six when his official journal came into being. He himself wrote little for it, leaving to his disciples, as he always had, the task of spreading his doctrine; but politically it was on his thinking that the review was based. A man of independent means, he had long ago devoted himself exclusively to the problem first of legal, then of general social reform. He had sought to approach the task systematically, to set a definite goal at the start, and to invent machinery for advancing society toward it. Back in his youth he had discovered that goal, the now famous slogan, "The Greatest Happiness of the Greatest Number"—the slogan in 1824 of the Philosophic Radicals and of the *Westminster Review*.

Intellectually a lineal descendant of eighteenth-century rationalism, he disregarded supernatural sanctions and supernatural rewards and punishments, and declared that the aim of law and all social organization should be to secure for people in this world the greatest possible amount of happiness, the smallest amount of pain. He believed that society would best secure this greatest happiness by allowing each individual to pursue his own interests. Far from promoting anarchy, this procedure would insure stability and order; a great deterrent to crime, for example, would be the pain incident to being generally condemned by one's fellow men. Benevolent conduct, on the other hand, would be stimulated by the love of praise and the pleasure derived from it. The proper working of such a plan depended largely upon the education of the people, especially of their "social instincts," but since all people were infinitely educable this was not an insuperable barrier.

In the history of thought, Bentham cannot be considered an innovator. He was much encouraged, as John Morley pointed out, by the work of Helvetius, with whom he had much in common: "interest the basis of justice, pleasure the true interpretation of interest, and character the creation of education and laws."[2] His psychology, his belief in the infinite educability of this human race, he derived from Locke and Hartley. There is some justification, then, for Carlyle's indictment of the Benthamite party as "the irremediable fag-end, so far in the rear of others as to fancy itself the van."[3] What makes Bentham a radical is that he actually set at work applying these near-commonplaces of eighteenth-century thought to conditions as they actually existed in the England of his day. In a nation where conduct was largely decided for the individual by an aristocracy making his laws and a church directing his motives, such application meant changes so startling and so fundamental that the appellation of radical did not appear inappropriate.

For years he worked on, alone and relatively obscure, scribbling off in his almost illegible hand scheme after scheme for the improvement of English law and society. Following his study of law, which he found himself conscientiously unable to practice, he first wrote a demonstration of the iniquity of Blackstone, completed in 1776. In numerous later works, most of them not published until long after they were written and until redacted by disciples such as Dumont, he continued to apply his pleasure-pain principle to details of law and legislation. He invented a model prison wherein convicts would be taught useful work. He also invented what he called a Chrestomathic School, a necessary adjunct to his plans for society, to be so organized that large numbers of boys might be educated at small expense. He worked out a "Table of the Springs of Action," a convenient chart listing possible pleasures and pains which might result from any action. He demanded electoral reform and attacked the Church and church organization, the laws hindering free speech, the laws against usury, and the use of the oath in legal proceedings. Seeing little good and much harm in the possession of colonies, he wrote a tract advocating their emancipation. If ever there was a professional thinker, it was Bentham; but he found time to enjoy music and to take regular exercise in his garden in Queen's Square Place, Westminster, which had been Milton's. He also made practical contributions to his own happiness by equipping his house with speaking tubes, central heating, and an ice box, which he called a frigidarium, for keeping his food cool and preserving it.

In 1808, he met James Mill, a born propagandist, though in no sense an undignified agitator like Hone or Carlile, who was to become his prophet. Mill, who had been earning a precarious living as a journalist, was for some years a virtual dependent of Bentham's, and it was only after the publication of his *History of British India* and his appointment in 1819 to a position in the India House, where he eventually was Chief Examiner, that he achieved independence. Francis Place, Charing Cross tailor, a man of genuine practical ability whose counsels directed radical action in Westminster, was associated with Bentham and Benthamism from 1812. In 1820, John Bowring, of whom more anon, came and sat at Bentham's feet. By 1824, there had grown up a school which derived its beliefs, as John Stuart Mill points out, from the sage's writings rather than his lips. James Mill, Bentham's oldest associate, was the visible head. He was loyally supported by several young men, little more than boys, who had formed themselves into a club which they called the Utilitarian Society. They had heard the term Utilitarian applied in a derogatory sense to the teachings of Bentham, and with characteristic youthful scorn for unenlightened opponents they decided that that was to be the name of their group. They would be a rationalist school, like the French *philosophes*, and make reason and the Utility of Bentham prevail. Sometimes they called themselves Philosophic Radicals. For their beliefs they did not go directly to Bentham, but to Mill, whose articles on government, education, liberty of the press, and prisons in the recently published supplement to the *Encyclopaedia Britannica* served as a very convenient handbook. They read omnivorously elsewhere, also, conscious as they were that they did not know quite everything, and met frequently at Bentham's house to discuss their findings.

The leader was their youngest, the slender, seventeen-year-old intellectual, John Stuart Mill, described by a turbulent visiting American, John Neal, as "a thorough-going radical with a girlish face and a womanly voice like that of John Randolph."[4] In his *Autobiograhy,* Mill gives an account of the founding of the group, stating that the idea was his as well as the name, that the Society started with three members and never reached ten. He lists as other members Eyton Tooke, son of the economist, William Ellis, George Graham, and J. A. Roebuck; and these were without doubt the most important. The idea of existing as a school lost its charm after about three years, but the Society was succeeded by another discussion group, of which John Mill was of course a prominent member, that met with George Grote, another young would-be *philosophe,* in the City, before business hours in the morning. The early hour and the miles of walking to reach the intellectual feast do not appear to have been even minor obstacles. Here was a group which admirably combined youthful seriousness with youthful ability.

Roebuck describes the first Utilitarian Society meeting he attended. He was fresh from Canada, having returned from the land to which his family had migrated to study law. With him he brought a letter of introduction to Thomas Love Peacock, an examiner under James Mill at the India House. "I think," said Peacock, "that I can introduce you to a young friend of mine in this house who belongs to a *disquisition* set of young men," and he took Roebuck around to John Stuart Mill. Roebuck joined what was so appropriately described as "the disquisition set" soon after.

My first visit to the Utilitarian Society [he writes], I shall never forget. It met in a low, half-furnished, desolate sort of room,—I believe the dining-room of the house, not Mr. Bentham's dining-room. The place was lighted by a few tallow candles. A desk was drawn across the end of the room, at which desk sat the chairman, and some half-dozen young men sat in chairs round the room and formed the society. The essay was a critique for some review of an edition of a Greek author. . .[5]

Thus the young Utilitarians settled the problems of the universe. The essay was probably intended for the *Westminster Review,* and it is not at all unlikely that most of the articles done for that journal by members of the Society were thus submitted to the entire group. The evident confidence and authority that characterize the papers which can be identified as written by these younger members of the *Westminster's* reviewing staff may be in part due to the assurance naturally supplied by this concerted thinking—the feeling that the writer represented not an individual but a school. Certainly the club, directing their boyish enthusiasm as it did toward unlimited speculation particularly on questions of politics and society, must have contributed much to the public usefulness for which its members were later distinguished. Perhaps the *Westminster Review* is more to be honored as the convenient vehicle of their apprentice efforts in thinking and writing than for its more obvious achievements. Nor was their contribution to the review inconsiderable. Ellis wrote four excellent articles and collaborated with the younger Mill on the fifth. Mill himself wrote thirteen articles. It is not possible to identify completely the work of the others, but they too contributed more or less frequently.

Another group of Benthamites who did reviewing for the *Westminster* were products of Cambridge, where a rationalist movement leading from Paley made students particularly susceptible to Bentham's doctrine. John and Charles Austin, both destined to be prominent in law, were the most important of these. Later came Charles Buller. All three were on friendly terms with the Mill group of Philosophic Radicals. Likewise there was a less reputable individual, but a no less confirmed Benthamite, Henry Southern, who had come down from Cambridge and in 1820 had begun editing the *Retrospective Review.* Between him and his brother-in-law, Charles Barker, also of Cambridge, we must divide the greater share of the glory and the shame of the literary reviewing in the *Westminster.* Cambridge also contributed the versatile T. Perronet Thompson, retired major, afterwards colonel, of dragoons, dabbler in mathematics, music, economics, and politics, as well as in journalism. He later became the owner of the review.

Other Benthamites contributed to the review more or less frequently. Peregrine Bingham the Younger, barrister of the Middle Temple, a somewhat talented individual who had attended Westminster School and Oxford, was one of these. At Westminster he wrote a prize poem, and he was later distinguished for his great interest in literature. How he came in contact with the Benthamites is hard to explain, except by the fact that intellectual London was a small place. At any rate he wrote much for their review, specializing in articles on Tom Moore. Albany Fonblanque was another important *Westminster* reviewer, somewhat outside the Benthamite inner circle. He was star contributor to Black's daily newspaper, the *Morning Chronicle,* which from 1820 showed decidedly liberal leanings, and in 1830 succeeded Leigh Hunt as proprietor of the *Examiner,* having done most of the work on it for some years. Thomas Love Peacock's connection with the review developed naturally enough from his position at that hotbed of Benthamite radicalism, the India House. Though he considered Utilitarianism ridiculous, he approved thoroughly of many of the Benthamite beliefs, and probably thought the Philosophic Radicals less ridiculous than either the Whigs or the Tories.

Another important contributor was Dr. Southwood Smith, famous as a humanitarian, whose articles on medicine are a distinctive feature of the review. He had begun life as a preacher, but later had become a doctor of medicine. A liberal, and, like Bowring and Southern, a Unitarian, his connection with the Benthamites was almost inevitable. Crabb Robinson, who contributed a few short articles at the solicitation of Southern, also probably formed the connection through Unitarianism, for he was by no means a Philosophic Radical. In the same way it came about that William Johnson Fox wrote the leading article for the first number.

Two friends of Shelley's besides Peacock, Walter Coulson and Thomas Jefferson Hogg, and Byron's executor, John Cam Hobhouse, were also among the *Westminster* contributors. Radicals of a respectable sort, as they all were, they naturally came in contact with members of the Benthamite group, and were all touched somewhat with Benthamite thinking, particularly Coulson, editor of the liberal newspaper, the *Globe-Traveller*. Probably through Bowring another liberal, Ugo Foscolo, contributed valuable articles on Italian literature.[6]

Some of the other contributors had even less connection with the Bentham coterie, securing editorial notice by submitting articles as aspiring magazine writers do now. Edwin Chadwick's first article, on life assurance, submitted in this way in 1828, marks the beginning of his association with the Benthamites. Their attention was also attracted by his article entitled "Preventive Police," which appeared not in the *Westminster* but in the short-lived *London Review* (1829), an enterprise of Whately, Blanco White, and Nassau Senior. From about 1827 until 1830, when he became literary secretary to Bentham, Chadwick, a student in the Inner Temple, appears to have earned his living as a free-lance writer, his articles appearing in the *Westminster*, the *London Review*, and the *Morning Herald*.

The authorship of many of the articles in the *Westminster* I have been unable to determine. Some were no doubt written by utterly obscure people. For instance, one John Kenrick, a tutor in languages and history in Manchester College, wrote the article on Niebuhr's *History of Rome*, according to his statement in a letter to Napier, editor of the *Edinburgh*, proposing that he become a writer for that journal.[7] J. A. St. John, assistant editor of the *Oriental Herald* and of the *Weekly Review*, who had started work as a reporter on a radical newspaper in Plymouth at the age of sixteen, wrote for the *Westminster*,[8] but what he wrote is unknown, probably immaterial.

The editor of the *Westminster Review* should have been James Mill. That had been the dream of the Benthamites when that group had consisted of only Mill and Bentham. But somehow the review was not founded while Mill was available, and he had done his work for the cause in occasional mild articles in the *Edinburgh Review* and in the essays in the supplement to the *Encyclopaedia Britannica*. In 1823, when Bentham decided to found the review, Mill as examiner at the India House did not wish to be officially connected with political agitation. Indeed, his situation would appear to have been precarious enough at best, Mill being known as a political opponent of both major parties. Hence he could not accept the editorship for which his position as virtual high priest to Bentham and source of light to the youth of the Utilitarian Society would have made him the logical choice. And unfortunately Mill did not like John Bowring, the man upon whom the mantle fell.

This antipathy alone should not count too heavily against Bowring, for Mill was an excellent hater of persons as well as of institutions—the sort of vigorous hater who attracts disciples and makes enemies. "When I know Mill well, shall I like him?" asked Coulson of Peacock on first meeting Mill, "—will he like what I like and hate what I hate?" "No," was the answer, "he will hate what you hate and hate everything you like."[9] Mill did not approve of the intimacy of his son John with Graham and Roebuck, because, says the highly sensitive Roebuck, they were of humble origin—for in spite of his democratic theories and his own humble origin he was temperamentally an aristocrat.

The charge of humble origin could have been made with equal truth against Bowring. He was a merchant of obscure birth; but he was by no means satisfied to remain an obscure merchant. Like the little but exceeding wise spider of the Proverbs, he took hold with his hands, and was in king's palaces. In 1818, at the age of twenty-six, he came up to London from Exeter, having already at least some smattering of languages, which he had presumably picked up from political refugees. His connections in foreign trade put him in touch with more of these impecunious idealists, with the result that he gradually became known as an accomplished linguist and a friend to the popular cause. In the 1820's and early '30's he brought out in rapid succession seven volumes of verse translations—his *Russian Anthology, Batavian Anthology, Ancient Poetry and Romances of Spain, Specimens of the Polish Poets, Servian Popular Poetry, Poetry of the Magyars,* and *Cheskian Anthology.* For the *Batavian Anthology* he owned to a collaborator, Harry Stoe Van Dyke. These volumes gave him a considerable popular reputation as a linguist, and the degree of LL.D. from Groningen in 1829.

This would appear to be a somewhat remarkable ten-years' achievement for an ordinary man, but it was nothing for Bowring. His foreign connections made him appear a logical member, along with Joseph Hume and John Cam Hobhouse, of the committee which coöperated with Byron in the dream that Greece might still be free; and we find Bowring leading Greek deputies about London, and dining, along with the deputies, with William Allen the Quaker. "It was a very interesting visit," Allen wrote, "and we conversed upon some important points. I must obtain for them the Scripture Lessons in modern Greek, and also send some seeds of useful vegetables. . . ."[10] Bowring was prominent in Unitarian circles, and in his spare time wrote hymns, the best known of which is *In the Cross of Christ I Glory*. He also contributed to most of the annuals—*The Amulet, Keepsake, Friendship's Offering*—religious verse of a quality suitable to the occasion.

Most important of all, he became, in 1820, what John Stuart Mill in the *Autobiography* terms "a sedulous frequenter of Mr. Bentham." This connection he could easily effect through his interest in foreign revolutionary movements. His personality apparently charmed the old man into forgetting the religious verse, and into counting him among the most enthusiastic and valuable of his followers. The two became very intimate, and Bentham was forever writing him notes, headed in his queer script, "J. B. to J. Bo." "For the last ten years of his life, I believe," writes Bowring, "not a thought, not a feeling of his was concealed from me."[11] Allowing for some exaggeration natural to one of Bowring's enthusiastic temperament, one still finds the statement indicative of their relations. Francis Place, who liked Bowring no better than did James Mill, wrote in his diary, regretting the ascendency of the young linguist,

Bowring also panders to him, is his toad eater, and can therefore command him, and as something of the sort is necessary to Mr. Bentham's comfort, to deprive him of Bowring without substituting someone would, if it could be done, make him unhappy.[12]

Apparently there was no convenient substitute.

Bowring's enemies hinted that, his business interests being in a bad way, he persuaded Bentham to found the review and make him editor. At least, Bentham did found the review, and Bowring as editor received, according to his own statement,[13] a good salary. Just how much he was paid he does not state; Jeffrey in 1815 received fifteen hundred pounds,[14] and in 1825 Murray offered Lockhart a thousand pounds for editing the *Quarterly,* with an interest in a paper which it was estimated would bring his total salary to twenty-five hundred pounds,[15] but Bowring may not have been so well paid. The job proved very fortunate for him, as a matter of fact, for his business ventures failed almost immediately.

An excellent characterization of Bowring in 1838 may be deduced from Caroline Fox's account of a call which he made at her home.[16] He came with Edhem Bey, Egyptian minister of instruction, the latter a phantom of delight "dressed in a large blue pelisse with loose sleeves, scarlet gaiters and slippers, a gold waistband a foot and a half wide. . . ." Dr. Bowring himself was "a very striking-looking personage with a most poetical, ardent, imaginative forehead, and a temperament all in keeping, as evidenced by his whole look and manner." During the call he contributed more autobiographic information than one would have believed possible in the time, as well as much about what Lady Georgina Wolff said to Sir Charles Lemon. He "gave an 'appercu' of his own radical views." He knew Shelley and Byron intimately, also Dickens and Cruikshank, also Mazzofanti. He seemed rather surprised at poor Miss Fox's ignorance of his *Matins and Vespers,* a volume of hymns which had been "the means of converting a poor Syrian, who on being shipwrecked possessed that and that only, which copy is now in the possession of the Bishop of Stockholm." For good measure, he advised everyone to visit the Holy Land, where "the first voices Dr. Bowring heard were engaged in singing his hymn, 'Watchman, Watchman, What of the Night?' " At "this very interesting party" the reporter was evidently a wide-eyed listener who wrote down without bias exactly what she heard.

This account agrees very well with that of John Neal, who met Bowring at Bentham's table and thus recorded his impressions:

I took rather a fancy to him. He was a good deal of a chatterbox, to be sure, but then he had a refined, intellectual face, a very pleasant manner, and just enough of modest pretension to make him an agreeable companion.[17]

Neal quoted from *Timothy Flint's Monthly* for November, 1833, a description of Bowring as "about five feet nine inches high, of slender make, with one of the most poetical faces you ever saw . . ." and a further reference to "eyes which in spite of golden spectacles and the distortion caused by their long use are capable of being lighted up as with an inward fire."[18]

But Neal did not like Bowring, and called him "the busiest of busy-bodies, and the slipperiest."[19] This attack is partly to be accounted for by Bowring's mutilation of an article of Neal's in the *Westminster,* and his statement that Bentham had declared of Neal that he had "as lief have a rattlesnake in his house."[20] Neal, stoutly maintaining that Bentham would not as lief have a rattlesnake in his house, denounced Bowring as a poseur, a plagiarizer, and an embezzler, and painted a sorry picture of his misguided patronage of foreign refugees in London, for which the refugees and Bentham paid in the end. Evidently this is a reflection of London gossip, and indicates the general attitude toward Bowring at the very time when he was editing the *Westminster.* Comments in memoirs and diaries are generally unfavorable. Harriet Martineau charges him with "vanity, unscrupulousness, and incompetence."[21] He is the Old Radical of George Borrow's *Romany Rye* appendix, wherein he is exhibited as a political jobber and a fake linguist, turning prose translations made by poor young refugees into English verse and claiming full credit for the work. This charge is also made by Neal, who states that it was generally known that Bowring did his books of verse translations in this way. Place referred to him once as "that wild poetical surface man," and what he called him at another time is indicated in his diary by a very neat rectangular excision, made by Place's literary executor. In 1826 he was generally believed guilty of unscrupulous handling of funds in connection with the Greek loan; "I doubt," Place wrote, "he will never again be quite straight with the Public. I have grieved greatly over it: it disgraces the Cause."[22] Crabb Robinson did not like him, agreeing in the general verdict on the Greek affair, and expressing his opinion that Bowring was guilty of plagiarism.[23]

It is hardly our concern to determine the character of Bowring, whose activities, for anything we know, were well intentioned if perhaps ill advised. But we must make note of his generally admitted incompetence, for he handled the business of the review; and we are even more concerned with his reputation, which must have proved prejudicial to the influence of the Benthamite journal and which disposed its contributors to quarrel with its unfortunate editor even more than contributors usually quarreled with editors.

Bowring's "understrapper," as Neal called him, did little to improve the standing of the *Westminster's* editorial staff. Henry Southern, whose name is now forgotten, was very active in journalism in the eighteen-twenties. At the beginning of the decade, when he was twenty-one, he began editing the *Retrospective Review,* a quarterly which summarized and commented on old books —*Urn Burial, Areopagitica, The Book of the Knight of the Tour Landry.* This rather able journal continued until 1827. Shortly after the death of John Scott, he became editor and later joint owner of the *London Magazine,* with which he was connected until a year before its discontinuance in 1829. On the founding of the *Westminster* he became literary editor, and held this position for some three years. "Southern was and is a man of sterling ability," Crabb Robinson wrote in his diary after their former intimacy had been broken off, "but he is a man of indulgence and neither delicate nor scrupulous in his conduct toward others."[24] By this he meant that Southern was seldom sober, and had not repaid him the £65 15s. he borrowed when he purchased his share in the *London Magazine* or the £15 he borrowed to become a member of the Athenaeum Club or the £30 he borrowed on another of the frequent occasions when he needed it. It is not surprising to find James Mill, at Place's Charing Cross establishment for a gossip, complaining of Southern's conduct, or Place himself, disgruntled at an inferior article in the *Westminster,* noting of it, "Written by Southern, I suppose when half drunk."[25]

Under such unfavorable auspices the review was launched in 1824. The members of its staff were divided into camps: James Mill, Place, and the younger Philosophic Radicals in one at open warfare with Bowring and a few straggling allies in another. Mill, his son states,

augured so ill of the enterprise that he regretted it altogether, feeling persuaded not only that Mr. Bentham would lose his money, but that discredit would probably be brought upon Radical principles. He could not, however, desert Mr. Bentham. . .[26]

Then there were those among the reviewers who had none too much affection either for Mill and his group or for Bowring, such as Peacock, Crabb Robinson, even Southern. It may be observed that among the major contributors only James Mill and Francis Place were men of maturity and experience, and Place was no literary genius. Bowring was in his early thirties and the others were younger. Not half of them had had university training, and none of them belonged to aristocratic families. Their circle offers a marked contrast to the brilliant Whig group centering about Lansdowne House, the bored Tories of the court, and the gay young Tories of *Blackwood's,* and likewise to the starved loud-mouthed radicals who could not always succeed in keeping out of jail. They were all middle-class men who proposed to get on by their own effort, men of remarkable energy and enthusiasm. And though they were devoted to the cause of Bentham each in his own way, there can be little doubt that they all found in the "greatest happiness principle" something to which they could subscribe with conviction.

But at least one of Bentham's old ambitions was to be realized, and the venerable reformer skipped more gaily than ever about his garden. There would be a radical review, "one-half," Bentham wrote, "consecrated to politics and morals, the other half left to literary insignificancies."[27] The literary insignificancies he had to admit if the journal was to be called a review, in spite of his feeling that poetry was of doubtful utility. Longmans, a most reputable house, London representative of no less a periodical than the *Edinburgh Review* and after the failure of Constable its sole publisher, had agreed to undertake the new venture.

The capital thing is [wrote Bentham] the circumstantial evidence this affords of the growth of Radicalism; for with their experience and opportunities of observation, the Longmans would never have launched into any such expenses without good ground for assurance that Radicalism would either promote, or not prevent the accession of a proportionate number of customers.[28]

Their risk, however, was considerably lessened by a fund, said to have been nearly four thousand pounds,[29] which Bentham provided. Considering its politics the Benthamites named their review most appropriately after that part of the metropolis represented in Parliament by two respectable radicals, Burdett and Hobhouse, and distinguished as the residence of Bentham.

An attractive prospectus, done in a neat script on white paper of excellent quality, was sent out:

In projecting this new Quarterly Review the conductors conceive that they are about to take possession of ground entirely unoccupied by any prior publication. The other critical works of the same kind are the powerful and efficient advocates of their respective parties, but it is the firm and decided determination of the Editors of the Westminster Review to take part with no faction, to support no body of men, and to perform the duties of the office they have undertaken, and in which they are not untried, as uninfluenced by personal enmity as by personal friendship.

Later in the elaborate prospectus this statement is in a measure contradicted.

The Editors have great satisfaction in stating that they are the organs of an able and active society of individuals, who have seen with regret and somewhat of indignation that the name of criticism has been usurped with sinister views, and that the interests of literature and of a wise policy, and through them those of the Public have been sacrificed to selfish and unworthy purposes, are resolved to establish a tribunal where a fairer and more unbiassed hearing may be obtained. . . It is their ambition to make this review the representative of the true interests of the majority, and the firm and invariable advocate of those principles which tend to increase the sum of human happiness, and to ameliorate the condition of mankind.[30]

For a sample of how these worthy acts are to be performed, the prospectus refers the eager public to the forthcoming first number, to be published by Longmans.

But the review was never published by Longmans. The article which most clearly defined the political and intellectual position of the new quarterly was James Mill's merciless denunciation of the *Edinburgh Review,* one of Longman's most profitable enterprises. So the publishers expectant hastily withdrew, and Mill as hastily persuaded his own publishers, Baldwin, Cradock, and Joy, to undertake the *Westminster.* Here apparently his instincts as a propagandist and his attachment to Bentham prevailed over his dislike for Bowring.

The first number of the radical journal appeared on time,* a somewhat unusual procedure for quarterly reviews and one which it was not often to repeat, in January, 1824. Contributors were to be paid ten to sixteen guineas per sheet of sixteen pages, but the price soon rose in conformity with the practice of the other reviews. "£20 a sheet would . . . be much below the price paid for either the *Quarterly, Edinburgh,* or *Westminster Review,* and not more than is paid by the *New Monthly Magazine,*" Place wrote in 1826.[31] With its neat grayish jacket the *Westminster* was more conservative in appearance than either of its opponents, and its single column format was more attractive. It was corpulent to the extent of almost three hundred pages, and sold at the usual price for reviews, six shillings a number—surprisingly high, it seems today, for such heavy and laborious reading as we of the present usually find them. But an edition of two thousand copies was quickly exhausted, and a second edition of one thousand followed; furthermore, as Bowring points out, "as its readers were, to a large extent, among the non-opulent and democratic classes, whose access to books is principally by associations of various sorts, the number of its readers was very great."[32] The *Edinburgh Review* itself, still the leading quarterly, was at this time selling on an average only about eleven thousand,[33] and the *Quarterly,* which appeared only twice in 1824,[34] was much weakened at this time

* John Stuart Mill states (*Autobiography,* p. 66) that the first number appeared in March, 1824. But cf. the announcement in *The Examiner* advertisements on p. 64, issue of January 25, 1824: "The Westminster Review, No. I, was just published yesterday (Jan. 24) . . ." Mill therefore must be mistaken.

by the illness of Gifford, who complained in a letter to Canning[35] that his review was moribund, and named the *Westminster* as one of the vultures waiting to devour its remains.

The *Westminster* reviewers were rightly jubilant at the success of their first number. Even the members of Mill's faction were pleased. Contrary to their expectations, they liked the review itself very much, and the attention that it attracted even more; "There could be no room for hesitation, and we all became eager in doing everything we could to strengthen and improve it."[36] The high quality and large sale of the first number was fortunate, then, in more ways than one, for it is not at all unlikely that except for this circumstance the Mill group, which contained most of the Benthamite ability, would have entirely withheld its support. The only article of note in the first number from the camp of the disaffected is James Mill's essay on the *Edinburgh Review*,[37] written out of loyalty to Bentham in accordance with their early plan of reviewing reviews—a practice common to several magazines of the 1820's, and not original with the *Westminster*.

This one article, however, probably did more for the review than all the other articles in the first number. A masterly attack on all rival parties, particularly the Whigs, it inevitably attracted much attention, and served to indicate the political position to be held by the Benthamite party and its new party organ.

III

POLITICAL PROPAGANDA

In his article on the *Edinburgh Review,* Mill, speaking, of course, not in his own person but as the authoritative "we," declared open war on the English aristocracy, the clergy, the law, and the reviews. Though the essay was devoted largely to one of those reviews, it was characteristic of its author's systematic mind that at the beginning he should make perfectly clear the place in the general scheme of things of the particular object of his attack.

First, the nature and function of periodicals:

For a considerable number of years this field has been to such a degree occupied by two rival, celebrated, and successful publications that the old have sunk into insignificance. . . Under the guise of reviewing books, these publications have introduced the practice of publishing dissertations, not only upon the topics of the day, but upon all the most important questions of morals and legislation, in the most extensive acceptation of those terms.

The most effectual mode of doing good to mankind by reading is to correct their errors; to expose their prejudices; to refute opinions which are generated only by partial interests, but to which men are, for that reason, so much the more attached; to censure whatever is mean or selfish in their behaviour, and to attach honour to actions solely in proportion to their tendency to increase the sum of happiness, lessen the sum of misery. But this is a course which periodical literature cannot pursue.

For periodicals, Mill continues, are under the disagreeable necessity of finding an immediate sale. The unpopular magazine will not find purchasers and must disappear. The writer for periodicals must therefore adjust his statements to the bias of his readers; he must flatter their prejudices. To question those prejudices for the sake of enlightening his readers would ruin his own career.

The class of readers among whom it is most important to secure popularity, if a periodical would succeed, is the aristocracy, who set the fashions—and, Mill might have added, can themselves afford to buy six-shilling reviews. It is therefore important that a periodical should please the members of this class and favor their continuance in power. "It will obtain applause, and will receive reward, in proportion as it is successful in finding plausible reasons for the maintenance of the favorite opinions of the powerful classes."

Mill points out that he is using the term aristocracy in a broad sense, meaning that group, small in proportion to the population, "sharing among them the powers of government, and sharing among themselves also the profits of misrule." That group, in England, is made up largely of the owners of the great landed estates, who "have the principal influence in sending members to the House of Commons." For the counties are controlled, and most of the boroughs admittedly owned, by great families. Electors who do not place their votes regularly at the disposal of their landlords sell them, obviously to some man of property; hence a few monied men gain admittance to the political aristocracy.

With the aid of two sets of retainers, clergymen and lawyers, this aristocracy keeps its position. The aid of the Church is necessary, because that institution has great power over the minds of the people. Hence the Established Church and its clergy are made dependent upon the state—that is, the aristocracy itself—for position and advancement. The priesthood, then, acts with its aristocratic patrons "and receives its share of the profits of misrule."

Lawyers are more difficult to control. The law is so complex that only specially trained men can understand it. Yet the rich, unfortunately for themselves, are dependent upon the law, and so upon lawyers, for the security of their property. There is nothing for it, then, since the law must be on their side, but to admit the lawyers to the governing class with their considerable share of "the profits of misrule." It is usually thus that men of talent find their way into the House of Commons—as the well paid servants of the landed aristocracy.

Of the two parties into which the governing class is divided, the adherents of the one think that they can profit most by preserving the present administration in power, accepting what they can get from it, becoming part of it in time. The adherents of the other hope to profit most by ejecting the present administration and gaining control of the government themselves. The first are the Tories, the ministerial party; the second the Whigs, the opposition. The tactics of the Tories and the Tory *Quarterly Review* are simple: they defend things as they are, and oppose all reform. This Mill demonstrated at length in a later article devoted specifically to the *Quarterly Review*.[1] The Whigs in their *Edinburgh Review*, on the other hand, must act warily.

Here it is that Mill launches his brilliant exposure of those who have been considered the friends of the popular cause, showing that they as well as the Tories have an interest in keeping the masses "brutalized"—Mill here using the same word that Matthew Arnold was to apply to the populace almost a half century later.

The primary object of the Whigs and their Review is to discredit the ministry and augment the favor of their own leaders with the aristocratical class. But in order to do this the more effectually, it is expedient to produce as much as possible of the same effects upon the public at large, including the middling and lower classes. Public opinion operates in various ways upon the aristocratical classes, partly by contagion, partly by conviction, and partly by intimidation: and the principal strength of that current is derived from the greatness of the mass by which it is swelled. It is the interest of the opposition, therefore, to act in such a manner . . . as to gain favour from both the few and the many. This they are obliged to endeavour by a perpetual system of compromise, a perpetual trimming between the two interests.

They attempt to persuade the aristocracy that their measures will be more advantageous to them than those of the ministry; and at the same time they affect liberal principles to gain the favor of the masses. They must recommend an empty compromise as "the middle course," and must use other high-sounding but vague and meaningless phrases to conceal their actual lack of principle. "The set of opinions, purely on the side of the aristocratical power, are called despotical. Those which support the demand of effectual securities in favour of the people are declared anarchical. . . ." Thus the political articles of the *Edinburgh Review* have always cleverly dodged all important issues in an effort to gain the favor of all classes. The Whigs and the Whig review have no more concern for the welfare of the common people than have the Tories and their *Quarterly*. They merely pretend interest in the people in order to advance their own interests. Actually, in accordance with their fixed policy, they do no more than play at seesaw. Instances culled laboriously from the *Edinburgh* by the younger Mill are quoted in abundance and at length to demonstrate this characteristic of the Whig journal. In fact, a second article on the *Edinburgh*,[2] by John Stuart Mill, was required to exhaust the supply of quotations.

Never had the Whigs been so mercilessly attacked by liberals, or the fair name of periodical literature so bitterly maligned. Not only Tory and Whig but even radical journals received their death sentence. In an incidental paragraph Mill points out that radical proprietors have been lacking either in goodness or wisdom, or in both; "the principal influence to which they bend is that of the favorite opinions, right or wrong, of those to whom they look for their reward." The masses being as badly educated as they are, it must do more harm than good to write for their approval. *Black Dwarf, Examiner, Political Register, Republican*—all are implicitly condemned. The *Westminster* alone is left to perform that perennial task of Englishmen—saving England.

Mill's case is admirable if you admit his major assumption, which is also a major assumption of the Utilitarians and so of the Utilitarian review, that self-interest is the basis of all human conduct. His repeated use of the phrase, "it is the interest," is notable. It is the interest of all periodical writers to flatter the prejudices of possible readers, for otherwise their journals will not sell. The major reviews have an additional interest, the profits of misrule, which makes them doubly corrupt. And what, then, one asks, of the *Westminster Review* itself? Will not its Utilitarian sponsors act likewise from self-interest?

Mill was too clever a logician to overlook this possibility, and in an explanatory paragraph he makes his apology, which, alas, might conceivably serve also as an apology for his opponents.

We have no claims to be trusted, any more than any one among our contemporaries: but we have a claim to be tried. Men have diversities of taste; and it is not impossible that a man should exist who really has a taste for the establishment of the securities of good government, and would derive more pleasure from the success of their pursuit, than of any other pursuit in which he could engage, wealth or power not excepted.

And we know that this is an accurate characterization of Bentham. Neither did Mill overlook the possibility that the *Westminster,* as well as the other reviews, might find an appreciative public.

We may be sanguine enough, or silly enough, or clear-sighted enough, to believe that intellectual and moral qualities have made a great progress among the people of this country; and that the class who will really approve endeavours in favour of good government, and of the happiness and intelligence of men, are a class sufficiently numerous to reward our endeavours.

By this class Mill meant of course the middle class; he himself, like the *Edinburgh,* was championing certain "outs" who wished to get in. He was no defender of liberty or equality in the abstract. The lower class, "brutalized," undiscriminating, the prey of violent demagogues, in his opinion obviously could no more be trusted than the aristocracy. Clearly the article was never written by a thoroughgoing democrat. Yet Mill was somewhat ahead of his times; not until eight years later would Parliament pass, and then unwillingly, a Reform Bill giving representation to those whom the *Westminster Review* said it hoped to please.

Yet if the leading article of their first number can be believed, the reviewers politically were not prophets crying in the wilderness. This article, a review of a poem entitled *Men and Things in 1823,*[3] is W. J. Fox's survey of English conditions at the time, and as such deserves notice along with James Mill's comment on the *Edinburgh Review.* It emphasizes most the increased importance of the people in national life; and in the term Fox includes the lower class, though it is to the other classes that most of his remarks apply. Political orations, he says, are now designed to secure the favor of the crowd. People everywhere are becoming interested in the popular cause everywhere: "It begins to be reckoned as good a thing for the Greeks to win a battle as for the Opposition to carry a motion." Books are written for ordinary readers: "Flattering dedications are defunct; the public is the best patron for your literary adventurer." And again, "All our great poets write for the people. Sir Walter Scott is the choicest specimen." Demonstration follows that Scott's poetry is well calculated for popular consumption. Byron, Wordsworth, Campbell, Moore, and Southey have all been affected by the new public: "They sing for the many; except that Wordsworth seems rather to chaunt a demonstration to the initiated few that the many should be sung to." Shelley and Keats are not mentioned.

Fox views the literary men, Tories, Whigs, radicals, for what they represent, and without political bias. So does he other phenomena of the times. Of particular interest are the remarks of this intelligent clergyman on the religious state of the nation. He points out that along with considerable sham and hypocrisy there exists in England much sincere interest in religion, which the upper classes have developed "very much out of loyalty to George the Third and hatred of the French Revolution," their inferiors through the operations of Bible and Tract Societies; hence both have been influenced by the new democratic tendencies. Religious enthusiasm, however, is the only national enthusiasm. Byron and the reviewers together account for a generally heartless and blasé tone, "the affectation of no feeling at all." This Fox deplores; and he deplores, too, the fact that England has become unduly mercenary—a lament which is to sound with increasing frequency, though seldom in Benthamite pages, throughout the century. He is concerned for the laboring classes, and with very un-Benthamite complacency prophesies the decline of individualism.

Our social arrangements may stop far short of the forms contemplated by Mr. Owen, but there seems good reason to expect that they will be modified by the influences of his favorite co-operative principle; that combination will in some measure supply the want of capital; and that the prodigious improvements in machinery which have been, and will be made, instead of merely enriching individuals already wealthy, will become directly subservient to the interests of the operative classes.

One reads at the end the few superficial comments on the poem about England in 1823, delighted with Fox's paper and convinced that here has been a strange leading article for the new organ of the Philosophic Radicals. Benthamite humanitarianism without Benthamite dogma, it proves that already Benthamism is coloring liberals outside the charmed circle, and that liberals outside the charmed circle are coloring Benthamism. It will not do, then, to expect absolutely consistent "profit and loss philosophy" from the *Westminster*.

It is vain, however, to search for further glaring departures from the Philosophic Radical tenets in the first number. Exciting articles there are several: Dr. Southwood Smith's attack on aristo-cratic education, Peregrine Bingham's attack on aristocratic litera-ture represented by Tom Moore, two separate defenses of democ-racy in the United States. To all these we shall allude in detail later. The number also contains a long and difficult article by Perronet Thompson, "On the Instrument of Exchange," which he said it took him eleven years to write; an article on special juries; an article by Bowring on Russia; an article on Edward Irving; and miscellaneous notices. Perhaps Fox's comment on Wordsworth, quoted above, is applicable here: the new review hardly speaks to the people, but it certainly chants a demonstration to the initi-ated few that the people should be spoken to. One would look far for a single number of an English periodical of greater gen-eral excellence, and it is not surprising that even the members of the hypercritical Mill faction were delighted with it.

Its reception by its rival periodicals, too, was surprisingly friend-ly. There is no evidence that either the *Edinburgh* or the *Quarterly Review* was overjoyed, but the impudent *Blackwood's* honored it with enthusiastic welcome, and the *Monthly Magazine* and the *Metropolitan Literary Journal,* lesser monthlies, praised it warm-ly. The *Monthly* expressed "high approval and commendation of the style in which it is written," and made "the unreserved declara-tion that, judging the character of this publication by the first number, we consider its establishment as a great public benefit."[4] "Timothy Tickler" in *Blackwood's*[5] liked it particularly, of course, for the *Edinburgh Review* article, agreeing most jubilantly with its charges against the Whigs, and pointing out that the article was written by an erstwhile *Edinburgh* reviewer. Timothy's seven double column pages should have proved valuable advertising. "In general," he says of the new review, "it is written well, with distinctness and vigour almost throughout, and occasionally with considerable power and eloquence"; and of the reviewers he states, "You have to do with a clever, determined, resolute, thorough-going knot of radical writers—a set of men, educated, some of them, as well as the Edinburgh reviewers—and quite as well skilled as the best of them could ever pretend to be in the arts of communicating with the intellect of the world as it is." Naturally *Blackwood's* detests the *Westminster's* radicalism; but it accepts the new journal as the third of the great reviews, and in succeeding months does battle with it as with the *Quarterly* and the *Edinburgh*.

Politically, as Mill's article on the *Edinburgh* made clear, the Utilitarians considered themselves distinct not only from Tory conservatism but from Whig liberalism and Carlile radicalism. Throughout its early years, and most effectively during its first four, which we shall now consider, the *Westminster* attempted to attain two closely related objectives—destructively, the general weakening of the power of the two major parties and the proportionate strengthening of the middle class; constructively, the accomplishment of certain specific reforms in government and society. And though the Philosophic Radicals considered themselves preëminent particularly in logic and abstract thought, their work on the smaller and more immediate tasks appears today their more useful contribution to the "greatest happiness of the greatest number." In this work they were materially aided by those on whom they had declared the most bitter war in their first number, the Whigs and the Whig journals, even the *Edinburgh Review* itself. It must be remembered, for example, that the *Edinburgh* had printed James Mill's articles before the *Westminster* was founded; that it had advocated moderate reform in the electoral system and had long since pointed out the inadequacy of the University curriculum; and that when the time came it supported the establishment of London University. It believed as firmly as the *West-*

minster reviewers in the authority of the science of political economy, and McCulloch, the most popular political economist of
the time, contributed regularly to it. One daily newspaper in particular, *The Morning Chronicle,* was distinctly liberal, and to it
the Philosophic Radicals, including Place and John Stuart Mill,
had contributed. The *Globe-Traveller,* a weekly owned by the
economist Colonel Torrens, was also friendly to reform, and it
was in its pages that John Stuart Mill first broke into print. Leigh
Hunt had supported in the *Examiner* many of the measures that
the *Westminster* proposed. Perhaps most important of all, Mac-
Vey Napier in preparing his supplement to the *Encyclopaedia
Britannica* (1816-24) had secured James Mill to write on such
important topics as government and education. In these articles
the Benthamite program is outlined and practically the entire political message of the *Westminster* is stated. By 1824, the ground
was well prepared. Politically the review represents not the growth
but the flowering of Benthamism.

The general tone is philosophic enough. All customs and institutions must be subjected to a thorough and unbiased scrutiny;
nothing must be accepted because it always has been accepted. The
test for accepting is very simple: does the institution best promote
the greatest happiness of the greatest number? During the first
four years of the review, Utilitarian logic very clearly demonstrated that whatever was was wrong. As Hazlitt with much justification observed, the *Westminster* approved of practically no established institution but the East India Company.

"In the present situation of Great Britain," wrote John Stuart
Mill,[6] "extensive and searching reforms are imperatively needed.
All half measures are useless, with reference to the production of
any great or permanent good." But reform, he says, will be difficult to effect, partly because of the short-sightedness of most public men.

A short-sighted man is ever timid. He sees that under the present system,
person and property are to a certain degree secure. Change the system,
and he knows not what will happen. Not knowing what will happen,
he fears the worst. And though he dreads great changes most, his opposition extends even to the smallest. Innovation once begun, though it
be but a trifle, he knows not when or where it will end.

Even from "the more manly and clear-sighted" little can be expected, for the party system, with continuance in office its highest ideal, will swallow them up. "They are dragged down to the level of the meanest animal who can give a vote; they dare not advance a step without *his* previous sanction. . . ."[7] Therefore, the nation should interest itself in measures, not men.

This is the way the *Westminster* at its best sounds during its first four years. The tone is evidently sincere. The logic is clear-cut if not always sufficiently careful of the full implication of its premises. As here, it often leads its votaries into trouble. Clearly Mill's analysis, just quoted, lays open to serious question the *Westminster's* cardinal tenet, democracy. But if he saw at the time that the quest for votes might vitiate politics fully as much if the number of voters were increased, he did not say so. It was not until later that he was to express grave doubts that the United States with universal manhood suffrage had, as the review stated, "the only good system of government."

This moderately disloyal statement appears in an article in the first number of the review,[8] one of several devoted to the praise of the United States, the *Westminster's* ideal commonwealth[9] and at this time a highly controversial topic in England. The *Quarterly Review* was a notorious enemy of the American republic; the *Edinburgh*, true to form, employed what Mill called its "see-saw." The *Westminster*, which never seesawed on this subject and seldom on any other, found little to condemn in the United States except "the absurdities of that legal system which they borrowed from their English ancestors,"[10] the tariff, and Negro slavery. But slavery, like the legal system, was a legacy left by English colonists; and, besides, England could not condemn the institution in the United States as long as she allowed it to continue in her own West Indies, or the tariff as long as she kept her Corn Laws.

Balanced against these major blemishes and a few minor ones, however, the virtues of the American experiment in democracy, as seen by the Benthamites, are many. The government belongs to the people, and so will not abuse their interests; the review points out in its first number[11] that "extensive suffrage and voting by ballot prevail," that taxes are low, and that education is available to the masses. There is little poverty, citizens being exempt from "suffering from the misgovernment and barbarous political institutions of Europe." Particularly the *Westminster* finds the United States useful as an example of a nation that gets along without an established church, without a vice society, without prosecutions for blasphemy or libel, and without king, Lords, and Commons. English institutions are clearly open to question, when without them the Americans, as Peregrine Bingham points out, "possess a greater amount of happiness than the same numbers have ever enjoyed before."[12] It is easy to see why the conservative journals, the *Quarterly* in particular, found it desirable to maintain an unfriendly attitude toward the radical experiment in America. It menaced the English government; and the *Westminster* by rejoicing in that menace made it all the worse. In its very first number it had taken pains to accuse the *Quarterly* of deliberate misrepresentations of America contained in Gifford's famous review of *Faux's Memorable Days*.[13]

If it was important that the Benthamites show democracy to be successful where tried, it was equally important to show that all other governments were iniquitous and did not promote the greatest happiness. A leading article by George Grote, his only contribution to the review,[14] attempted to refute Mitford's Tory *History of Greece*. Grote, writing with assurance in his own special field of Greek history, asserted that ". . . the Grecian democracies secured, to no small extent, the happiness of the people under them, while the Grecian oligarchies did not even aim at securing it." He attributed Greek preëminence in literature and philosophy to "a strong desire of the public applause: there are many motives which suffice to produce mediocrity, but this alone will give birth to excellence." And here one thinks of Milton and Browning, and begins to regret that the Utilitarians insisted—and following good precedent they did insist—on carrying their politics over into literature and philosophy. But it was important to attach the ancient Greeks to their cause rather than to that of the English aristocracy.

The melancholy tale of France most admirably served the reviewers' political purposes. First and best, there was the aristocratic government before the Revolution. In the articles "Court of Louis XIV and the Regency,"[15] "Private Memoirs of Mme de Hausset,"[16] and "Memoirs of the Countess of Genlis,"[17] the reviewers, quoting at length, demonstrated with great glee the evils of monarchy. Here was their chance to indulge in the grand game of calling their political opponents immoral, for all monarchs and aristocrats, dead or alive, were their political opponents. It was very fortunate that they could find a book of which the authoress

fearlessly and freely plunges into a very sewer of corruption as the natural element of the court of France, and from every dive into this loathesome sink of impurity drags up a prince or princess, a duke or duchess, reeking with pollution and steaming from the stews,

and another which

exposes all the machinery of an absolute anarchy; and, if people will not determine to be blind, must show them that under such a government they are in a worse state than the very sheep in the pen of the butcher.

And, as a result—"Can we be surprised that a deluge of blood at length swept the land so long cursed and polluted by these iniquities?" The iniquities do not "excuse the blind ferocity of the revolutionists," but they account for them, render them inevitable.

To the Revolution itself the review devoted little space, John Stuart Mill's short article on Mignet[18] being its only contribution of importance. Mill shows an interest not only in Mignet's story but in his style; objects to him for straining after brilliance of expression; commends him for his sprightliness. Politically, he contributes only one thrust at the conservative point of view— that people of his own time were unduly panic-stricken about the Revolution because they knew too little about it.

What the Tory prints choose to tell them of this most interesting period of modern history, so much they know, and nothing more: that is, enough to raise in their minds an intense yet indefinite horror of French reforms and reformers, and as far as possible of all reforms and reformers.

For the rest, the reviewers disliked Napoleon, certainly no democrat, and the succeeding royalist government, and thought that except for the overthrow of the aristocracy, of course a great achievement, the Revolution had accomplished little.[19] They did not approve of the English participation in the Napoleonic Wars; but this was not strange, for they approved of very few things that England had done aside from producing those prophets of the new age, Locke and Hartley and Priestley and Bentham.

Regarding the evils of England's eighteenth century, the review had little to say; but the Restoration supplied them with one important article and sundry lesser sneers. The article was a review[20] of the Lord Braybrooke edition of Pepys's *Diary,* just published. The reviewer found all the personal details amusing but slightly irrelevant, and concentrated his attention on political corruption. He found much of it in the *Diary,* and rejoiced in it all. He found a king "governed only by his lust, and the women, and the rogues about him," constantly in debt, at the head of a council silly and incompetent; a Commons voting great sums to support this king, and to carry on a war with the Dutch which had no excuse for being except the whim of the court: "a love of excitation and novelty, that impatience of quiet, to which vacant minds are subject." This material he used to refute all talk of "the wisdom of our ancestors" and to counteract sentimental devotion to Merrie England.

The Benthamites were no friends to Charles I and liked but moderately the Commonwealth government, as was amply demonstrated in their favorable review of Godwin's *History of the Commonwealth of England,*[21] and better still in John Stuart Mill's paper on "Brodie's History of the British Empire."[22] Most of his article is concerned with proving Charles the First an evil and silly despot, the Commonwealth men also despots, but as admirable as despots can be. Mill, believing in democracy, could not admire the methods of the Long Parliament, but he found much good to say of the measures which it enacted. The reviewers did not approve highly of Cromwell. Sometimes, indeed, as in the article on Godwin, they were very severe with him, ranking him with Napoleon as a "hateful oppressor," and regarding his protectorate as treason to the cause of representative government. They had little to say about the Tudors. But groping further back, in medieval times, they found the knights, and were happy.

For they simply could not endure a knight. They regarded him and his age with loathing and scorn. Even the enlightened eighteenth century did not excel the *Westminster* reviewers in sublime contempt for Gothic barbarism. Political reasons for this attitude are not far to seek: "The age of chivalry was the age of aristocracy in its most gigantic strength and wide-extending sway; and the illusions of chivalry are to this hour the great strongholds of aristocratic prejudice." This is John Stuart Mill's statement of the case, in his remarkable *Westminster* essay, "Age of Chivalry."[23] Basing his observations on the research of Dulaure and Sismondi, he points out that the ideal knightly virtues are wholly admirable, but that the knights did not have them. They were irascible, cruel, and relatively uncourageous; their wars were undertaken through cupidity and ennui, and their crusades through ennui and selfishness. By slaughtering infidels they hoped to placate God for their gross misbehavior. It was personal vanity that made them fight duels for ladies. Yet these knights are idealized, "and so delighted are we with our own romantic conceptions that we are ready to fall down and worship their imaginary original"—a highwayman, who for the sake of plunder led his practically unarmed retainers to almost certain death in battle, himself on horseback and encased in armor so that there was very little chance of his being hurt. If there was any bravery or decency in the Middle Ages, it was to be found among the low-born burghers and peasants, for whom the knights had nothing but contempt.

The *Westminster* during its early years frequently reminded its readers that it was dangerous to honor knighthood. In another article devoted to the subject,[24] chivalry was again blamed for many existing ills: it left as legacies an absurd code of honor and a tradition of loyalty which now aid materially in preserving the iniquitous institutions of Merrie England. The glamor which the *Quarterly Review* on occasion saw in the Middle Ages was rudely attacked. "The superiority of chivalry is that of a chevalier, a horseman, or one rich enough to purchase oats, hay, and straw to maintain a horse. . . . Those who teach that we have derived any good thing from the Middle Ages deceive themselves and us."[25]

Reading James Mill's "while the stupidity of the Middle Ages was still in its perfection, the fetters of the clergy upon the human mind were easily preserved from relaxation,"[26] and similar contemptuous allusions to the days of knighthood, one begins to wonder whether the Benthamites considered the whole romantic revival of medievalism as part of a wicked Tory plot to keep the aristocracy in power. There is no evidence that they did; but they certainly saw very clearly that the charm of the Middle Ages was capable of exerting great force against their political dogma of democracy.

The reviewers found the knights' descendants, the contemporary aristocracy, fully as bad as Carlyle found them a decade later, but, unlike Carlyle, they had no expectation that such a class could ever be useful. A leading article on the Game Laws,[27] ostensibly reviewing several pamphlets and reports on the subject, pictures the aristocracy as principally concerned with hunting and "preserving their game," and, by enforcing the laws against poachers, starting honest but hungry boors in a career of lawbreaking. The suspected poacher has no fair chance at his trial, because the plaintiff is also the presiding magistrate. And neither the game nor the presiding magistrate matters much.

Assumption the first: alter the law, and you destroy the game. Destroy the game, and there will be no resident gentry; this is assumption the second, and a curious one too. A resident gentry is of vast importance; this is the grand assumption of all. If we were content to refute them out of their own mouths, we might ask what great good can come out of the residence of a country gentleman, whose sole motive for residing upon his estate is, by their own confession, the killing of game?

The specific charges of the Utilitarians against the aristocracy of their own time are perhaps best summarized in James Mill's leading article, "State of the Nation," which appeared in the *Westminster* for October, 1826.[28] As he and other reviewers said many times, the only ambition of the members of the upper class was to keep themselves in power, because, he pointed out here, they lived upon the taxes: "upon the labour of others without rendering them an equivalent." Because of their wealth and influence, they determined to a great extent the standards of national morality.

> . . . the disposition to live upon the labour of others is diffused throughout the community: The moral sense of the nation is perverted; the distinction between what is right and what is wrong . . . is lost. . . Assuredly among the items in the state of this country may be enumerated, as standing in the first rank, prodigal expensiveness on the part of the government; and consequent upon this, and inseparable from it, the vice, in the aristocratical class, of living upon the labour of others.

The prodigal expensiveness of government Mill attributed in large measure to the effects of the war with France, a war into which the English aristocracy, out of fear of ideas, forced the people. To the English, observing France,

> it became apparent the party demanding extensive changes . . . would prove the stronger. Then it was, and not till then, that the government of Great Britain struck in, and took part in the civil war of France; struck in to prevent the success of the party demanding extensive changes. . .

For the changes included "the extinction of those privileges of the aristocratical class, by which that class were enabled to perpetrate bad government for their own advantage." Obviously the aristocracy would not wish such an event to take place in England, so they convinced the English people that the French had "horrid ideas," and now the people could pay for the war. "No such monstrous case of gulling, no such inordinate swallow of delusion, we verily believe, is to be found in the history of civilized man," Mill wrote. Moreover, he found that the war had accustomed the nation to extravagant expenditure:

> Enormous fleets and armies during the war paved the way for enormous establishments during peace; the nation was inured to such a state— the aristocracy to hold the lucrative posts, the people to pay the expense.

It would be better, Mill said, to pension the aristocracy than to keep whole armies and navies for the sake of giving them colonelcies and admiralships.

He thought that even the Corn Laws, "a tax upon the rest of the community for the benefit of the receivers of rent," the landed aristocracy, were less pernicious than the support of heavy armaments, but of course he disapproved thoroughly of the Corn Laws, finding the special protection of grain-growers evil in itself and productive of general economic instability as well as of high prices for bread. Unlike such radicals as Cobbett, he was more concerned about the economic instability than about the misery of underfed laborers. He also thought the usury laws contributory factors in the economic instability, and the cost of colonies a part of the national extravagance. He considered reform in the legal system and in parliamentary representation necessary, pointing out the absurdity of a House of Commons relatively owned by the House of Lords through aristocratic control of electors and the continuance of rotten boroughs. With emphasis and assurance he declared that parliamentary reform would come within a few years. In Ireland he found the evils of aristocratic government represented in their worst form, and advocated Irish independence as best for both England and Ireland.

Yet, in spite of many obstacles, the nation, Mill thought, was improving. The industrious middle class was growing richer; and if the laborers were not richer, they were at least no poorer.

We are not among those who think that their condition has greatly deteriorated, because we see no reason to suppose it was ever good . . . we can have no doubt that their state of servitude when lords were still more lordly, and squires still more squirish than they are at present, was, though in another form, even harder and more corrupting than at present.

Their condition would follow the trend of the times and improve, were it not for the fact that "where a given amount of produce is to be divided, and the numbers among whom it is to be divided are too great, the share of each cannot but be small." The fault lay in the nation's failure to teach them this basic truth, and in the example of social injustice set by the aristocracy, who considered it proper "to live upon the labor of others." Hence the laboring man did not consider it infamous to beget children whom he could not support and who would become a charge on charity and the state.

All this must have been familiar doctrine to the consistent readers of the *Westminster Review*. At every possible turn, it denounced the uselessness and expensiveness of the aristocracy. Its pronounced pacifism at a time when wars were generally regarded as a matter of course is most remarkable, even though the position is maintained for political and economic rather than ethical reasons. An article entitled "War Expenditure"[29] was devoted to refuting the theory that wars bring prosperity because they produce a market for goods and employment for men. The reviewer of Mill's *Political Economy* pointed out the wastefulness of wars: ". . . every war, however glorious, however grateful to an ambitious ruler, or profitable to the members of an aristocracy, must inevitably occasion a decrease of wealth, and hence a diminution of public enjoyment."[30] Opposition to war expanded itself in 1827 into a whole article,[31] condemning the military policy of the past fifty years—the war against the American colonies, the war with France—a frequently recurring topic in the *Westminster*. Here the reviewer developed at length the theory, later to be urged by Ruskin, that wars are waged for the benefit of rulers, not of the people, who are inveigled into fighting. The army is a convenient place for younger sons of the aristocracy to find employment without much risk; other occupations, except law, would cause them to lose caste, and law is out of the question because it requires mental effort.

Thus the army is really the sole vent for the youth of the higher classes, and it is perfectly conceivable that they should deem it the business of life, and that, favorably situated as they are for influencing the affections of the lower orders, these latter should be persuaded to engage in it under their auspices. All the arts by which vulgar minds are wrought upon are brought in aid of the delusion: Music, dress, gallantry, display, banners, emblems of triumph, parade, all lend their charms to captivate the inexperienced.

The reviewer further points out that the horrible features of the enterprise commonly receive little publicity. Then follows a résumé of a book called *The Eventful Life of a Soldier,* strong anti-militarist propaganda which does include the horrible features with an enthusiasm not frequently to be equaled until a century later.

Taxation to support the aristocracy almost directly some reviewers found even more iniquitous than indirect taxes in the form of military organizations. Four articles,[32] one of them a review of their reviewer Thompson's work on the subject, were devoted to the injustice of the Corn Laws. The Benthamites objected to this form of taxation not alone because it enriched the landowning aristocracy at the expense of the rest of the nation, but because it violated the general principle of free trade fundamental to what they considered the precise science of economics outlined by Adam Smith and Ricardo, which along with the doctrine of Malthus was a vital part of the Utilitarian creed. They defended free trade in three distinct articles.[33]

This is one of a number of definite measures which they advocated. Here we may conveniently leave for a time their general attacks on the Whig and Tory aristocracy and all pertaining to it, and consider briefly some of these specific proposals, the adoption of which they considered necessary for the reform of the English government. Most of these proposals are closely connected with their hatred of aristocratic rule, for their purpose was to set up a society calculated to promote the welfare particularly of the middle class, and incidentally of the laborers. Living as they did before Darwin and Galton, and believing in the possible perfection of every individual, they had no doubt that their Utopia could be actually realized by a proper application of the theories of the economists, of Malthus, and of Bentham, legislation and education to be necessary instruments in the work. They would teach the people the principles, and would effect a reform in Parliament so that the laws would be made by the people's representatives. Laws so made would of course apply the principles in which the people believed. Hence a democratic government, as we have seen, was indispensable in carrying out their program, and they frequently hinted that the Crown and the House of Lords might well be done away with.[34] But unlike the founders of their beloved United States, they were not tainted with the theory of natural rights, and advocated democracy purely on the principle of expediency. They favored universal manhood suffrage, believing according to James Mill's ill-fated theory of identity of interest that if everyone had the vote the lower classes, to be educated in this theory, would see that their welfare would best be secured by choosing middle-class representatives. A very satisfactory middle-class civilization would result.

Two articles pointed out the necessity of the Smith-Ricardo political economy, one a short tribute to the work of McCulloch,[35] the joint production of John Stuart Mill and William Ellis, the other a long paper on James Mill's *Elements of Political Economy*.[36] Both articles recommended emphatically that everyone read the books being reviewed. The latter sketched briefly the main tenets of the political economists, and pointed out that the science was exact and consistent and humanitarian, concerning itself with the means whereby the greatest amount of wealth "as an instrument of happiness" might be obtained. The reviewer defended the well-known principle of laissez faire in trade and industry:

It is now pretty generally acknowledged that the legislator can do no more than guarantee to each individual the fruits of his own industry. Should he attempt more than this, should he give to anyone something more than the fruits of his own industry, he can only do so by encroaching on the property of others, or, in other words, by discouraging *their* industry.

The same reviewer sketched the relation of capitalist and laborer under the principle of the wage fund. The employer must make the profits of his enterprise as great as possible, for then his share of them, distinct from that of the laborer and that devoted to upkeep, will be great; his savings will be proportionate; and the result will be the possession of added capital. "Every addition to his capital furnishes fresh employment for laborers. Other things, therefore, remaining the same, the rate of advancement of a country in wealth and population is determined by the rate of profits." Furthermore, as to the employees, "the command of the laboring classes over the necessaries and conveniences of life depends upon the ratio which their number bears to the means of employment." Hence "whatever tends to increase their numbers without proportionally increasing capital must be mischievous in the extreme." In addition to these major tenets, the ones which principally provoked the wrath of prophets of later decades, the reviewer pointed out that supply and demand always regulate price;

that machinery by increasing the quantity of produce and so the amount of wealth furnishes additional employment for labor; and again that wars are wasteful.

In numerous dull and didactic articles before and after this résumé of Mill's textbook, the reviewers preached one or another of these beliefs, and along with their Edinburgh rivals provoked their own colleague, Peacock, to write into *Crochet Castle* the absurd Mr. MacQueedy, for whom they had to chide him mildly a few years later.[37] As in William Ellis's laborious defense of the employment of machinery,[38] it was customary to begin the case by reference to "the early stages of society, when the instruments employed in the cultivation of the earth were few and rude"— precisely MacQueedy's irrepressible procedure. The constantly recurring theme, in Ellis's article and elsewhere, that everything can be done better and more profitably by the use of machinery, must have suggested Peacock's Steam Intellect Society, his name for an organization dear, as we shall see, to the Benthamites—the Society for the Diffusion of Useful Knowledge. The style and method of most of the *Westminster's* articles on political economy, as well as the content, surely justified Carlyle's much later denunciation of this doctrine as "the dismal science."

Ellis's reasoning in his article on machinery is very simple: machinery increases profits; increases therefore the wage fund, the total amount available for the payment of laborers; increases therefore the wages of each worker. If wages are still too low, if there is much unemployment, the reason must be that there are too many workers. In an earlier article[39] he fiercely attacks one existing practice that the Benthamites held largely responsible for the ills of working class: state and individual charity. Outside aid encourages laborers to have larger families than they can support, to commit the crime denounced by James Mill as "living on the labor of others." Moreover, there are too many workers already, and anything that tends to increase their numbers should be discouraged.

New labourers grow up, procreate, and in their turn become expectants of the rich man's bounty. In whatever manner the alms are distributed, a premium is held out for want of foresight. . . Where an immediate pleasure is in question, a just estimate of consequences is seldom made. The pleasures of marriage are immediate. That a proper value should be put upon the corresponding drawbacks is of essential importance to the happiness of the parties, as well as to that of the whole community.

Better not to relieve the indigent, but "to so order things that there shall be no indigent to relieve." Private charity, practiced usually by members of the upper class, is often not exclusively altruistic: alms-givers enjoy hearing " 'God bless your honour,' and similar terms of adulation"; and it is fashionable to visit the poor. Even the genuinely benevolent must beware of "making their feelings the instruments of mischief."

Charity schools which furnish support as well as instruction are bad, for such support not only encourages incautious marriage, but also reduces mortality among indigent children. "The schools provide a more liberal allowance of food and clothing to the children, the medical attendance is better, and the children enjoy all the benefits of cleanliness and pure air." Ellis does not object to these advantages in themselves, but he finds that "the derivative effects are tremendous—the lowering of wages and the misery of the people." For the same reasons he disapproves of charity-supported lying-in hospitals, foundling hospitals, and dispensaries. Thus the Benthamites proposed to settle the perplexing question of unemployment by a stern Malthusianism which naturally appeared incredibly cruel to those not trained to live purely by reason, though according to their usual cautious policy they never openly advocated birth control in the *Westminster*. That even their own reviewers did not unanimously endorse their solution of the problem of poverty is indicated in a flippant note of Walter Coulson's to Leigh Hunt:

The Utilitarians are fast reforming the world by a new Review called the Westminster Review, the object of which is expressed in this motto, "the greatest good of the greatest number," which is to be effected by reducing the numbers to a few and their pleasure to nothing—so wonderful are the ways of providence.[40]

Their other efforts at reform were more patently benevolent. Their dogmatic political economy aroused not only flippant comment, but also violent opposition, from many thinking people of their own day and of the Victorian era just ahead, but no one could offer serious objection to their proposals for law reform, except with regard to their Malthusian opposition to any legislation giving public aid to the poor. In this department the name of Bentham gave the reviewers added assurance, and they spoke out boldly in almost every number.

The aim of criminal law is to prevent crime and reform criminals; vengeance is unknown to the law, the object of which is to promote the greatest happiness of the greatest number. This major principle of Bentham's is emphasized particularly in two articles, one on Edward Livingston's proposed penal code for Louisiana,[41] the other a review of James Mill's article on prisons in the *Encyclopaedia Britannica*.[42] The exposure in these two articles of existing evils in the operation of English criminal law, including the injustice and absurdity of imprisonment for debt and the unwholesome condition of prisons, substantiates all the later charges of Dickens, express and implied, against such abuses. There also appeared in the review an entire article attacking debtors' prisons.[43] The administration of justice in the provinces under a system of unpaid magistrates, and the resulting incompetence, unfairness, and delay, particularly aroused the reviewers' indignation,[44] and they supported enthusiastically Peel's proposed creation of the office of public prosecutor.[45]

Many of the articles on civil law, too, anticipate Dickens. Here the reviewers insisted, following Bentham, that simplicity and promptness of execution should always be sought, and condemned the legalistic mind that glories in needless complications. Their first number contained an attack on the law's delays as witnessed in the Court of Chancery.[46] Two articles, both presumably by Graham, the second, a continuation of the first, being certainly his, exposed the absurdities and abuses of the English system of pleading,[47] preserved because so productive of lawyers' fees. In the number for October, 1826, Bentham himself in the one complete *Westminster* article from his pen[48] advocated simplicity in the method of transferring property. The number containing this article, not announced until January, 1827, was unusually late in appearing, perhaps because of Bentham's delay in writing the article, on which he worked until December 10, 1826.[49] On printing it, Bowring in an editorial note at the beginning stated that Bentham was the author, thus making it the first signed article to appear in a nineteenth-century review. It is also the earliest written in the first person. Other articles advocating law reform are an attack on primogeniture,[50] John Austin's only contribution to the review, a favorable notice of Bentham's attack on the oath in legal proceedings,[51] an attack on laws against usury,[52] and a demonstration of the probable unfairness of special juries appointed by a judge.[53]

The Benthamite organ also contributed to the greatest happiness in the field of medicine. Here the Utilitarians were most fortunate in having as a reviewer Dr. Southwood Smith, who had become a close friend of Bentham and who, according to that prophet's will, presided at the ceremony of receiving his body for dissection in the cause of science. Dr. Smith, generally regarded as one of London's most competent physicians, wrote frequently for the review, attempting to present controversial medical questions in their true light, with the obvious aim of educating the nation on very important and much neglected subjects. His articles are all clear and vivid, easily understandable to the layman, and today fascinating to anyone interested in the state of medical science a hundred years ago. Many of them are illustrated. Particularly valuable is his "The Use of the Dead to the Living,"[54] the only important article which he devoted primarily to advocating a specific reform. Pleading that dead bodies should be made legally available to medical students for dissection, he sketched the history of the growth of knowledge in medicine and demonstrated that students should have specimens to dissect. "Ignorant physicians and surgeons are the most deadly enemies of the community." Only by the practice of dissection could that ignorance be overcome. He pointed out that since there was no legal method whereby students might procure dead bodies, they had to resort to employing "resurrection men" who did not scruple to indulge in the revolting and criminal practice of exhumation. The bodies of persons dying in prisons and workhouses, if unclaimed by immediate relatives, and in fact all unclaimed bodies, Dr. Smith maintained, should be sold to medical students. This article was widely reprinted in England, and also appeared in pamphlet form in the United States, where, as Dr. Smith pointed out, the same conditions obtained, and it was largely influential in securing the needed reform.

As physician of the London Fever Hospital he contributed two papers[55] on those mysterious diseases, typhus, yellow fever, and what he called plague. In these articles he maintained stoutly that such fevers are not contagious like smallpox and measles, but spread by some other means, evidently "exhalations" rising from marshes and from badly drained and unsanitary urban regions. Dr. Smith pointed out that "it was common to see four, six, or even eight individuals of the same family simultaneously affected; that is in the same day, the same hour, the same instant. This might have arisen from an exposure to a pestilential air; it could not have arisen from contagion."[56] These articles, though they do include propaganda for sanitary regulations, the work to which Dr. Smith was later to devote much attention, are written primarily from the point of view of the scientific popularizer.

Later essays in anatomy and physiology[57] preserve this same point of view, and should have been extremely valuable to readers of the *Westminster*. It must have been fascinating and perhaps startling to learn of the similarity in cellular structure existing between lower animals and man, and to be told of studies in embryology leading to the conclusion that "the form of the brain in man, as its exists in this early stage of his foetal life, is precisely similar to the form of the brain in fish as it exists in its permanent and adult state,"[58] and that "the elementary parts of the nervous system in all the classes are identical."[59] Though there were many medical journals available at that time to members of the profession, the *Westminster* alone provided such information for laymen, before the Society for the Diffusion of Useful Knowledge began publishing its pamphlets.

Other distinctly humanitarian enterprises of the review are represented by Ellis's able articles supporting the movement for the abolition of slavery in the West Indies and suggesting plans for the gradual manumission of the slaves,[60] and an acutely logical paper by Charles Hay Cameron exposing the absurdity of dueling and the code of duel.[61] Edwin Chadwick's first identified article in the *Westminster*[62] demonstrated with the aid of very adequate statistics that in view of increasing longevity the rates charged by life assurance companies were too high. Ostensibly reviewing the 1819 *Catalogue of the British Museum,* the review published in 1827 a spirited attack on the regulations of public libraries which made them generally inaccessible to the public.[63] Anticipating much agitation on the subject in succeeding decades, the reviewer stated that "we cannot believe that any nation under the canopy of heaven can equal, much less surpass us in locking readers out of libraries."

The review was far from provincial, and concerned itself much with affairs abroad. Regarding England's own colonies, it generally followed Bentham and advocated emancipating them. This position was emphasized in a leading article on Canada,[64] which stated that the people of that country were "waiting but for a favourable opportunity to rescue themselves from our subjection and throw themselves upon the protection of the United States,"and that such an event would be good for both England and Canada. "No nations on the face of the globe are so well governed, or so prosperous as the United States," the faithful *Westminster* reviewer declared, so Canada would lose nothing. England's trade with Canada was so trifling that England would lose nothing, and emancipation would save the expense and trouble of maintaining the colony. Best to emancipate Canada and let her do as she liked. As we have noted, the reviewers favored treating Ireland in the same way; but meanwhile they found it desirable to propose measures for reform there. They pointed out that the governing aristocracy of Ireland was incredibly corrupt, and that absenteeism was consequently a splendid thing and to be encouraged;[65] in a leading article[66] they advocated for the Irish much instruction in the doctrine of Malthus, this to take the place of state aid provided for in poor laws. In their one article on India[67] they demonstrated at length the evils of English misgovernment there, but gave the impression that a reformed English government would be best for all concerned.

The reviewers evidenced interest in the popular cause everywhere

—in Spain,[68] France,[69] and particularly Greece, Bowring's connection with the Greek Committee providing two articles[70] on the subject, as well as a defense of the Greek Committee from the general charge of fraud and mismanagement.[71] They were strongly anti-Russian and bitter enemies of the Holy Alliance, as is evidenced by a violent article[72] and, as we shall see, by Bowring's rejection of an article on Prussia because it contained opinions not uncomplimentary to that empire.

Throughout they proved themselves thoroughgoing rationalists, insisting that all political measures should be considered in the pure light of reason, and that emotion or prejudice should not be allowed to stand in the way of arriving at the truth. Their paper on Bentham's *Book of Fallacies*,[73] a work more ably treated in the *Edinburgh* by Sydney Smith in his "Noodle's Oration,"[74] demonstrates their passion for clear thinking. "The wisdom of our ancestors," the reviewer points out, is no valid reason for accepting or rejecting a method of procedure, nor is precedent. Every question must be settled on its own merits. Several fallacies stand in the way of intelligent action—"Nobody complains, and therefore nobody suffers"; "We may pave the way for mischievous propositions hereafter"; and "Why should we disturb the tranquillity of affairs?" Then there are the fallacies transferring emphasis from the measure to the man advocating it; and there is fear of a proposal because someone calls it a theory. The reviewer goes on to demonstrate further that extraneous elements are allowed all too frequently to enter into a discussion and obscure the true issues. To do the Benthamites justice, it should be stated that in the *Westminster* before 1828 one finds few glaring examples of the fallacies which the reviewer deplores.

Glancing back over the work of the political department of the review, we find its position on affairs of the day generally clear-cut and uncompromising, its comments emphatic but never undignified. In its criticism of the government it was outspoken, but it carefully kept within the law and avoided prosecution. On the whole there is much justification for the praise bestowed upon it by the *London Magazine*,[75] even though Southern's interest in both the *London* and the *Westminster* casts over the eulogy something of a shadow. Discussing the three reviews, the *London* found that the *Westminster* preserved even more effectively than the others the ideal of uniformity and consistency; that the personality of its contributors was completely submerged in the authoritative "we." Furthermore, declared the *London,*

The writers in the Westminster are men of clear ideas, powerful language, and with a considerable portion of disputatious bitterness and tenacity. They possess peculiar opinions; and by their consistency and skill in maintaining the tenets derived from the premises from which they set out, they are formidable adversaries. The grand distinction between the Westminster reviewers and the Edinburgh is that the former have a system. . . The Edinburgh reviewers have, as a class, imagination; the Westminster reviewers are destitute of it, but they are acute, logical, and energetic. The strong writers support their system, while the system makes the feeble among them strong.

And, discounting generously this bit of puffing, we cannot deny that *Westminster* reviewing was sufficiently intelligent and vigorous to warrant enthusiastic praise. Of course it is impossible to estimate its share in bringing about the reform movements for which the nineteenth century is distinctive, but it surely did all that a dignified propagandist could to promote in politics what it considered the greatest happiness. Even at the risk of offending the shades of its anti-chivalric contributors, we must remember the *Westminster Review* as the most important crusader of the decade.

IV

THE NEW CULTURE

Suppose the political objectives of the Benthamite intellectuals attained: suppose the aristocracy displaced; the middle class, in power, rendered more comfortable and prosperous by the official adoption of the specific reform measures for which the reviewers had fought. The Utilitarians and their liberal allies might well count such innovations a considerable achievement. But the picture would still be incomplete, for the Philosophic Radicals desired results of much broader scope than mere political success, important as that was.

From the winter of 1821, when I first read Bentham, and especially from the commencement of the *Westminster Review* [writes John Stuart Mill in his *Autobiography*], I had what might truly be called an object in life; to be a reformer of the world. My conception of my own happiness was entirely identified with this object. The personal sympathies I wished for were those of fellow laborers in this enterprise.[1]

Nothing, then, short of a far-reaching transformation of the human scene would satisfy this boy-idealist, the founder of that most unusual club of young men, the Utilitarian Society. The *Westminster Review* itself contains clear evidence that the other members of the Benthamite group were infused in varying degrees with the same lofty idealism, obviously not the sort of aspiration to be content merely with the transference of political power from one class to another.

In considering what the reformers did want, it may be helpful here to restate briefly the social gospel that inspired them. According to Bentham, their efforts should be directed toward the increase not primarily of humanity's wealth or holiness or intelligence, but of humanity's happiness. Other achievements are important only so far as they assist in the realization of the principal objective. This objective, "the greatest happiness of the greatest number," is to be

attained by instructing each individual in the pleasurable and painful consequences of various actions, teaching him to think for himself, and then as far as possible relieving him of restrictions and
inhibitions. The instruction is manifestly important, for without
it man will not know what his best interests are. The removal of
restrictions is equally important, for without it man may not be able
to achieve his best interests however clearly he may know them.
Reflecting on this far-reaching and comprehensive program, we can
see how closely Benthamite propaganda must relate what may be
broadly termed the political with what may be broadly termed the
cultural. We have pointed out the relationship between political
bias and literary judgment in the earlier reviews of the century, the
Edinburgh and the *Quarterly;* in the *Westminster* we shall discover
a very close connection between politics and something broader,
the concept of the good life as a whole, literature included.

The review does not contain any single articles in which a reviewer undertakes to describe the Utilitarian cultural ideal in detail,
to define clearly what the Benthamites considered the attributes of
the good life, or to state precisely in what the greatest happiness
of the greatest number was to consist; but all this may be pieced
together with some accuracy, though it should not be assumed that
every reviewer would endorse fully all the parts of the composite
description. So let us turn again to the pages of the *Westminster
Review,* from 1824 to 1828.

In reading an iconoclastic article entitled "Present System of
Education"[2] we make discoveries, among them that the reviewers
are not interested in political agitation alone. In education the English still hold, says the writer of this article, to

the imperfect machinery which we have received from our ancestors.
From these same ancestors we received the distaff, the horse-mill, and
the coracle. Those we have converted into the cotton-engine, the steam
engine, and the three-decker. . . We have despised our ancestors, and
we have proved their wisdom folly. And, as we have despised them, we
have risen and flourished.

Thanks to progress and reform, he goes on, we are no longer
"marching, under the influence of insanity and a red rag, to war on
Palestine and pestilence."

Instead [continues the same reviewer], we have invented steam-engines and parliaments; and, what is more, we persist in attempting to improve both. Yet we neglect that fundamental engine, that very machine of all machines with which we must work out these results. We forget that, in all this, man himself is the first mover; and while we labour to reform and improve his actions, and to profit by his action, we neglect his principle of action, and forget to cultivate or create those powers, of which we would still reap the effects.

Clearly this reviewer realized that man himself must have a place in "our glorious gains." Clearly, too, the future welfare of humanity was closely associated in his mind with what we have come to regard as a characteristic Victorian cult, the cult of progress, which has firm roots in a characteristic eighteenth-century doctrine, the doctrine of perfectibility.

In nineteenth-century England, the *Westminster* reviewers were the first systematic popularizers of this cult, which in its intellectual phase secured among their contemporaries the appellation of "the march of mind," a phrase employed sometimes with reverence and sometimes with contempt. The Benthamites were alert enough to have at least some intimation of the general revolutionary influence of the age of invention, in the early years of which they were aware they were living. Already mechanical progress, effecting unprecedented and to the middle class extremely pleasant changes in society, appeared to justify a belief that the world was about to be transformed—as indeed it was. The eighteenth-century psychology that was accepted by the Utilitarians naturally led them to suppose that intellectual progress likewise might be unlimited, since the mind grew mechanically and by the activity of Hartley's vibriatiùncles[3] could digest anything that was fed it. The growth of the mind, then, depended only on its getting enough food, and the quality of its growth could be determined by the quality of the food provided for it. Its functioning, according to these associationists, was as mechanical as its development. Hence the reviewer wrote advisedly when he referred to man as "that fundamental engine, that very machine of all machines." Furthermore, it naturally would appear shameful to him that the human mind should stand still when he had reason to hope that progress was almost a law of the universe, and when everything else was being improved. "The march of mind" was a well-justified dream.

As we have seen, the training of the intellect was fundamentally necessary in the working out of the Utilitarian program; and the cult of progress made it appear doubly important. Man must grow intellectually in order to perceive his best interests, and to keep in harmony with the scientific development of his times.

Before the constructive tasks of education could begin, however, two nuisances had to be abated. One was the Church of England. The other was censorship of the press. Both institutions being regarded as foes to intellectual liberty, it is not surprising that their chief antagonists among the reviewers were the two Mills.

The Church was a pet antipathy of the elder Mill, for it seemed to him to stand squarely in the way of all reform, political as well as cultural. On this subject Mill spoke for the Utilitarian group in two long, vigorous, and carefully reasoned articles. The first is an attack on the *Quarterly's* principal reviewer, the famous renegade Robert Southey, and his *The Book of the Church*.[4] The book, Mill maintains, is an attempt to charm the unwary by a recital of the past glories of the establishment. He finds that in it Southey has committed almost all the crimes against logic as set forth in Bentham's *Fallacies;* the crime of appealing to prejudice and not reason, of employing abusive language against all dissenters, of utilizing the glorious past to excite loyalty to the inglorious present. Mill points out incidentally that the past actually holds little for Southey to boast of:

it is one of the most remarkable things about the Church of England that she has produced so few men eminent for anything, even the priestly virtues. . . For one martyr that the Church of England can produce, the Church of Rome can produce thousands.

He makes a particular point of demonstrating the unsaintly qualities of Laud, whom Southey adopted as his leading saint.

But Southey's book, according to Mill, is more than a sample of the bad reasoning of the defenders of the Church, more even than a demonstration of the intellectual poverty of its past. It is most interesting of all for

the full evidence which it exhibits of the hostility which the church has displayed, so constantly as to show that it is one of the elements of its nature, to the great interests of mankind, to all those securities which are necessary to save the Many from becoming the victims of the Few. . .

This statement admits of explanation and justification, and Mill hastens with very effective logic to supply the need. "A corporation of priests is indeed unfortunately situated with regard to all the higher moralities. They have an interest in degrading the human mind; and of any considerable number of men the majority are always governed by their interest." First, they form an alliance offensive and defensive with the civil government to secure themselves against all competitors for their places. Thus to obtain government protection, it is necessary for them to support the existing order in the state in all respects, injustice not excepted, and to discourage all free thought. The more degraded the human mind, the more secure the monopoly. Then, not content with mere freedom from competition, they increase their power still further by acting upon the ignorant fears of their individual victims.

The fears which the priest has to act with, are the fears of invisible powers. But these fears are always most intense, when the human mind is most degraded. When illuminated and strong, it completely excludes those fears; it ascends to just conceptions of the laws of the universe, and admits no idea of a God, but that of a perfect intelligence, the object not of fear, but of love.

To the mind in this enlightened state, knowing the kindly will of a just God,

the idea of a priest as a teacher of this will, still more as a mediator for averting the wrath, is merely ridiculous. The priest has therefore the strongest conceivable interest in preventing the human mind from acquiring this clearness and strength. . . It is his interest to perpetuate the reign of ignorance and darkness, to prevent the diffusion of education among the people, and if that cannot be done, to get the management of it into his own hands, and to fix it as completely as possible upon frivolous objects; above all things, to prevent the diffusion of good books, especially every book that criticizes him and his system;

to prevent the freedom of the press, if possible, altogether; but if that is impossible, perpetually to decry it, and reduce the liberty allowed it, within the narrowest limits.

It appears to us, for these, and for many reasons . . . that a corporation of priests, dependent upon the government, is entirely Antichristian. . .

Throughout this declaration of war upon the Established Church, Mill shows no mercy toward either the institution or its defender, Southey, whom he accuses of gross misrepresentation at practically every turn.

Strangely enough, the article evoked no comment from any of the numerous ecclesiastical journals of the time, or indeed from other organs of orthodoxy. Yet the anti-clerical tone of the *Westminster* was by no means unnoticed. Probably typical was the resentment of the governing board of the circulating library at Leeds. According to the story told by the provincial liberal, John Marshall, in a letter to Bentham, the committee excluded the offending journal from the library, which had "a large income and six hundred subscribers." Marshall twice endeavored without success to have it restored, being on one occasion "opposed by a clerical gentleman . . . on the grounds of the intemperance of the language and the virulent attacks on our establishment in church and state. It was conceded that the work was conducted with great ability, but the prejudice excited against it could not be overcome. . . ."[5] There is no record of greater tempests than this directly brought on by the reviewers' opposition to the Establishment. It was not until the passing of the Reform Bill made the menace of liberal thought immediate that any of the clergy took decided steps to defend the Church against the influence of such opinions as those expressed by Mill. When the new government, made bold by that influence, laid hands on certain Irish bishoprics, John Keble responded with his famous Sermon on National Apostasy, from which Newman dates an event far-reaching in its consequences, the beginning of the Tractarian Movement. So indirectly Mill may have had a slight influence on the Church in a way that he would scarcely have predicted.

Incidentally, the utterances of the reviewers on religion itself appear today notable rather for orthodoxy than for radicalism. Not only did they avoid an open break with Christianity; they took pains to appear definitely Christian. Such an attitude must have been due in part to the real devotion of the hymn-writing editor, who may have somewhat augmented the journal's apparent religious faith by his emendations. However achieved, a distinctly Christian tone is preserved throughout so consistently that even a spirited defense of the new geologists[6] does not assert their right to be heterodox but declares their science consistent in large measure with orthodoxy. While contending that "it is a most mistaken view of the purpose of revelation to consider it as intended for the discovery or communication of physical truths," the reviewer yet finds geology affording "many and beautiful proofs of the Divine power and superintendence." Yet consistent and violent hostility to the Establishment must have made the reviewers appear wicked to many of their contemporaries.

Mill's second attack on that institution, published in April, 1826,[7] restates and expands much of the material outlined in his earlier paper. Particularly it emphasizes the hostility of the clergy to freedom of the press.

Journalistic propagandists themselves, the *Westminster* reviewers did not underestimate the importance of the press in the campaign of education. Their careful examination of their rivals, the *Quarterly* and the *Edinburgh,* and their valuable articles on the newspapers of the time,* aim to safeguard their readers against pernicious journalism and to direct them toward the reliable in periodical literature. Their first article on newspapers, published July, 1824, contains a paragraph prophetic of the vast changes which the press was destined to effect and was at that time effecting in the new reading public.

The newspapers . . . are the best and surest civilizers of a country. They contain within themselves not only the elements of knowledge but the inducements to learn. There is no one so uninstructed, there is no one so ignorant, who cannot find in them something which he can learn. . . The understandings of their readers are led on by degrees

* Important articles on newspapers of the 1820's are: Vol. II, pp. 194ff, "Newspapers"; Vol. X, pp. 216ff, "Newspaper Press"; Vol. XII, pp. 69ff, "Provincial, Scotch, and Irish Newspaper Press."

from the simplest domestic occurrences to those which affect their remotest interest, or appeal to their noblest sympathies: from the overturning of a coach to the overturning of an empire. . . The instruction is conveyed, not by the direct inculcation of opinions, but by the habit of looking beyond the narrow circle of one's personal observation to the results of a more enlarged observation.[8]

Hence the reviewers demanded freedom of the press as another important step in the process of setting up the new intellect machinery. The principal articles on this subject were written by the younger Mill, who was as hostile to restrictions on the press as his father was to the monopoly of the Church. The two topics were closely related, James Mill having pointed out clearly that the clergy had an interest in preventing free discussion "if possible, altogether." His son's first article on liberty of the press deals with the prosecution of the radical, Richard Carlile, for publishing and selling the works of Tom Paine. Carlile had been heavily fined and imprisoned, and though the Benthamites did not approve of his brand of radicalism, Mill defends in this article the desirability of allowing every man to print what he chooses.[9]

Adopting a cause for which he later became famous, he demonstrates the uselessness of attempting to prevent by legal action the free expression of opinion. A typical *Westminster* reviewer and an astute practitioner of the Aristotelian rhetoric, he protests his loyalty to Christianity* while insisting that belief must not be imposed by law. He emphasizes the usefulness of public discussion in establishing truth, and argues that attacks on Christianity, if freely permitted, will cause Christians to provide a reasoned defense of their creed. Such a defense, if the champions have truth on their side, will lead all thinkers to a sound and sincere faith in the Christian teachings. Freedom to attack the Church will exercise a salutary influence on the clergy, who, fearing the possible exposure of corruption and inactivity, will lead godly, righteous, and sober lives even against their will. "The honour of the church is

* II, 4: "Nothing can be more desirable, nothing could be more felicitous, than for every member of a civil community to be completely under the influence of Christian principles." Or again, II, 9: "Christianity is the only true faith in our opinion."

better looked after when all her faults are 'set in a note-book, learned, and conn'd by rote, to cast in her teeth.' " One pauses to admire the effectiveness of the youthful reasoning machine, and his facility in quoting Shakespeare to his purpose. By figures on the sale of Paine's *Age of Reason,* he shows that prosecution excites popular sympathy for the prosecuted and increases his influence over the uneducated, whom it is desired to protect from it. The article is a masterly demonstration of Mill's cardinal position, that "freedom of discussion has generally the happiest effects on the mind and manners of the people, on the progress of intellect, and the diffusion of knowledge."

This article was followed by a second,[10] treating the law of libel as applied generally to freedom of political discussion. The government as well as the Church, one learns, has an interest in degrading the human mind;

. . . there are many subjects, and these the most important of all, on which it is the interest of the government, not that the people should think right, but, on the contrary, that they should think wrong: on these subjects, therefore, the government is quite sure, if it has the power, to suppress, not the false and mischievous opinions, but the great and important truths. . . It is the interest of rulers that the people should believe all their proceedings to be the best possible: every thing, therefore, which has a tendency to make them think otherwise, . . . government will use its most strenuous exertions to prevent.*

When it is considered that the law of libel is entirely a judge-made law, Mill argues, and that the government decides what opinions may be expressed and what may not, the injustice of the situation becomes apparent.† The government decides what the

* Cf. Cobbett's *Political Register,* particularly 1810-12, for constant repetition of the identical message.

† Mill supports his contention that the law of libel is judge made and conceived in tyranny by careful reference to Holt's authoritative treatise on that law. See *Westminster Review,* III, 314f: " 'Everything,' says Mr. Holt, 'is a libel, the purpose of which is, to misrepresent and find a handle for faction.' But what is faction? Every man opposing ministers. What is misrepresentation? Falsehood. Who is to judge what is falsehood? The government: and the government, therefore, is to judge its own cause; the government is to decide upon the truth or falsehood

people may legally believe, and thus "possesses absolute control over their actions, and may wield them for [its] own purposes with perfect security." Fortunately the exercise of this tremendous power over the press is controlled to a certain extent by the government's fear of public opinion, otherwise there would be no more freedom of expression at all.

Mill then tears up and casts to the winds the argument that the people are incapable of forming correct opinions, that the government must protect them.

An ignorant man [he points out], even if he decide at haphazard, has a chance of being sometimes in the right. But he who adopts every opinion which rulers choose to dictate, is always in the wrong, when it is their interest that he should be so, that is, on the most momentous of all topics.

Another question [he continues] which it does not suit those who make the ignorance of the people a plea for enslaving them to put, is, why are they ignorant? because to this question there can be only one answer, namely, that if they are ignorant, it is precisely because that discussion, which alone can remove ignorance, has been withheld from them. And although their masters may find it convenient to speak of their ignorance as incurable, we take the liberty of demurring to this conclusion, until the proper remedy shall have been tried. The remedy is, instruction: and of instruction, discussion is the most potent instrument.

Such was the case of the *Westminster* reviewers in behalf of general enlightenment, against the pernicious combination of Church and State which was selfishly trying to prevent the march of mind. It was obvious to the Philosophic Radicals that the monopolists were afraid of the march of mind, knowing that once it had produced what for the sake of convenience we may christen "the New Man" it would send the aristocracy the way of "the distaff, the horse-mill, and the coracle." The *Westminster's* readers would not mourn because of that. So the review attracted a loyal following for its educational program, consistent as that was with the material aspirations of the middle class. The potential New

---

of a charge of error against itself, and if it pronounces the charge to be false, it is to have the power of inflicting punishment, to any extent, upon the accuser."

Man would believe in the new intellect as much as the reviewers wished if by doing so he could hope to enjoy the privileges of a noble lord. Thus, for some ten years, a distinctly intellectual group was allied with the middle class, and the members of that class did not object so long as the intellectuals were getting them what they wanted. They would even read the *Westminster Review* (in coffee houses), in spite of the heavy logic and the quotations in Latin, Greek, and French.

It does not appear to have occurred to the reviewers at all generally that the New Man might be recruited to any extent from the so-called lower orders. The younger Mill did see the possibility and state it. Writing of the dangers to the uneducated of a free and uncensored press, he says,

Give them education. Let them have it as extensively and rapidly as possible. Every body allows that there is no danger now to the educated class. Let there be no other class. This may not be an immediate remedy; but it is the only effective and permanent one.[11]

Yet it was not until 1830, after the Philosophic Radical group had withdrawn from the review, that the truly oppressive Taxes on Knowledge were honored with an article of their own. The stamp tax on newspapers and periodicals made the price of reading matter almost prohibitive to all except the upper and middle classes, and prevented the dissemination of knowledge even more effectively than the law of libel. But when finally the matter was treated at length, the emphasis was rather on the dangers of machine-breaking as a result of lower-class illiteracy, than on the illiteracy itself or the degraded condition of the illiterate.

The laborers, one learns, should be taught the laws of political economy and kept in their place. As we shall see, they were to be trained primarily as servants of the New Man. In things cultural as in things political, Benthamite idealism burned chiefly to enlighten the middle class. That to us such idealism seems outworn is a good commentary on the march of mind. In 1824 a middle-class culture seemed attainable; beyond that no clear-headed radical thought of going. As late as 1840 a Tory could refer to the mild Reform Bill as the "Act for Giving Everybody Everything."[12] If the

Utilitarians had been what we today would call radical, they would have accomplished nothing except perhaps a revolution.

The views of the *Westminster* on the education which was to produce the middle-class culture, and on that culture itself, are expressed frequently throughout the journal: sometimes tucked away in reviews of such works as Dupin's *Commercial Power of Britain* or the latest parliamentary report on charities. The substance of these remarks is accessible in three articles[13] dealing specifically with this subject and well worth reading by anyone interested in the history of nineteenth-century English culture.

We have observed that the reviewers considered man to be a "fundamental engine." One of them, Dr. Southwood Smith, defined education as "the process by which the mind of man, possessed with powers but unfurnished with ideas, is stored with knowledge and enabled to apply this to the business of life."[14] The business of life he considered it unnecessary to state, remarking that "at every stage of society, and in our own very decidedly, it is understood by the enlightened community."[15] Furthermore, "the business of life is no longer what it was."[16] In other words, education must adapt itself to prepare the young for whatever new social conditions they will have to face in their own age.

Elsewhere in the review we find the statement of a more inclusive aim in education:

to cultivate and enlarge the human faculty to its utmost verge, to elevate and improve the moral faculty to the last extent of its susceptibility, to store the mind with knowledge, and to render the corporeal powers that which nature designed them, under exertion, to be.[17]

One suspects that in most particulars the reviewers would have approved of T. H. Huxley's famous description of the liberally educated man, whose body, it may be remembered, "does with ease and pleasure all the work that, as a mechanism, it is capable of," and "whose intellect is a clear, cold logic engine."[18] Their ideal seems generally virtuous as far as it goes, but does it include enough? These reviewers were partially determining the culture of Victorian England, though they had no assurance of that fact. What sort of culture will it be?

The answer is generally known from the event; but let us compare it with the prophecy, which, fortunately or not, was in some respects unfulfilled. Particularly important are the remarks of Dr. Smith, who in the first number of the journal, at Bentham's request, reviewed that sage's plan of education for the middle and upper classes, the *Chrestomathia*.[19] It should be remembered that Dr. Smith, a close friend of Bentham's, was himself a man of sense and culture, having prepared for the Unitarian ministry before entering medicine, and especially that according to all accounts he was an unusually benevolent gentleman and a genuine humanitarian.

Education, Dr. Smith states, "has not hitherto accomplished all the wonders it is capable of producing." He regards this deplorable circumstance as due largely to the fact that Westminster and Oxford are proceeding under the same system that obtained there at the time of Edward the Confessor. They taught Latin and Greek then; they still teach Latin and Greek, and little else. Education has not progressed; "no plan of instruction has been adopted for those who are to be engaged in the active business of life." In school they can learn only language, and for this learning the only available instruments have been the "execrable" Westminster and Eton grammars.

Here the reviewer pauses for a remarkable explanation. We do not want, he says, to be considered hostile to the study of classical literature.

. . . It has great value, especially as a means of exercising the intellectual faculties, and is conducive to the formation of a pure and correct taste; to a gentleman it is highly ornamental; to a member of the learned professions it is indispensable: but we object altogether [he continues] to the mode in which it is taught; we object still more to the space which it is allowed to occupy in the common course of instruction; and we object to its forming any part of the education of a very important class of the community, to whom, at least as it is at present communicated, experience proves it to be utterly useless.

Certain things, then, to "a very important class in the community," those "who are to be engaged in the active business of life," are neither requisite nor necessary. The "great value" of the classics as a means of "exercising the intellectual faculties" does not concern them. Neither does "the formation of a pure and correct taste," a process in which the classics also have great value. There will be a distinct intellectual gulf fixed between "those who are to be engaged in the active business of life" on the one hand, and the "gentleman" and the "member of the learned professions" on the other. This distinction is clearly drawn later in the same article.

For the lawyer, the physician, the divine, the scholar, the senator, and the statesman, Latin and Greek are indispensable. To men who are to be occupied in the ordinary business of life, whose main object is to become acquainted with things, and who are to think only in order to act, Latin and Greek are comparatively useless. . . . They have nothing in common with the business of the world as it is transacted now: they do not enter into men's thoughts: they do not form the topic of conversation in society: they are obsolete: they no longer have an habitation or a name, except in some degree in literature; and they possess no power of developing the human faculties which is not at least equalled by other branches of learning.

It is surprising that Matthew Arnold, then a mere infant in his second year, survived at all the atmospheric disturbance incident upon the publication of this piece of Philistinism. On the other hand, it may of course have served a useful purpose in hastening the birth of Huxley, who first saw the light the year following. If we ourselves could be transplanted to 1824, we should certainly agree with the reviewer in considering the almost exclusively classical curriculum of school and university quite inadequate. Yet we should question the extreme earnestness which excluded from the common man's education everything not immediately useful, and should wonder whether "the greatest happiness" were really best to be achieved thus.

Returning to Dr. Smith's article, we find that the middle class, described as "the strength of the community," the class which "contains, beyond all comparison, the greatest proportion of the intelligence, industry, and wealth of the state," is to be educated, not by a Greek distaff or a Latin horse-mill, but appropriately enough by a modern invention, Bentham's *Chrestomathia*.

The successful operation of the new plan depends largely on what Dr. Smith figuratively describes as "a machine of immense power capable of producing the most extraordinary effects"—the system originated by Lancaster. This system, which the schoolmaster whom Brougham had officially declared to be abroad in the land was already using generally, provided that by a varyingly complicated arrangement of student monitors the bright boys taught the dull ones while the master merely supervised the process. Somewhat ill-advisedly, as time has demonstrated, the reviewer declares the machine to be "an improvement in the art of teaching . . . of more importance to the advancement of knowledge than any discovery that has been made since the invention of the alphabet itself." Bentham in the *Chrestomathia* extends the system beyond elementary instruction to a complete plan of education, including "the whole field of knowledge."

The "Chrestomathic Instruction Tables," which fulfill this generous ambition, could have been designed only by a Bentham. There were two of them, one describing the new system, the other applying it: both admirable, though the march of mind has rendered them amusing antiques. The reviewer outlines the first in detail. It is divided into five columns.

The first column states the advantages which are to be derived from intellectual instruction; namely, that it is a security against idleness, considered as a source of sensuality and mischievousness; that it is a security against ennui; that it is a security for admission into good company, &c.

This part of the mechanism, it is evident, will teach the raw material why it ought to be educated, undeniably "a question to be asked." The second column concerns itself with grounds for determining the order in which subject matter should be taught, such as "the natural pleasantness of the subject." The third and fourth columns present the curriculum. What the fifth column presents the reviewer neglects to state.

The curriculum is divided into stages, five in all, and the stages in turn into subdivisions in appalling numbers. After the Chrestomathic child has acquired the three R's, his real instruction will begin with "natural history," including mineralogy, botany, zoölogy, geography, geometry in its simpler phases, "historical chronology," and "biographical chronology." Drawing is to be used extensively in this instruction. He will then advance to natural philosophy: this, the second stage, includes mechanics (hydro-statics, hydraulics, mechanical pneumatics, acoustics, optics), or-ganic and inorganic chemistry, magnetism, electricity, galvanism, and ballistics. The work of the first stage will be continued in more advanced form. At this stage also the New Man will pick up his comparative philology. The later stages continue the instruction of the first two, with appropriate additions. The third stage con-tributes geology, architecture, husbandry, and physical economics, "mechanics and chemistry applied to domestic management, and other common purposes of life." History will be included here, and the comparative philology will be continued. The fourth stage adds "hygiantics or hygiastics." The student in his last stage is to be exposed principally to higher arithmetic, geometry, and algebra, along with "uranological or astronomical chronology" and book-keeping. Here he will receive also a kind of trades orientation course, and will learn "the advantages in regard to the dispatch and perfection of which the principle of the division of labour is productive."*

That the system is entirely practicable the reviewer has no doubt. The machinery has been tested and proved to possess "immense power." To a thoroughgoing perfectibilitarian, "the most extra-ordinary effects" waited only on the efficient use of that power. The proposed curriculum he considers ideal. "The subjects them-

---

* The salutary results of such a course are described as follows: "Thus the Chrestomathic school would become a source of general communica-tion, a channel through which the several sorts of artists might receive from one another instruction in points of practice, at present peculiar to each. The carpenter, the joiner, the cabinet-maker, the turner in wood, the ship-builder, the white-smith, the black-smith, the metal-founder, the printer, the engraver, the mathematical instrument maker, the taylor, the shoe-maker, the collar-maker, the saddler, the distiller, the brewer, the sugar-maker, the bread-maker, etc.; the respective tools and other imple-ments of the several artists, together with the operations performed by many of them, would thus be compared together, and a comparative and comprehensive view be given of the points of resemblance and difference."

selves are naturally interesting to the human mind," concrete and tangible, stimulating to the curiosity. Best of all, they have a real value in "the business of life," altered as that has been by the new industrialism. The teaching of history, economics, and political science will insure the achievement of "the ultimate object of all education," the formation of "enlightened men and virtuous citizens." History and political science, taught, one gathers, as a single course, called history but conducted as political science, will assist in the creation of true standards of social values. Economics will demonstrate

the capital advantages of commerce, the manner in which it produces those advantages, the circumstances on which its power of increasing the wealth and prosperity of a country depends. . . . There is no subject [the reviewer continues] in which this class of the community is more deeply interested . . . than that of political economy.

Of this there could be no manner of doubt, as later intellectuals were to learn to their sorrow by actual observation. The Philistine was a foe to sweetness and light because there was no subject in which he was more deeply interested than "the capital advantages of commerce."

The *Chrestomathia,* Dr. Smith believes, will contribute not only to intellectual but to moral growth. The system includes student self-government, whereby discipline is to be maintained exclusively by the boys themselves. It is by this phase of the instruction that the students will secure very necessary practice in the ways of justice and in the pleasure-pain sanction of morals. In studying hygiastics and ballistics they should form habits of industry and well-doing, and emerge from the machine paragons of virtue.

Their time is completely occupied: their attention is constantly fixed: they are never idle: they never deviate from a regular and steady course. . . . If the temptation to bodily listlessness and mental dissipation occur, they are immediately roused to exertion by the active spirits around them, and compelled to put forth their strength, in order to keep pace with companions, by whom they would feel it an intolerable disgrace to be outstripped. . . . The mind is induced to postpone its gratification as often as its temptation to yield to it recurs, and is stimulated to the steady performance of its duty.

Such an ideal might well cause the playboys of *Blackwood's* to view with alarm, as they did, the neglect of "the emotions" in education. There would be no more idle boys; they would all be highly competitive boys, already seriously engaged in "the business of life," which, even for childhood, should be no longer what it had been. Yet such a consummation appeared desirable to a genuine humanitarian, and might have been distinctly useful at the time. Unfortunately the doctrine did not take effect until later, when the doctrine needed was not competition but coöperation.

The crime of encouraging idleness is one of the more serious charges against the public schools and the universities, particularly in the second of the *Westminster* articles on education.[20] This article, a thorough demonstration of the debility of the old machinery, should have annihilated Westminster and Eton, Oxford and Cambridge, completely and for all time. At these institutions, "life and money, labor and industry, are expended on what is unproductive." The prospective citizen is taught "Ovid and Catullus, Homer and drinking, driving curricles or stage-coaches, and rowing boats." After spending his time and money he starts work, having decided perhaps to become a lawyer, and finds that he has to educate himself. Yet pleasant memories, the reviewer states, inspire him to become what we know as the devoted alumnus, though "if the heart of age throbs with recollected delight at an ode of Horace, so might it have throbbed at the movements of a steam-engine, had useful science occupied the place of nonsense-verses." It is difficult to decide whether the reviewer is more bitter against the Eton grammar and "propria quae maribus" in the schools, or "rowing boats" in the universities. The schoolboy learns only to repeat Latin rules parrot-fashion, and the university student develops nothing but a gay and vulgar indifference to thought and information.

The reviewer discovers another bad feature of things as they are: circumstances have conspired to create a monopoly in the educational business and place it in the hands of that despised race, the unscrupulous clergy, who did not themselves create the monopoly but who, finding it, are eager to preserve it. "The system is contrived to support the monopoly, as the monopoly defends the system. It is a profitable trade." Thus there is more than mere inertia to be overcome before a reform can be effected. The *Westminster*, however, pursuing its mission in life, proposes to alter this commercial situation. Readers of the review have already learned that the clergy, interested in "degrading the human mind," have formed an alliance with the existing political order. This reviewer points out that money acquired in degrading the mind further by teaching boys Latin, Greek, and idleness, will enable the Church to defend the *status quo* more effectively. It is possible that the old educational machine would not have appeared so despicably weak to these radical .idealists if it had not been operated by members of the opposing political party. Certainly it would not have appeared so weak to the readers of the radical review. Here is another point of liaison between the new culture and the new politics.

Two years later, a publication of the Society for the Diffusion of Useful Knowledge—Peacock's Steam Intellect Society—furnished the occasion for still another assault upon the powers of intellectual darkness, this time in a leading article.[21] The offensively middle-class reviewer considers the Steam Intellect Society a promising ally in the building of the new civilization, its contribution to be the diffusion of knowledge among the lower classes.

For to the diffusion of knowledge, he points out, we owe all "our glorious gains." Without it the world would never have even begun to emerge from its former state of "feudal despotism and ignorance." "The gradual education of a few effected for them, in time, a certain emancipation, and, successively, wealth, power, and the means of resistance." They became the middle class, whose praises the *Westminster* never tires of singing. From the dawn of civilization until now progress has been slowly making headway.

Suddenly the reviewer becomes inspired with belief in a theory destined to become almost a religion later in the century, moral evolution. In sober Utilitarian prose he says

> Move upward, working out the beast,
> And let the ape and tiger die:

And did Providence send that animal, man, into the world that he should remain what he was born—a fit associate for tigers and lions? Was not

man created for other and higher ends? . . . He who does not aid the
conversion of the human animal into man . . . is immoral, inasmuch
as he is negligent of a serious duty: he who opposes it, is criminal and
sinful, since he counteracts the design of the moral Governor of the
world. . . .²²

The inspiration lasts for only a paragraph. He recalls himself
to the more immediate effects of the diffusion of knowledge among
the lower orders, stops thinking of new possibilities and reverts to
the old radicalism. He suggests that the lower orders may be taught

that early marriages cause low wages and starvation, that industry and
economy are preferable to poor rates and workhouses, and finally, perhaps,
that it is better to work voluntarily in a crane than compulsorily in a
tread-mill. They will learn also to discover when laws are their friends
instead of their enemies; . . . they will even learn to know that there
are unavoidable evils; that some evil must be endured for the sake of some
good; that among conflicting interests, some one must yield and someone
rise; and they will not be in haste to pull down a machine which does
its work, because it does not do this in a perfect manner.

In the lower class it is ignorance, not knowledge, that is dangerous to society. The only reason anyone supposes knowledge dangerous is that it has in the past sometimes become wealth and cast
down the mighty from their seat. The reviewer declares himself
quite willing that with knowledge some individuals among even
the lower classes should climb the ladder to wealth and power, so
long as they climb according to the rules of the game, laissez faire
and constant competition. Those who do not climb, also obeying
the rules of the game, will be quiet and not break up machinery
or annoy their betters with demands for factory legislation. "They
will learn to know that there are unavoidable evils," wrote the
reviewer in justification of certain evils perhaps not quite unavoidable; while Carlyle, still in Edinburgh writing articles on the
Germans and wondering about the business of life, was preparing
himself to create a *Chartism* and a *Past and Present*.

Education, according to the reviewer, will make the lower classes
good and peaceful citizens. Better still, it will enable them to contribute more generously to the wealth of England. Already, thanks
to useful knowledge, much has been accomplished. "It is through

men of science and art, that Britain is the most wealthy, the most powerful, the most naval, the most colonizing, and the most shop-keeping, of nations." How have such men achieved all this, when education has been systematically denied them? No one knows. No thanks to the millions spent on the present system of education that the English are "so clever, and so opulent, and make such beautiful steam-engines." The workers of the past have become the middle class of the present, the backbone of England. The workers of the present are destined also to progress—

That which they have done but earnest of the thing that they shall do. For now they have the *Chrestomathia* and the Steam Intellect Society.

The latter, it is hoped, by training the lower orders to do more skilful work in all the crafts, will fit them to increase the nation's commerce. With proper instruction they will be able, for instance, to make all kinds of mathematical instruments, from which some merchant will derive substantial profits. Perhaps, too, they will learn to make pottery, weave carpets, print cotton, and work in metals—activities "which belong to art purely, as much as they do to what is called simply manufacture." In this type of manu-facturing France has been driving England out of the market, because the French lower orders know the fine arts and have good taste. "An abundance and cheapness of prints, a public exposure of statues, and an universal reading of their own best writers, pro-duce that insensible education which displays itself in matters of art, and which . . . has even rendered them the arbiters of dress in Europe." Such contact with art serves also to improve the character, "to divert them from those brutal and coarse amusements which are the acknowledged disgrace of our populace," even to render them honest and law-abiding. The reviewer becomes so much interested in exposing statues in public that once he refers gaily to "works of mere utility"; but he soon recovers his balance and his under-standing of the true place of the fine arts. "Let art and taste once become common among the people, as it is in France, and com-petition would ensure low prices, or at least fair ones, to both parties: while the effect could not fail to be to increase the demand for our productions of numerous kinds." It would even be well for stonemasons to become familiar with good architecture, to absorb its atmosphere, for thus they would become more useful stonemasons, the builders of medieval cathedrals being good workmen because they were also artists. Ruskin might have been considerably annoyed to encounter this doctrine in the files of the Utilitarian review, though he could have preserved a measure of self-respect by maintaining that the reviewer was putting his cart before his horse.

The *Westminster* abounds in other remarks on the degeneracy of the English plan of education, all expressing the same Utilitarian tendencies, all decided and vigorous, few contributing anything new to the discussion. James Mill in his article entitled "State of the Nation"[23] supports the projected London University, where "utility and dignity" are to be substituted for "ease and dignity." A sentiment later expressed by none other than Carlyle is stated in a paper on legal education:

All persons who have attained to eminence in learning must be sensible that their proficiency was not attained through the aid of their pastors and masters, but in spite of them; that they bolted out of the prescribed course; that they contrived to get into some neighboring library, notwithstanding the vigilance of those that had the care of it; that in contempt of advice and authority, they managed to read some really instructive books. . . .[24]

In April, 1828, the last number before the withdrawal of the Philosophic Radicals, the review devotes forty-seven pages to the "Scientific Education of the Upper Clases."[25] It proposes definitely that the Society for the Diffusion of Useful Knowledge should set itself at work upon the aristocracy. With customary scorn of the elegant as opposed to the useful, the reviewer suggests that it would not hurt the Lords to know something, though Gilbert's peerage by competitive examination appears to have been beyond his imaginative powers.

In the glorification of the march of mind the *Westminster* was not without assistance from its contemporaries. The *Edinburgh* from time to time published "strictures" on Oxford,[26] though these were always less iconoclastic than those of their Radical opponents. Though Cobbett, spokesman of the lower orders, was uniting with the Tories in decrying an educational policy calculated primarily to adapt the laboring man to an industrial civilization,[27] the *Edinburgh* along with the *Westminster* raised its voice in defense of the new London University and the Society for the Diffusion of Useful Knowledge,[28] both pet projects of the Great Whig, Brougham. In general agreement with the Utilitarians on matters of education were Thomas Campbell's *New Monthly Magazine*, and the *London Magazine* under the editorship of the *Westminster's* own Henry Southern.[29] Yet in the campaign for educational reform the leadership of the *Westminster* is noteworthy. Particularly is this true of its utterances on the education of woman and her place in society. Though the reviewers personally were not all in agreement on the question of the rights of women,[30] there is no dissenting opinion expressed anywhere in the review.

The group of younger Radicals headed by John Stuart Mill favored complete intellectual, political, and social equality of the sexes. Good Chrestomathic youths, they were no worshippers of Horace or Catullus, and for them the classical poetic conception of the vine wedded to the elm had no charms. They thought of women as individuals, who, like men, might be improved almost if not quite to the point of perfection. Hence the intellectual welfare of woman and her social rights and privileges, as well as the effect of her subjection upon society as a whole, appeared very important to them.

The younger Mill was the first to approach the subject. His discussion of the *Edinburgh Review*, in the second number of the *Westminster*, contains two paragraphs notable for their advanced views on the position of woman. "He who is restrained by indolence from improving himself, has a direct interest in the non-improvement of others; since, if others improve, and he does not keep pace with them, he must necessarily lose his rank in their estimation. But he is most of all interested in the non-improvement of his wife." It would be humiliating "to rely on her for protec-

tion and guidance"; moreover, were she instructed, she might see
that other men were superior to her husband, or at least his
equals, and would cease to idolize him.

To these causes [Mill continues], must be ascribed the morality which
is usually chalked out for women. . . . The qualities which are said to
constitute excellence in a woman, are very different from those which
constitute excellence in a man. . . . In a woman, helplessness, both of
mind and of body, is the most admired of attributes. . . . To be entirely
dependent upon her husband for every pleasure, and for exemption from
every pain; to feel secure, only when under his protection; to be incapable of forming any opinion, or of taking any resolution without his
advice and aid; this is amiable, this is delicate, this is feminine: while
all who infringe on any of the prerogatives which man thinks proper to
reserve for himself; all who can or will be of any use, either to themselves or to the world, otherwise than as the slaves and drudges of their
husbands, are called masculine, and other names intended to convey
disapprobation.[31]

The *Edinburgh Review,* Mill states, has consistently favored
this deplorable attitude. Perhaps he is hardly fair in this statement,
for as early as 1810 the *Edinburgh* published a long article on the
education of woman which, though it appears to admit that she
is the vine, maintains that she will be a better vine if she is educated
as men are and that the education of woman will stimulate the
desire for education among men.[32] This article Mill does not
mention, but he does cite many cases in proof of his point. He
goes on to accuse the *Edinburgh* of believing the only morality to
be sex morality: "it has affected even prudery." He points as
examples to the articles on Moore's amatory poetry, including the
translation of Anacreon, and the condemnation of Plato "for having expounded, in his *Republic,* the footing upon which he thought
that the marriage contract could most advantageously be placed."
Yet in all other respects, particularly in regard to common honesty,
the *Edinburgh* has been shown to be most immoral.

Among all conceivable methods of atoning for the offense of leaving all
other virtues to shift for themselves—to lay an excessive and dispropor-
tionate stress upon those which are of least importance to society, is surely
the most extraordinary.

For this unintelligent emphasis on a relatively inconsequential matter the fault is laid at the door of the clergy, that diabolic race who have "laid down, not that system of rules which is most conducive to the well-being of the two sexes, or of society at large; but that which is best calculated to promote *their* ascendency."[33] To relegate sex morality to a position among the virtues "which are of least importance to society" is bold doctrine, which the middle class in general was not soon to adopt, and which during the century secured adherents rather among intellectuals and rebels against the social order founded by the Benthamites.

Gallantry toward ladies, an important factor in the encouragement of uselessness as a desirable feminine attribute, the reviewers point out, originated in unalloyed male selfishness. It was no more noble, no more idealistic, than the knights themselves who first displayed it. Here again the Utilitarians find that medievalism has deposited a weight of darkness on the intellect. Chivalric gallantry, John Stuart Mill maintains in his remarkable paper entitled "Age of Chivalry,"[34] was "a species of foppery." Knights fought, "not to make a woman happy, but to make the whole world acknowledge the pre-eminence of her charms." It does not appear to have occurred to Mill that perhaps no useful knowledge would make the lady as happy as this acknowledgment. He declares that such fighting was conceived in male vanity and pride of possession, and that actually medieval woman was not well treated. Proper consideration for women "does not consist in treating them as idols to be worshipped, or as trinkets to be worn for display; any more than in shutting them up like jewels in a case. . . ." Such treatment proves that they are valued; but "the value set upon them is quite compatible with perfect indifference to their happiness or misery." No, the wicked knights were flattering them not out of real regard for their welfare, but because in their half-savage state of knighthood, blessed neither with the active life of the barbarian nor the intellectual excitement of the Chrestomath, their sexual desires were very strong, and "to obtain the woman who was the object of desire became often a matter of extreme difficulty." So the attractive woman of high birth was fought for in tourna-

ments, while "if a baron happened to be smitten by the charms
of the daughter of one of his vassals, he demanded of her father,
as a matter of course, that she should be yielded up to his em-
braces." There remained "the large and unattractive majority" who
were "altogether neglected." This is a painful circumstance, for
"it is the treatment of them, and not that of their more attractive
sisters, which is the test of civilization."

So we see the younger Mill already the sovereign champion of
intelligence and self-reliance in woman, impeded as these qualities
were by her position upon a decorative but thoroughly rotten
pedestal. He was not, however, the only knight-errant in defense
of the probably unattractive. The author of the review of Mills's
History of Chivalry, for example, anticipates Mill's remarks on
gallantry, declaring it bad for both sexes.[35] Women should become
"our companions and coöperators in intellectual pursuits," working
with men "towards the advancement of society in knowledge and
happiness," and never "bestowing their approbation" on those
who treat them as "helpless, dependent, and frivolous." One of the
principal grievances of the reviewers against the popular Letitia
Landon (L.E.L.) is her acquiescence in what Mill was later to
call the subjection of women.[36] The author of an article on the
Louisiana penal code quotes with approval the statement that the
code should not be "exclusively the study of our own sex." He
declares "that the youth of both sexes, before the usual period of
leaving school, are perfectly capable of understanding these subjects," and that this opinion the reviewers "have repeatedly and
earnestly stated to be our own."[37] This is not precisely true; the
phrase "of both sexes" has not been "repeatedly and earnestly" included in similar context. But the writer evidently wishes to give
his review credit for the early and unqualified endorsement of
such an opinion. Four years later, placed by Macaulay's brilliant
debating, it is true, between the horns of a dilemma, Perronet
Thompson was to commit the review definitely to votes for
women.[38]

This completes the sketch of the Utilitarian cultural program
except for one element to be considered later in detail. Though of
course it does not provide a complete explanation of the Victorian

era just ahead, it does in many respects foreshadow both the good and the bad in that era. Reverence for the middle class, faith in education almost as a panacea and in science almost as magic, worship of progress and even belief in moral evolution, above all, earnestness and insistence on individual effort along practical lines —these we have seen to be characteristically Benthamite. According to the prescription of the *Westminster,* the New Man should have been a peaceful, law-abiding citizen and a hard worker, wasting no time on trivialities, his material wants generously supplied; he should have been well informed on many matters of everyday interest and a clear thinker on all topics, easily able to adapt himself to new conditions and happy to assist in the progress which the law of the universe decreed.

Dr. Smith, reviewing the *Chrestomathia,* predicted of the members of the new middle class to be formed by useful education that

above all, their minds would be independent. Understanding everything taught them—they would have taken nothing upon trust, they would have believed nothing upon authority. Knowledge would be communicated to them, the materials of thinking afforded them, and their minds would be left to their own operations.[39]

People so trained, he continues, would at once see the injustice of Negro slavery, of wars stirred up by selfish rulers and fought by their innocent and unoffending subjects, of capital punishment for minor offenses, of the double standard of morals for men and women. Their intelligence would bring about the millenium in government. "What good burgesses, what pure voters, what capital special-jurymen, what admirable judges of libel"[40] they were to become! The result would be happiness for all.

On the whole, the plan of the reviewers might have produced a tolerable culture if it could have been realized in its entirety. Its major emphases reduce to two: intellectual ability to be developed by proper education and free discussion, and energy and earnestness in applying this ability to useful effort. Arnold, writing to reform the ways of the Victorians, once said that culture consisted in knowing the will of God and making it prevail. This is not precisely what the Utilitarians had prescribed, for knowing the will of even Arnold's liberal God was not what they meant by intellectual ability. But their ideal man would not have been so different from Arnold's as the average middle-class Victorian turned out to be; for what they desired was not what happened.

The readers of the *Westminster Review* and their descendants liked certain aspects of Utilitarian thought, but not others. They desired material prosperity, and to achieve this they gladly accepted the doctrine of effort, toward which they were already favorably disposed by training and heredity. They agreed "never to be idle, never to deviate from a regular and steady course." From an excess of this at least tolerably admirable quality which effectively preserved them from "Double-barreled Dilettantism" they were to develop into the Philistines that they are generally admitted to have been; meanwhile they were to remain untouched by high intellectualism and devotion to clear thinking. The New Man, not detecting utility in these virtues, was not much interested in them. All he really demanded of intellectuals was philosophic justification for getting rich. Having found that, he had no reason to search the pages of the *Westminster* further.

Perhaps the fault lay partly in the fact that the New Man never had a chance to be exposed to Bentham's ideal education, which might have improved him even if it could not fulfill the hopes of its advocates by perfecting him. Perhaps the emphasis of his would-be instructors was wrong when they declared that his main object was "to become acquainted with things" and that he was "to think only in order to act." The *Westminster*, it is true, said very little about not living by bread alone, and its doctrines appear today a curious mixture of splendid inspiration, truth, and benevolence with an almost incredible blindness and indifference to human suffering. But the indifference was philosophic rather than deliberately cruel, the result of too unquestioning a belief in the exactness of political economy as a science. The reviewers, moreover, were excusably concerned with living by bread when, as they often pointed out, bread was so dear that many people could not buy any.

If they proposed treating schoolboys after a system that today seems reminiscent of one Gradgrind, their admiration for the practical and their belief in hard work provided an antidote much needed at the time. Their account of conditions at the universities agrees well with the statements of such observers as Mark Pattison, who wrote of his Oxford undergraduate contemporaries of 1832: "If I was lazy, selfish, greedy, and rapacious, these youths were so to a degree that disgusted me."[41] Furthermore, Pattison found

lectures regarded as a joke and a bore, contemned by the more advanced, shirked by the backward; Latin and Greek regarded as useless, except for the purpose of getting a degree; and as for modern literature, the very idea of its existence never dawned upon these youths, none of whom knew any language but English.[42]

The first four chapters of his *Memoirs* emphasize particularly his intellectual loneliness as an undergraduate and the wretchedness of the training he received. Considering the quality of the exclusively clerical teaching staff, such observations are not surprising. "I could certainly keep ahead of my pupils," wrote Thomas Mozley, commenting on the same period in Oxford's history, "which was all many tutors ever did. . . . In matter of fact, a tutor did no more than half of the class could have done quite as well."[43] If after such testimony we are still disposed to charge the reviewers with heartlessness for their rigorous scheme of education, we should remind ourselves that they demanded the abolition of flogging in the schools, a practice notorious during the first half of the century.

So, considering the needs of their age, we cannot blame them for the sternness and aridity of their program or for its having turned out badly, even though the results may be partly due to serious weaknesses in it. Yet at the same time, as we reflect on the highly competitive boys learning ballistics, we may allow ourselves a moment of sympathy with the misgivings of the *bon vivant* Christopher North. He, commenting in his *Noctes* on the new theories of education, moves his quaint puppet, the Ettrick Shepherd, to a poignant prophecy: "O Sirs! in anither century or less, 'twill be a maist monstrous world, fit only for your Utilatawrians —and in less nor another century, no fit even for them."[44]

It is of course unjust to suppose that the New Man's Philistinism was entirely the contribution of the Utilitarians. His champions though they were, his teachers though they wished to be, their exact influence is of course imponderable. Carlyle, their avowed enemy, proposed nearly the same solution as theirs to the problem of living: man was not to know himself, he was to know his work and do it. Here also is the creed of effort. The obvious work for the members of the middle class, which was to become dominant perhaps sooner than even its champions of the 1820's supposed, was what the reviewers called "realizing the capital advantages of commerce," a phrase likely to be translated "making money" unless the translator were extremely well versed in political economy. The Philistine would have wanted to bestir himself energetically in the quest of material prosperity even without much encouragement. So we can merely say that in 1850 there was the New Man, in 1824 the *Westminster Review*.

V

LITERARY INSIGNIFICANCIES

It was inevitable that the *Westminster* should have a literary as well as a political department, for without one it could not be a review or possess that influence in politics which the name of review had come to carry with it. Faithful to the precedent established by the older reviews, the criticism of this department was colored largely by political bias. Southern, to whom fell the task of editing the part of the journal devoted to what Bentham disparagingly called literary insignificancies, was a radical, a Benthamite though not a member of Mill's Utilitarian group. It remains to study the *Westminster's* treatment of the so-called works of imagination, unfortunately not numerous, which were published during his reign, from 1824 to 1827.

It also remains to study the place which the Philosophic Radicals assigned to literature in the life and culture of the Chrestomathic Man. The impression now long prevalent that the Utilitarians were hostile to literature is in general correct. The reasons for that hostility and the limitations of it—and there were limitations—are not so generally understood. Actually they had a positive ideal for literature, a New Literature to fit the New Man in the New Age. The championship of this ideal led the reviewers for political and social reasons to attack much which men have found pleasant and beautiful; and it so happens that the destructive attack rather than the constructive ideal is what we remember.

At the beginning of his paper on chivalry the greatest of the young *philosophes,* John Stuart Mill, outlines very clearly the characteristics of the new and useful literature. English literary men, he asserts, attempt merely to be decorative, and incidentally do not succeed even in that. This is a matter which is ordered better in France, where they write as if they were conscious that the reader expects something more valuable from them than mere amusement. Though many of them are highly gifted with the beauties of style, they never seem desirous of showing off their own eloquence; they seem to write because they have something to say and not because they desire to say something.[1]

Thus Mill declares that Sismondi's history of France "when completed, will supply an important desideratum in literature."[2]

No sane critic will deny that such an ideal is legitimate, no scholar will grudge to consider it of great potential value to the literature of the late 1820's. True, it is not the union of strangeness with beauty, or, in a sense, the renascence of wonder. Neither does it encourage expression of the ego, that god of individualists with aspirations toward art. It implies thoroughgoing hostility to album verse, sentimental songs, polite essays, fashionable novels, and Fourth of July orations. It does not rule out as literature all the work of so-called creative artists or even all the writings of the romanticists; the younger Mill himself at precisely this time was discovering that Wordsworth had something to say, something of great moment in the life of one machine-made intellectual. It is not destructive of literary activity, though it led to destructive comment, mostly sound, on almost all the literary activity that then was. Yet, as we shall see, there were good reasons why the ideal and the resulting destructive comment were likely to be understood by Benthamite disciples as hostile to all poetry and works of imagination, and above all to be regarded by opponents of the school as convincing evidence that Utilitarians were sworn enemies to all that was to be termed sweetness and light. Thus in the literary department as elsewhere the reviewers nourished Philistinism among undiscriminating middle-class readers, while among their opponents they aggravated opposition to all phases of the Utilitarian program. Here the foundation was being further laid for the Mid-Victorian struggle between God and Mammon, the soul and the machine.

The reviewers customarily employ the word "literature" to connote not their ideal, but, properly enough, what their contemporaries would regard as literature—Horace and Catullus, Tom Moore and Walter Scott. It is with the relatively light and trivial if thoroughly pleasant work of such authors in mind that they commit themselves to denunciations of literature as a whole more sweeping than would appear necessary or intelligent.

In the program of education for the New Man it is made very clear that such literature is to play a distinctly minor part.

Directly and immediately [writes the author of the article entitled "Present System of Education"], we have risen to the station which we occupy, not by literature, not by the knowledge of extinct languages, but by the sciences of politics, of law, of public economy, of commerce, of mathematics; by astronomy, by mechanics, by natural history. It is by these that we are destined to rise yet higher. These constitute the business of society, and in these we ought to seek for the objects of education.

If, as in past ages [continues the same reviewer, now in the clutches of an enthusiasm unworthy of a rationalist], the whole attention of youth is not or is not to be directed to the mere acquisition of two extinct languages, neither ought it to be directed to mere literature. . . . Literature, we have said before, is a cant word of the age; and to be literary, to be a litterateur, . . . a bel esprit, or a blue stocking is the disease of the age.* The world is to be stormed by poetry and to be occupied by reviews and albums. He is to be a statesman because his Greek verses carried the prize; to conduct a political journal because he is a poet; or the excise perchance; or an embassy, or the secretaryship of Bermuda, or that of the Admiralty. All this is extremely pleasant and entertaining. . . .

But ledgers do not keep well in rhyme, nor are three deckers built by songs, as towns were of yore. . . . Literature is a seducer; we had almost said a harlot. She may do to trifle with; but woe be to the state whose statesmen write verses, and whose lawyers read more in Tom Moore than in Bracton.[3]

Poetry and literature will not help England spin cotton or abolish the poor laws or institute free trade.

Such comments may be extreme, startling, but they are by no means unique or thoroughly unjustifiable even if applied to the whole of imaginative literature. A *Westminster* reviewer, Peacock, had succeeded in drawing fire from a radical poet by maintaining

---

* A glance at a list of so-called "literary" periodicals published at this time tends to substantiate the charge. The *Literary Sketch Book,* the *Literary Magnet,* the *Literary Chronicle and Weekly Review,* the *Metropolitan Literary Journal,* are but a few of them.

a similar position, and Shelley in refutation had asserted that the reading of poetry aids the individual by stimulating inward growth, that the pleasure he gains as a result is "durable, universal, and permanent," and that "whatever strengthens and purifies the affections, enlarges the imagination, and adds spirit to sense, is useful."[4] Thus the reader of poetry, his personality made deeper by the cultivation of his imagination, will be of proportionately greater benefit to society. But Shelley's argument seems not to have converted the Utilitarians, depending as it does on the remote operation of intangible forces. As we know, many clear-headed people likewise have regarded literature as useless, and many still do regard it thus. We are reminded of Carlyle, who urged Tennyson and other poets to abandon their craft for prose and social uplift, and of reformers of our own day who regard the writing of poetry as an almost criminal waste of brain and energy. We are reminded at the same time of the New Man, to whom "the business of life" meant "realizing the capital advantages of commerce."

The charge of uselessness in practical affairs is the first but not the only point in the *Westminster's* indictment of literature. The Utilitarians were troubled as Plato had been by the fact that literature is often untrue and misleading, hence dangerous and sometimes pernicious. This position is most fully defined in Bingham's article on Moore's *Fables for the Holy Alliance* in the first number.[5] "This article," says John Stuart Mill, "did a good deal to attach the notion of hating poetry to the writers in the Review." However, Mill continues:

The truth was that many of us were great readers of poetry; Bingham himself had been a writer of it, while as regards me. . . . I disliked any sentiments in poetry which I should have disliked in prose. . . . And I was wholly blind to its place in human culture as a means of educating the feelings.[6]

It is not surprising that the Bingham article in conjunction with similar statements in other articles did give the impression that the reviewers hated all poetry. "Unfortunately," says Bingham, "the *exclusive* culture of the faculty of the imagination has but too strong a tendency to impair the powers of judgment." The poet's business, he continues, is to select from the facts at his disposal those which will stimulate the imagination and to state them in the most impressive way possible. "It is evident that an habitual process such as this cannot but tend to disqualify any man for the severer exercise of his reason," for truth is found by a laborious consideration of all details, not merely of the striking ones. This process of slow and painful thinking is incompatible with the poetic temperament. Hence

there are few poets that have been good reasoners. They are the mere creatures of sympathy and antipathy; their heart tells them this, and their heart tells them that; their love and hatred, their approbation and disapprobation are measured by no intelligible standard. Their fine feelings supply them instinctively with all the rules of morality. In their view, logic has indeed a closed fist and a scowling aspect, and the tune of *"triste raison"* is always foremost in their ears. They love to carry us back to days of yore when the mind of man was still cradled in infantine weakness; and appear almost to regret the passing away of the blessed days of chivalry, with all their darkness and *donjons,* violence and insecurity. . . .

Clearly if they saw anything good in medievalism, when democracy was not in flower, there must be something wrong with them. And indeed it is undeniable that lovers of the age of chivalry were often poets and never good Utilitarians. At least Moore, though not particularly prominent in the renascence of medievalism, was, according to Bingham, "a *poet,* and therefore *not a reasoner."*

In reviewing Moore's *Irish Melodies,*[7] Bingham displays the same attitude toward poetry. Referring to the early Irish bards he quotes Spenser on the activities of these beloved vagabonds:

. . . they seldom use to choose unto themselves the doings of good men for the argument of their poems; but whomsoever they find to be most licentious of life, most bold and lawless in his doings, most dangerous and desperate in all parts of disobedience and rebellious disposition; him they set up and glorifie in their rithmes; him they praise to the people, and to their young men make an example to follow.

He continues to quote at length to the same effect, stressing the wrong which may result from "evil things being decked and attired with the gay attire of goodly words"; and at the end of the quotation comments in this paragraph:

"It little occurred to Spenser that in thus reprobating these poor bards, he was giving an admirable analysis of the machinery and effects of almost all that poets have ever done." One wonders why the learned Utilitarian did not go directly back to Plato to complete his argument by authority.

In the article entitled "Vocal Music,"[8] Bingham points out another evil for which poets were sometimes responsible. They encourage "depression of spirits, discouragement, despair," as Moore in the *Irish Melodies* often does.

Instead of pointing our hopes to the future, they are eternally damping our few enjoyments with unavailing regrets for the past, and conjuring up every image which shall constantly remind us of the brevity of life and the transient nature of human enjoyment: setting suns, fading colors, dying leaves, moaning winds, broken vows, departed friends, lost pleasures, and voices from the tomb.

Clearly such writing has no utilitarian value: "The man who exerts his powers to aggravate our misery is, so far, an enemy of the species." So we should not be surprised to find the New Man, if he reads fiction at all, clamoring for tales with happy endings and decrying the inclusion of the unpleasant or the pessimistic.

Bingham is not alone in his distrust of literature or his fear of "the gay attire of goodly words." The Utilitarians naturally realized that anything which has the power to affect people may harm them. Bowring, as we have seen, objected to the oratorical tendencies of the Americans, and Fonblanque, reviewing Moore's life of Sheridan, pointed out that eloquence should be viewed with suspicion. "Ignorance presents the widest field for declamation, and in exact proportion to the spread of knowledge we observe a diminution of what is called eloquence."[9] The younger Mill, who was to demonstrate the bad effects of romance on Walter Scott's thinking, committed himself to this position also in commenting upon Hume as a writer of history.

His mind was completely enslaved by a taste for literature; not those kinds of literature which teach mankind to know the causes of their happiness and misery, that they may seek the one and avoid the other; but that literature which without regard for truth or utility seeks only to excite emotion.[10]

Later in the same article he declares that "romance is always dangerous" and that one who writes for effect, as literary men usually do, is never too cautious about the truth of his statements.

A third point against literature is closely connected with the other two. The aristocracy were its owners. This relationship, the reviewers say, accounts in large measure for its uselessness, its failure to attack evils, its fiddling while England starves, and the frequent instances of untruth in its teaching. The evils of aristocratic ownership are set forth with particular emphasis in the review of Washington Irving's *Tales of a Traveler*.[11] The British reading public, the reviewer points out, is divided into two classes, those "who are Somebody" and those "who are Nobody." The Somebodys have hereditary wealth and send their children to public school and university, where the serious student is the object of contempt and "the man who shares the greatest quantity of consideration" is "the man who feels no necessity to study and has plenty of money to spend upon his pleasures." They do their best to render "the cultivation of the powers of mind unfashionable, partly because of their own indolence, partly through fear that "a spirit of examination and intellectual exertion" may become diffused throughout the lower orders and lead to the loss of their own monopoly and privilege.

Hence a substitute must be found and has been found for useful inquiry. This substitute is *Polite* Literature, and what are called the fine arts; in other words, the cultivation of the powers of imagination, at the expense and almost to the destruction of the powers of judgment. The value of these pursuits, that is, their effect upon human happiness, their capability of affording pleasure or diminishing pain, are therefore upon all occasions prodigiously overrated, and a due taste for them inculcated as the main business of existence. Your true fiddle-faddle Somebody who would be in high repute among his fellows, will occasionally misquote a line of Horace, will perfectly idolize Shakespeare and hold in sovereign contempt the wretch who cannot discuss all his characters from Macbeth down to Caliban; he will assert that the reading of poetry is the highest of human pleasures; and gravely maintain that twenty lines of Virgil will assuage grief and alleviate the pangs of disappointment. . . .

There is much more in this vein.

The reviewer, now somewhat bitter, proceeds to characterize the literature which has developed under aristocratic tutelage. It must include

nothing that can excite controversy, nothing that can occasion dissatisfaction, all pensive, gentlemanly, and subdued, all trifling and acquiescent as a drawing-room conversation; prevailing errors in morals and legislation carefully upheld or at best left unnoticed: a little pathos, a little sentiment to excite tears as a pleasurable emotion for those who see them on no other occasion, a little point and a little antithesis to tickle the ear and divert the attention from the lamentable deficiency of solid matter.

This, says the reviewer, is literature, dangerous because useless, useless because aristocratic. "Gentle Geoffrey Crayon" has achieved his fame by conforming to these standards; he is popular because he is trivial and does not make anyone think. Thus Utilitarianism at times generated somewhat penetrating criticism as a sort of by-product.

Sir Richard Phillips's *Monthly Magazine,* which generally professed most enthusiastic admiration for the *Westminster,* took this article as a point of departure for reading the reviewers a lecture on the practice of dragging politics into literature.[12]

We should be sorry [says the *Monthly*], to see the cause of politics confounded or associated in this country with the *Hebertism* or *Vandalism* that makes war upon everything which can give splendor, elevation, and refinement to that leisure and that luxury which inevitably result from so advanced a state of society in which it is our destiny to be placed.

This warning the author of the same article applies also to the *Westminster's* approach to the problem of education. The *Monthly* returned to the subject frequently,[13] and Buckingham's *Oriental Herald* expressed similar fears in its comment on Bingham's article on the *Fables for the Holy Alliance.*[14] Ridiculing that article, *Blackwood's* indulged in reductio ad absurdum, and declared that "he who invents a new spinning jenney is, of necessity, a wiser and better man than he who makes a new Iliad," and that "York minster should undoubtedly be made into a cotton mill."[15] To such criticism the Utilitarian reviewers would have replied that "splendor, elevation, and refinement," qualities for the most part monopolized by the aristocracy, were not desiderata in their plan of the universe, particularly when achieved at the expense of clear thinking on social and political questions.

One sympathizes with *Blackwood's,* yet admits if at all candid that under certain circumstances the inventor of the spinning jenny might contribute more to the alleviation of human misery than the maker of the new *Iliad.* Such a contribution would obviously increase human happiness. Certainly, though starving genius in 1824 might have been inspired and aided in the quest of liberty by Shelley's odes, which even the *Westminster* might have considered useful literature, the mass of starving talent derived more good from Bentham's utility. For most people of the early nineteenth century the achievement of the greatest happiness depended largely on securing a decent living; nor are many anti-Utilitarians happy for long while clothed in rags, living in squalid cellars, sleeping six in a bed, and eating only by good fortune if at all. The intelligent philanthropist first devises means of improving bad physical conditions. He does not spend his life reading poetry to the indigent, and when times are particularly hard he is likely to suppose that all writers of imaginative literature are merely indulging a Nero-like virtuosity. Such appears to have been the belief of the Benthamites, whose motives were not altogether at fault if misery continued to exist long after their own voices ceased to cry out against it.

If a decorative literature took no part in furthering the reform movement that was so imperatively needed, the Utilitarians had reason to attack it as useless. If, by corrupting national thought or lulling it to sleep, such literature made reform more difficult, they were justified in regarding it as positively vicious. True, they did not see all sides of the picture, but one side they saw very clearly: that in 1824 literature in the commonly accepted sense of the word was on the side of their political opponents. Most of their contemporaries, indeed, concurred in this opinion, regarding literature as a polite ornament for members of the leisure class, as the *Monthly's* allusion to "splendor, elevation, and refinement" indicates. Such being the case, the attitude of the *Westminster* reviewers was almost inevitable. Furthermore, they had excellent precedent, in the conduct of the two older reviews, for adjusting literary criticism to political bias, and it must be recorded in their favor that they waged their battles by fair argument, without resorting to malicious dealing in personalities.

The importance of political bias in *Westminster* criticism is best illustrated in the case of Scott, who now for the first time received thoroughly scathing reviews. There was no reason for the Radical reviewers to condone faults or to let bad work pass. There was every reason for them to attack him. As a leading Tory, he should rank as chief of seducers.

The reviewers, however, lead up to this position gradually. John Stuart Mill opens the attack with one tiny depreciatory paragraph, in his paper on the *Edinburgh Review,* April, 1824,[16] asserting that Scott has never written anything useful. The Great Unknown is first treated at length in a review of *Redgauntlet,*[17] which is not a general essay on Scott but a vigorous attack on the weaknesses of that particular novel. At the beginning, the author of the review does comment, however, on Sir Walter's amazing fecundity. This quality, he asserts, does not astonish him as it does most of his contemporaries. Instead, he wonders that Scott does not write more rapidly, considering the enthusiastic reception accorded such obviously inferior works as the later "Waverley Novels." *St. Ronan's Well, The Abbot, The Monastery,* are characterized as "books of the stamp and order of the Minerva Press." The remainder of the review is occupied with a crushing comment on *Redgauntlet* itself. The materials are slight, the plot is weak. The letter form of the first part renders the introduction of the story unduly tedious. The characters are as absurd and impossible as the situation. The best that can be said for it is that "it is superior to its immediate predecessors." *Redgauntlet* received no such devastating comment from any other source.

The wrath of the reviewers was not to descend in its full force, however, until the publication of *Woodstock,*[18] "a story," the *Westminster* states, "in which there is but little nature of any kind, little spirit, scarcely any feeling, and no historical truth." The reviewer, moreover, denounces it not for its own defects alone; he uses it "to illustrate the character of these English historical romances." The author had much better, he maintains, have stuck to the Scotch.

The dialogue is bad. "It is curious to remark how the speakers in these romances express themselves after the same manner, however various their degrees of rank and remote from each other the periods of their existence." Gurth the Swineherd and Sir Harry Lee, the Cavalier Ranger of Woodstock, talk much alike, both somewhat like Shakespeare, always with an affectation of quaintness, yet with a modern tone which renders the whole effect absurd and unconvincing. Characters always display a tendency to speak with poetic diction, using abundant similes and metaphors. This eccentricity of Scott's dialogue, as well as the others, is carefully illustrated by examples chosen from the "Waverley" series.

The reviewer then passes to a consideration of Scott's ability in inventing plots and in characterization. "The story of *Woodstock* is singularly unhappy in its conception and is barren in great and agitating events." Moreover, Scott shows himself "a careless and inexpert mechanist in the construction of a story." In these respects the reviewer finds *Woodstock* typical of the "Waverley Novels," all mere "successions of scenes" which are usually connected "at the expense of glaring improbabilities." The characters are no better than the situations. The reviewer takes them one by one and demonstrates that they are absurd and historically inaccurate, particularly Cromwell, to whom Scott's obvious Cavalier sympathies have rendered him extremely unfair and who in the novel is thoroughly weak and unconvincing. His one ambition is represented as the possession of the person of Charles, a notable untruth. Scott's account of the plan for capturing the Stuart leader and of its execution is an insult to Cromwell's intelligence, and in general his treatment of the character of Cromwell is grossly libellous. Actually, the reviewer maintains, Cromwell was not ferocious or cruel in temper; he was famous, indeed, for his gentleness. To support this contention he cites many instances of Cromwell's kindness and benevolence. Scott's account is finally declared to be nothing but Tory propaganda insidiously imposed on the people in the guise of fiction and with protests of impartiality, obviously the work of a writer who admires only men of family, who casts a glamor only over their activities, and who in the debasement of a political opponent is capable of representing Cromwell, in a fit of cruelty, ordering the hanging of Sir Harry Vane's otherwise unoffending

Cavalier dog.* "Such," concludes the reviewer, "is an HISTORI-
CAL romance by the author of Waverley."

The final blow in the Philosophic Radical attack on Scott was
John Stuart Mill's review of his life of Napoleon, the leading
article of the number for April, 1828.[19] This is Mill's last contribution to the first dynasty of the review, written after the bitter years of self-examination during which he had finally found
truth in the Tory poet, Wordsworth. He is trying very hard,
therefore, to do full justice to merits in Scott's work which he
may have previously overlooked. He opens the article with the
statement, "Sir Walter Scott cannot write anything which as a
literary composition cannot be read with pleasure." He notes with
approval the narrative of Napoleon's first Italian expedition and
praises Scott for having maintained throughout "so lively, rapid,
and spirited a style that the interest never flags, the attention never
is wearied." Thus in spite of the hard and fast rule of consistency
which Bowring had laid down, he revokes the judgment which
earlier reviewers, possessed of a more partisan spirit, had passed
on Scott as a literary man. Yet, though penitent for past sins, he
is still a friend of popular reform, still a Radical; and he has
devoted much hard study to the French Revolution. It does not
take him long to turn his praise of Scott into censure. One soon
gathers that as a work of history the life of Napoleon is splendid
fiction and that it excellently illustrates the thesis that literature
is dangerous.

By careful citation Mill convicts Scott at point after point of
errors of fact and judgment. He declares that the work "has all
the defects of a book hastily written; it is utterly without research,"
and that, furthermore, Scott's Tory prejudice has rendered him
incapable of interpreting rightly such facts as happened to come
to his hand. A historian, says Mill, must be a sound philosopher,
and Scott's philosophy, quite unsound, completely incapacitates
him for writing well on the French people or any popular move-

* But for a bad piece of editorial inconsistency, cf. IV (October, 1825),
306. *Tremaine:* "Cromwell could cant and pray when he was ancle deep
in innocent blood, and pursuing his ambitious ends by whatever means,
it was sufficient that he was doing the work of the Lord."

ment anywhere. "In political and social philosophy his principles are all summed up in the orthodox one, that whatever is English is best, best not for England only, but for every country in Christendom, or probably the world." Therefore Scott condemns all proposed variation from contemporary English practice as untried theory. Such a position is certainly not that of the *Westminster Review* or of Mill himself, and he demonstrates clearly its disastrous effect on the writing of good history. Scott has been liberal and indulgent toward royalist defenders of the *status quo,* and has misrepresented all the measures of the revolutionists. Mill implies that the Tory novelist's scorn for what conservatives call the visionary has a local application to contemporary reform agitation in England.

Scott's theory of society being wrong, his powers as a novelist render him all the more dangerous when he attempts to write history. His account of the Revolution itself "conveys none but false impressions. It is a story skillfully and even artfully constructed for a purpose." The purpose is to entertain, and entertainment demands the consistent and the dramatic, involves "the art of so dressing up a fact as to make it appear to mean more than it does." An aristocrat who thus cuts his facts to fit his plots will write good literature, but bad and dangerous history. Scott

has committed the very common blunder of ascribing to persons what was the effect of circumstances and to settled design what was the result of immediate impulse. Every one of his characters has a part premeditated and prepared, and is ready to march upon the stage and enact it at the precise moment when his entrée will produce the most striking scenic effect.

Mill's demonstration that Scott has "thoroughly misunderstood and misrepresented" the first epoch of the Revolution, which occupies the remainder of the sixty-three-page article, though itself written with a bias, is interesting reading. The entire essay is indeed one of the outstanding papers in the review.

Though in the periodical press the chorus of praise for the later works of Scott was by no means unanimous, the *Westminster* took the lead in pointing out their defects. In general, unfavorable comment by other reviewers on the life of Napoleon consisted of

wise remarks on doubtful elegance of diction. It appears to have
been generally agreed among critics that any "Waverley Novel"
should receive a long and favorable review. Of such novels as
Redgauntlet and *Woodstock* it was conventional to say, "Not so
good as *Waverley,* but of course a masterpiece," and then to synop-
size. Careful examination of Scott's method and tendencies oc-
curs only in the *Westminster* and to a lesser degree in the *New
Monthly,* in both of which such criticism was to be expected. The
latter periodical was edited by Campbell, who in politics leaned
gracefully toward the Radicals, and owned by Colburn, who published many novels but not Scott's. It pointed out before the *Westminster* the Tory bias of the Great Unknown,[20] but did not attack
his writing as bad literature or indulge in such thorough annihila-
tion of the "Waverley" series as did its Benthamite contemporary
in the review of *Woodstock.* The penetrating observations of the
Utilitarians in their three articles on Scott lead one to conclude
that he was not a novelist or a historian, merely a Tory. There is
nothing to indicate that Scott or his friends were deeply grieved,
however, by this verdict, or even that they knew anything about
it. Lockhart does not notice it.

Not so dangerous a seducer as Scott, Tom Moore, pampered
darling of the Whigs, was yet likewise considered a menace to
the cause of truth. He received no less than six articles before the
break in 1828, the first four evidently by Bingham, the last two
by Fonblanque and Peacock respectively. With one exception the
papers by Bingham were, as Moore himself expressed it in his
journal, "half and half." The exception is *Fables for the Holy
Alliance,*[21] already referred to, in which Bingham takes the author
to task for being "a poet and therefore not a reasoner." The particular ground for this assertion is Moore's alleged dislike for
Americans because they have no aristocratic drawing-rooms.
Though they are "exempt from the evils of poverty and misgovernment," though "there exists among them a greater amount of
happiness than the same numbers have ever enjoyed before," yet,
says Bingham, "in the estimation of a sentimentalist they are a
coarse, calculating, matter-of-fact people," and this proves bad
thinking on the part of the sentimentalist. Bingham cites several

further instances of the disastrous effect on clear thinking of the "Whig aristocratical atmosphere in which Mr. Moore dwells," and might have concluded with better consistency, "Mr. Moore is a Whig, and therefore not a reasoner."

Moore did not allow this review to go unanswered. He had met Bingham—indeed, in some aristocratic drawing-room— where it appears that they had become good friends and had both been guilty of singing sentimental ballads, though one gathers that Moore drew more tears than Bingham.[22] At any rate, Bingham sent Moore the appropriate copy of the *Westminster,* with a note admitting that he was the author of the offending article, and Moore replied, as any good Englishman should, with the request that Bingham insert an inclosed letter in the *Times.* This letter, denying that Moore disliked Americans, was duly inserted. Bingham, however, had his revenge. In Moore's journal under the date of March 30, 1824, we find this entry:

Dined with Bingham at Gray's Inn; company, Mrs. Austin, Mr. Gattie, and another gentleman; all Benthamites and quite different from other people. The lady talked political economy. . . .[23]

Apparently no one sang. Yet their relations continued amicable, probably partly because of Bingham's generally favorable notice of the *National Airs* in an article in the same number.

Captain Rock[24] and the ninth number of *Irish Melodies*[25] received fair and judicious notices. The reviewer's chief charge against the former was the unspeakable pedantry of its recondite allusions; his chief point in its favor, its tone of sympathy for oppressed Catholics. Fonblanque's review of the *Life of Sheridan,* however, was in the main unfavorable. Moore's faith in the English aristocracy (particularly out of place in a work on Sheridan), his faulty inferences, his failure to discover obvious facts, his retailing of unverified suggestions and bits of gossip, his absurdly figurative style—all are pointed out as serious defects in the work. The tone of the review, however, is judicious. Moore thought that the subsequent attack on the same work in the *Quarterly* "added but little to what was in the *Westminster,*"[26] but replied only to the *Quarterly,* that being of course the more generally read in the circle of Moore's friends.

It was Moore's novel, *The Epicurean,* which supplied the occasion of Peacock's becoming himself one of the wicked race of reviewers.[27] The essay fulfills admirably his own demands as to what a review should be. It is both amusing and sound, more amusing and more sound than most reviews one reads in these present days. Peacock had read Moore's book through very carefully, and he knew a great deal about Epicureanism. With no preliminary formalities whatever, he set to work and gave Moore thirty-four pages of thorough and artistic trouncing. Gaily he castigated him for absurd and improbable incidents, absurd and unhappy figures of speech, absurd and inexcusable errors of fact resulting from total absence of thought and ignorance of the Epicurean philosophy, for plagiarism, and for omitting the iota subscript in quoting Greek. Though political bias played a smaller share than usual in the *Westminster,* Peacock's interpretation of Epicureanism fitted well into that journal's boasted unity:

Thus Epicurus first taught that general utility, or as Bentham expresses it, "the greatest happiness of the greatest number" is the legitimate end of philosophy; and it is curious to see the same class of persons decrying the same doctrine as impracticably dry when the word utility precedes the word pleasure, and as too practicably voluptuous when the word pleasure precedes the word utility. So much are small minds the slaves of words.

This paper represents *Westminster* reviewing as it should more often have been, and Bowring deserves praise for having for once given an assignment to precisely the right man. Moore was hardly unprovoked when he inserted in his squib entitled *Thoughts on Editors:*

> With Doctor Bowring I drank tea
> Nor of his cakes consumed a particle,
> And yet th' ungrateful L. L. D.
> Let fly at me next week an article.[28]

Later, having first asked Hobhouse to do it, the LL.D. gave Peacock Moore's *Life of Byron,*[29] and here, too, Peacock did an admirable piece of work,* which has as much to do with Utilitarian-

---

* Hobhouse, to whom Bowring introduced Peacock, made a few suggestions. He wrote to Peacock (Peacock Papers, British Museum Addl.

ism as Carlyle's essay on the *Nibelungenlied,* which the *Westminster* published soon after.

Another work of mere literature which inspired a particularly striking Utilitarian review was Johnson's two-volume edition of Cowper's correspondence.[30] This paper, an excellent example of how much utility can be condensed into twelve pages, is simply an essay on Cowper with a formal allusion to Johnson as editor attached. The reviewer, after paying his respects to the earlier work of Hayley for whitewashing his subject, launches into an attack, which in a Benthamite journal appears inevitable, on Cowper's ascetic philosophy.

> In judging the merit of human action [declares the reviewer], there can be, we conceive, but one standard according to which praise and blame should be dispensed—the test of utility, or conduciveness to the greatest happiness of the greatest number. This is the only directive rule which is safely applicable on every occasion of life without exception. . . .

Cowper's only criterion of good and bad, on the other hand, was "his own conjecture of what would be pleasing or displeasing to the Deity." Of his belief in the renunciation of happiness, the reviewer asks, "If individuals are thus called upon to give up their respective shares, what becomes of the mass?" One must renounce even the pleasure of helping others to happiness if happiness is wrong.

Furthermore, under Cowper's system, the march of civilization would come to a standstill. He not only objects to pleasure; in his devotion to contemplative retirement he objects to utility. "He forgets how essential it is to the welfare of society that there should be individuals actuated by motives of another kind, to engage in commerce, in the business of government, etc." Thus, "disparaging the labours of by far the most useful members of

---

36815, f. 50 & 51): "The worst part of the book is the appendix—that is, the most catchpenny portion of it, for it is cooked up with materials not worth a farthing in any way and what are called anecdotes are for the most part lies." For example, Hobhouse declares that the narrative of the residence at Milan in 1817 is "all but a romance," and that everything which "poor stupid Galt . . . says about Byron's life and adventures and conversations with him is absolutely a fiction."

society," he obviously is deserving of censure. Along with his asceticism he had that "belief in the imaginary superiority of ancient over present times which always characterizes the weakest minds." In short, though the reviewer does not say so, he was a romanticist. So, in spite of his having been personally a very pleasant individual, it was inevitable that "the habit of admitting propositions into the mind unsupported by evidence" finally led to insanity.

So much for William Cowper, on whose philosophy all good Utilitarians would agree. They would fail as completely to comprehend the merits of his way of living as he would have failed to comprehend the merits of theirs. He had succeeded admirably in detecting the unsatisfactory in the Utilitarian spirit without witnessing its apotheosis in the *Westminster Review;* they succeeded as well in detecting weakness and absurdity in his. The paper in which they did so has decided value for one who wishes to understand Utilitarianism and the ideal Utilitarian civilization; and the surprising thing about it for those trained to hold the doctrine in disdain is that so much of it is not only sound reason but high idealism.

One is no less surprised at the general excellence of Utilitarian literary judgment. The criticism of Scott, as far as it goes, is remarkably sound. The pronouncements on Moore are equally good. A diatribe against James Hogg's *Queen Hynde*[31] is the only unjustifiable and really bad piece of reviewing which resulted from the Radical bias, and this may be excused as an attempt to repay *Blackwood's* in their own coin without possessing the coin. The judicious advice to L.E.L.[32] to stop being merely pretty and try to say something is undeniably appropriate. Later a long and excellent review using the "touchstone method" was devoted to an exposure of the same lady's absurdities.[33] This paper, assuming a typical Benthamite position, takes her to task for agreeing with the popular belief that women should be subordinated to men, and "bestowing admiration upon those qualities which fit them for being useful and agreeable slaves." This attitude of hers is found to be altogether consistent with her apparent acceptance of the code of chivalry, which also encourages warfare and generally debases the individual. The complaint that Landor did not learn political economy before he wrote *Imaginary Conversations*[34] is likewise typical. The reviewer shows the Utilitarian spirit further in quoting with approval Landor's statement that we should have few friendships and no intimacies to distract us from the business of life. Like so many, the review as a whole is judicious and certainly not unfair.

A few other valuable essays in the literary department of the review have almost no conceivable connection with the business of life, and consistency should have demanded that they receive no place in a periodical sacred to utility. Yet even Bentham had admitted that the review must contain literary insignificancies, and perhaps it is more remarkable that so many of the literary articles bear the marks of Utilitarian influence than that a few of them do not. It is even possible that the atmosphere of persistent skepticism maintained by the Philosophic Radicals, their insistence upon independent thinking, had its effect upon the work of such men as Southern and Barker. Here and there, in articles which are not at all Utilitarian, appear startlingly new and wise observations on literary problems, much wiser than one finds in the journals which claimed devotion to literature.

For instance, the reviewer of Milman's dramatic poem, *Anne Boleyn*,[35] in an otherwise pedestrian notice, postulates the same theory of playwriting which animated the revival of English drama at the close of the century. The theory is not new, but its expression in the *Westminster Review* in 1826 is somewhat remarkable. The reviewer attacks the poetic drama and does it so well that he deserves quoting at length:

> Thus to jumble together poetry and the drama, shews an utter misapprehension both of the proper aim of a dramatic writer, and of the means by which that aim can be attained. The end is, to excite emotion by a representation of the emotions of others; to call up our sympathies, to raise our hopes and fears, by a representation of the hopes and fears, of the joys and miseries of other men. But to render this representation effective, it must be true to nature; it must be a correct imitation of the actions and language of mankind in the drama of life; a faithful exhibition of human passion; the language of real joy and sorrow.

A play, it must be remembered, is composed entirely of what men say and do: it is not a *relation* of actions, but the actions themselves. From hence originates a most important distinction between a poem and a play. The language of poetry is not the language of real life: it is real life, however, that the dramatist must portray. He must write as men would speak, and must vary with the variations of time, and place, and character. The thoughts his characters utter, must be the thoughts of men in such situations; and the language in which they are expressed must be the language in which such men would express them. The poet and his characters are separate persons; they have no connexion one with the other, and should invariably be kept carefully distinguished.

A poet in his own proper character is not confined to this strict delineation of life. As a poet, he may call all the charms of fancy to his aid, may display every beauty of his brilliant and fascinating art; but, as a dramatist, never. In real life, more particularly when under the influence of violent emotions, men are never poetical. A man, for instance, in the agonies of death, is not very likely to indulge in a trope; nor a thief or a murderer to pause in the perpetration of his villainy, to enunciate a well-turned and elegant simile. It has never been our fate to hear a woman in sorrow liken herself to a fountain, or any other water-dropping thing in nature; nor a disconsolate widow point out the resemblance between a spouseless doe's condition and her own; nor any similarity whatever between the antlered partner of her proto-type and her own departed lord. We never have had the fortune, good or bad, to know any lady

> 'Who plighted to a noble youth her faith
> When she had given her honour to a wretch;'

but we will take upon ourselves to say, upon the knowledge a few years' experience of human nature has given us, that no lady, upon such an accident being discovered, would ever think of poetically comparing herself to a ship in a storm. Such things may be found in our plays, though never heard of in life.

This is indeed radical doctrine. By implication, the reviewer is casting a stone even at Shakespeare, that idol of contemporary critics, and he is not unaware of the fact. Shakespeare, he says, "often deviates thus from nature," yet in general he has "the ease and simplicity of real life." After this partial retraction he proceeds to demolish Milman, who as a *Quarterly* reviewer as well as a writer of poetic drama could expect little mercy.

Another literary form investigated by the *Westminster* is the didactic novel. Southern inserted two articles on this subject, one in October, 1825, the other in April, 1827. Unfortunately for the oracular infallibility of the sacred review, he evidently forgot what was in the first before he inserted the second, or perhaps he neglected to read one or the other or both before insertion. At any rate, the first, a review of Ward's *Tremaine*[36] declares against the *genre*, while the second, treating of a novel quaintly entitled *Truth, by the Author of Nothing,* is equally emphatic in favor of it. One feels that in the last analysis the position of the *Westminster Review* on the didactic novel depended entirely on what lesson a particular book taught. *Tremaine* teaches religious conformity; *Truth* teaches candor and free thinking.

The reviewer of the former work maintains stoutly that if one wants to write a sermon one should write a sermon, not a novel. This, he complains bitterly, is not the generally accepted belief.

The pill is to be gilded with a due quantity of adventure, of love and seduction, that it may go more smoothly down. We are invited to a theatre to see a comedy, and it proves to be a meeting house and a sermon. We doubt the value of trickery and manoeuvering in most of the matters of life; and while we cannot give high praise to the manoeuverer who would trick us into religion, we do not set much store on that religion which is produced by trickery.

Furthermore, the reviewer does not believe that such novels are really conducive to religion, "that right feeling of devotion can be excited in the midst of a warm pursuit of worldly interests and associations."

By "a warm pursuit of worldly interests and associations" he has something very specific in mind—the actual purpose which he thinks the religious novel serves: namely, the retailing of "warm descriptions of love and adultery." His views on this subject, abominably expressed, are yet alarmingly like those of our own twentieth century.

The warm or hysterical, half hysterical female, the young female whose disappointed wishes keep her in constant excitement; the more aged virgin who regrets the lost hours of youth, are consoled by the very name of love; and it is too true a picture of enthusiasm that the term divine love is often associated with human desires, and that the current phraseology, which a sense of propriety forbids us to quote, is but the vent of passions that have been painfully restrained and that seize any opportunity for indulgence, even in words.

The majority of readers of these books are women, and three-fourths of them are written by women, following the lead of "the moral Richardson himself." They are all interested, the reviewer thinks, more in the sinning than in the retribution and repentance which follow. His case is well thought through and in his treatment of it we detect some vaporous contribution to the clouds of glory which Freud came trailing.

The author of the review of *Truth*[37] takes the opposite position from that of the reviewer of *Tremaine*, and looks with favor on the efforts of didactic novelists. He is, indeed, considering the didactic novel in general, not its subclass, the religious novel, but in approving of didactic novels he repudiates the earlier condemnation of the use of fiction to sugar-coat serious teaching.

He repudiates also the confirmed Utilitarian position on the place of literature. He admits that the attention which the author of a didactic novel must devote to his moral will inevitably weaken his work in a higher artistic quality, "the imitation and delineation of manners, and as affording an accurate picture of human life." In placing didacticism lower than characterization he is in substantial agreement with an earlier reviewer, who, in an essay on the Italian novelists,[38] had declared that the creation of individuals is the greatest triumph of a story-teller. Here, says the same reviewer, is the great weakness of Boccaccio, "the acknowledged prince of the Italian novelists"; he has placed his emphasis on narrative. "Distinction of character," he continues, "and the tracing of the conduct of individuals as modified by their respective dispositions, are the highest walk of the imagination, and the web of a story comes in the second place." It remained for a woman, a later assistant editor of the *Westminster Review,* to put this excellent doctrine into practice for the nineteenth-century English novel.

The reviewer of *Truth,* admitting that the didactic novel is artistically an inferior production, yet believes that it serves a useful purpose. It catches the attention of two classes of people, both of whom benefit by it. "One class consists of serious persons who are ignorant of the vast importance and value of cultivating the fancy and who from various scruples would not condescend to read a mere novel." He might here be referring to the habitual readers—or indeed the writers—of the *Westminster Review.* "They will notwithstanding," he continues, "venture into the precincts of a doctrinal novel for the sake of the doctrine; they are accordingly cheated into a perusal of the inventive part, and unconsciously and in spite of themselves and their consciences, they thus take a salutary draught of refinement." The reviewer might almost as well have praised the didactic novel for inculcating the quality that Bentham most detested, good taste.

In the other class are the devotees of frivolity, who would not read a serious treatise, but may gather an idea from a novel, "are perhaps induced to think on serious matters or tempted to entertain hospitably new ideas." Such novels must be inferior to Smollett in humor and as pictures of life; but they may be useful. So let the work go gaily on. *Coelebs* and *Tremaine* may have their honorable place. Here, indeed, is heterodoxy in the camp of utility, the statement of a belief in "the vast importance and value of cultivating the fancy."

It does not often happen that the *Westminster* in its earlier years contains passages like this, admitting the usefulness of the imagination. In fact, the considerable number of literary articles still unmentioned are notable only for their dullness and lack of merit. They are, like many reviews in all periodicals then and now, merely "notices"—uninspired synopses of unimportant books. Reviewers had, however, relatively little real literature to notice between 1824 and 1828, and it is surprising rather that some of the reviews are interesting than that many of them are dull.

One article, somewhat too general to be regarded as a mere literary insignificancy, should, however, be noted here. It is concerned with the effect of advertising on literature and reviewing.

Macaulay, it will be remembered, denounced the practice of puffing in his review of Robert Montgomery's *Satan*.[39] He was in splendid form, full of righteous indignation and reveling in it. Never were the sins of the puffing press more effectively exposed. They had been exposed two years earlier, however, in an article in the *Westminster* on this same Robert Montgomery.[40] The *Westminster* reviewer was much less vigorous, much less amusing, than Macaulay; but he pointed out the same absurdity in his victim's work.

It appears likely that Macaulay read the *Westminster* article. It is highly improbable that he neglected, as part of his preparation for his celebrated attack on the Utilitarians, to familiarize himself thoroughly with the Utilitarian review. The distinguished Whig, then, may have had a literary as well as a political indebtedness to the Philosophic Radicals.

The *Westminster* attack possesses a breadth and thoroughness of approach, lacking in Macaulay's, which makes it more than a literary article. Anticipating the speculations of social observers of our own time—not to mention Ruskin—it begins by pointing out the dangers of advertising, whatever the article for sale. The advertising business, says the reviewer, possesses "Herculean proportions even in its cradle. . . . Beauty may be purchased; deformity converted into charm; the colour of the hair may be converted into the glossiest of favourite colours. . . ." Horse dealers, real estate men, wine-merchants, all advertise and misrepresent. Booksellers are not far behind. Advertising destroys literature and corrupts criticism, but it sells books.

Competition between business houses is so keen that they cannot depend for sales solely on the intrinsic merit of books. They must advertise, spending large sums which will come back to them only if they sell books in great numbers. Hence they encourage the writing of two-volume novels, because it costs no more to advertise two than one, and the price charged for the two may naturally be higher. They cannot afford to advertise a book which does not promise to be a best seller; and "it is needless to say that books of readiest sale are not likely to be the best." Hence it is difficult to secure a publisher for a good book. It is the old story; good books are not written because good books are very likely not to sell. Writers who are capable of producing something better are forced by economic pressure to grind out best sellers.

The corruption of criticism through advertising funds has also become the old story. Here is the *Westminster* reviewer's description of the situation as it existed then:

Newspapers are in the hands of men, generally speaking, whose sole object is merchantile. It is a truth that they look to the advertisements as their first and best source of profit; and of these advertisements the booksellers supply a large and preponderating share. A publisher in a large way can put in or divert from the pockets of any newspaper proprietor many hundred pounds a year. . . Here is the secret of laudatory critiques, of favourable quotations, of sly allusions and grossly eulogistic paragraphs. . . A tacit contract subsists between one trade and the other; the one to pay, the other to praise. Criticism, false but fair-seeming criticism, has thus become one of the disguises in which the monster Puff stalks abroad seeking whom he may gull.

Thus thoroughly does the reviewer account for the development and popularity of the Robert Montgomerys of his time. He devotes less space to the exposure of his victim's actual absurdities than Macaulay. He has none of Macaulay's verve. But he has the honor, whoever he may be, of having written the first systematic description and explanation of a disease with which literature has been afflicted from his day to our own.

A striking characteristic of the *Westminster* is that few of its reviews are favorable. These reviewers at least would appear to be quite clear of the charge of puffing. There is no attempt on their part to sell the books published by Baldwin, though it may be significant that in their orgy of unfavorable reviewing, very few of Baldwin's books are noticed at all. The same number of the journal in which appeared the devastating notice of Ward's *Tremaine,* published by Colburn, contained eight pages of Colburn's advertising. However, if a reader suspecting the *Westminster* to be an example of literary integrity should compile a list of favorable reviews, he might be somewhat startled to discover that his titles consisted largely of the works of Bentham and James Mill. He might, however, console himself, and with justice, by the reflection that in matters of opinion the review was published frankly as the organ of the Benthamites, and that no one need have been surprised that books written by men of their party should receive long and favorable notices. It is legitimate to distinguish a coterie eager to advance ideas common to them all from a group of reviewers whose object is to sell the works of their personal friends for the mere pecuniary advantage of those friends. Still more one should distinguish the puffing of a friend's ideas from the puffing of a publisher's commercial enterprise. The *Westminster* reviewers honestly believed that the writings of Mill and Bentham represented the high point in the useful literature of their day, if not the entire body of it.

Aside from Mill and Bentham, indeed, the Radicals did not possess distinguished authors. They had had one poet much though not entirely to their liking, Byron, the only useful Lord; but he had died immediately after the review was founded. The Utilitarian organ was published in time, however, to pay its tribute to his work in Greece in an ostensible review of *The Deformed Transformed*.[41] The only reference to *The Deformed Transformed* is in the first sentence: "This then is the last work we are to expect from the pen of this great poet." The reviewer, who must have secured his information through Hobhouse and Bowring, and may have been one of them, then sketches Byron's activities in Greece, and concludes with Fletcher's invaluable account of his death.

On the publication of Dallas's *Recollections* and Medwin's *Conversations,* the review devoted a leading article to the defense of Byron against the misrepresentations in those volumes. The article is by Hobhouse,[42] who wrote it with a view to publication in the *Quarterly*, whose publisher, Murray, had also been Byron's publisher. The *Quarterly*, however, would have none of it, and so it appeared in the *Westminster*, the natural place for it. Hobhouse spares neither of these early detractors. His method of treating Medwin is particularly effective: he presents in parallel columns Medwin's statements and his own corrections. For example, as opposed to Medwin's quotation from Byron, "I will give you a specimen of some epigrams I am in the habit of sending Hobhouse, to whom I wrote on my first wedding day," the fact that

"Mr. Hobhouse was with Lord Byron on his wedding day," is rather conclusive evidence of misrepresentation. The value of the entire article is much increased by the knowledge that Hobhouse wrote it, a piece of information which the readers of the review could not have possessed.

The *Westminster* did its best for Byron, and in so doing it drew fire from one of the many ecclesiastical organs of the day, the evangelical *Christian Observer*,[43] which was pained to think that any writing should tend to "screen this impious and licentious author from the just punishment of being repudiated and consigned to oblivion." Aside from Byron there were no poets, licentious or otherwise, whom the Radicals were called upon to defend. They had no occasion to revert to Keats, though he is occasionally mentioned with respect.[44] Wordsworth is referred to only by implication, and the implications are not flattering.[45] What they might have done for Shelley remains problematical.

It appears that they rejected an essay on Shelley by Leigh Hunt. Mrs. Shelley, according to Dowden,[46] approved of its being printed, until Peacock, who was also consulted, pointed out to her that Hunt's article was based on the erroneous theory that Shelley and Harriet parted by mutual consent. Then, seconded by Mrs. Shelley, Peacock advised Southern against accepting it.

So evidently we lost a paper by Leigh Hunt on Shelley, which would have been interesting, probably friendly to the dead poet, but perhaps not of immediate Utilitarian value. In that respect, however, it would not have been alone. For the despised but inevitable literary department of the review frequently fell short of the standard of strict Utilitarianism. The *Westminster Review* itself was not always useful literature.

One wonders, for example, how the editors could justify the publication of reviews of Latin and Greek lexicons and render them consistent with the equally frequent attacks on the classics. Many of these articles, says Bowring, were written by "Hogg, a barrister." This would be Thomas Jefferson Hogg, the friend and early biographer of Shelley, who belonged to the outer fringe of the Benthamite group, and who was in the habit of writing on the classics for reviews. He did the article on Niebuhr's *History of Rome* for the *Edinburgh*.[47] Which of the articles in the *West-minster* are from his pen I am unable to discover. Bowring says that they were not so good as Hogg himself thought them; al-lowing Hogg credit for even the best of them, the reader is in-clined to agree with Bowring, whatever may have been Hogg's estimate of their value. The only serious offense against utility included under this class before 1829 is the article on Doctor Jones's Greek and English Lexicon,[48] which enraged the Doctor and evoked a reply from him that was reviewed in the number following.[49] After 1830, however, classical articles are as plenti-ful in the *Westminster* as in the *Quarterly*. Volume XIII alone contains no less than five of them.

Other articles which sin most grievously against utility are Bowring's disquisitions on foreign literature. These articles like-wise appeared more frequently after 1829. They evidently were *Westminster* filler, always at hand on those frequent occasions when space was at a discount. It is true that they add to the im-pression of striking cosmopolitanism for which the *Westminster* is outstanding. It is also true that Bowring, who never let ap-parent obstacles stand in the way of action, worked out, probably to his own honest satisfaction, a clever proof that these articles had a place in the review. With this proof he was in the habit of beginning the articles.

Typical of his prefatory protests of utility are the opening sentences of his paper on Servian poetry.[50]

We think it is a very interesting and a very delightful thing to be enabled to share in the sympathies and to understand the habitual thoughts and feelings of any large portion of our fellow men; to watch the dawn and progress of civilization among them . . . When the first step is taken; when knowledge begins to circulate; when books become the receptacle and standard of language; when tradition gives place to history and all the vague and misty fables which one barbarous age communicates to another are superceded by the record of authentic facts, the impulse is given which is now acting . . . upon the intelligence, the virtue, and the happiness of the whole world. . . We are convinced that our readers will participate in the pleasure with which we have contemplated the vigorous simplicity, the popular and passionate spirit, the fresh and fruitful energy of a poetical literature which has only now found a voice or even an echo beyond its earliest birthplace.*

Thus does the editor modestly drape with a garland of Utilitarian cant the fifteen pages of specimens and philological notes which follow. It is only a drapery. Never again is one led to suspect any interest on the part of the reviewer in the intelligence, the virtue, the happiness of the whole world; in the dawn and progress of civilization; or even in knowledge when it begins to circulate. Nor is one convinced by the specimens of the vigorous simplicity, the popular and patient spirit, the fresh and fruitful energy. Least of all is one convinced that James Mill would have liked the article or the specimens. Take for instance the poem thrillingly entitled *Kod Popova Dvora,* concerning the activities of turtle doves:

> Hark! they coo together
>   One alone is silent;
> Of his mate the turtle
>   Asks in anxious language,
> "Blessed God assist thee,
>   My beloved turtle,
> When I coo to thee, love!
>   Why not coo to me, love?"

Such articles as these of Bowring's are useful only under a widely different conception of utility from that of the Philosophic Radicals. It is not likely that "the greatest number" would ever read them, or that they would derive any profit or happiness from them if they did.

The reviews of books of travel which appear with painful frequency after the first two years are even more open to the same suspicion. In general, they are mere digests of the books on which the reviewers have fed, seldom exhibiting any independent knowledge. From them, of course, the reader could secure considerable information, most of it unreliable, on the geography of distant parts and the ways of the un-English. Thus, in the number for January, 1826, the interested Utilitarian could learn many cheer-

* Compare *Living Poets of Holland,* X, 36f, and *Living Poets of the Magyars,* XI, 29, where Bowring makes practically the same apology. An article on the runes of Finland, VII, 317 ff., stands forth naked and unashamed, however.

ful facts about Arabs and Persians from Colonel Thompson's forty-six-page article,[51] of which about half is quotation from the travel book reviewed and which contains in its midst twelve pages quoted without a break. This strikes one as a delightfully easy method of filling up the pages of a journal which was always hard pressed for money and material. Most of these résumés were probably done by Southern or some office boy; we know that the article on Chile and La Plata was by Southern,[52] and in style and method many of the others are much like it.

Though they appear to be, and unquestionably are, very obvious padding, they do possess some Utilitarian value. They save the reader the expense of buying the travel books, which were then as now appearing in hordes, and the time required to labor through them. This service is one which all magazines and reviews in varying degree performed. James Mill in the *Westminster*,[53] before its own evil days had come, pointed the finger of scorn at the *Quarterly* for this custom of synopsizing travel books. He might have objected less to the corresponding work in the *Westminster*, where travel reviews sometimes contain pleas for sympathy with oppressed and unfortunate peoples. For example, the article "Arabs and Persians," referred to above as a flagrant example of a filler, includes, notwithstanding, such an appeal; and, for good measure, goes out of its way to declare that the *Song of Songs* is more voluptuous than anything in the Koran. Such instances of thinking, however, do not occur frequently in these reviews. It appears pertinent to inquire how the knowledge that after breakfast African women "blacken their eyes with Kohl and stain their teeth and the inside of their lips yellow with the goora, the flower of the tobacco plant, and the bark of a certain root," will assist the readers of the *Westminster* to make more goods at a greater profit.

Among the more unutilitarian features of the review, we should note in passing an erudite article on ancient and modern wines[54] and, in the same number, an equally erudite article on Egyptian hieroglyphics; the proposals for reforming the antiquarian society[55] which led to Crabb Robinson's break with Southern; and a curious attempt to introduce Egyptian architecture into

England, though this last project, as the reviewer demonstrated, had the Utilitarian advantage of saving the expense of the more ornate Greek and Gothic. The reviewer admits that "an inclined wall" may look queer at first, but maintains that the people will get accustomed to it and like it. In this statement no sarcasm is intended, in spite of the Radical bias of the publication.

Perhaps the most astonishing piece of apparent inconsistency is to be found principally in the articles of the orthodox Utilitarians, particularly of James Mill himself. In a publication intended avowedly for the use of the people, not primarily of the intelligentsia, there is no hesitation in quoting Latin, Greek, French, and Italian at length and in important context without translation. This custom appears to reflect startlingly on the genuineness of the democracy of the Mill group. They must have known that a large number of their readers would be ignorant of foreign languages, yet they made no concessions to that ignorance. James Mill, for instance, in his article on the Church, quotes Bayle's *Critique* on Mainbourg's *History of the Calvinists* for three pages without translating. Perhaps he did so partly to keep the *Westminster* as dignified in tone as the older reviews; perhaps he wished to stimulate his readers to learn the language; or perhaps he had no hidden motives at all.

To one tenet of their program for the increase of usefulness in literature, the reviewers, however, were all faithful. They wrote unadorned prose, the quality of which depended entirely on its clarity and on the value of what the writer had to say. Their articles cannot be considered decorative or ornamental; when they are not useful, they are simply bad. The reviewing staff included no Hazlitt and no Macaulay, and neither Bowring nor Southern had a tenth of the literary ability of Jeffrey. We are not surprised to find McCulloch advising Francis Place, who was thinking of writing an article for the *Edinburgh*, "Will you permit me to say that I think your article will be improved by avoiding those asperities of style in which you sometimes indulge and which are the great blemish of the *Westminster*."[56]

Many of the articles are very dreary and difficult indeed. For the brave soul who proposes to read through Place's paper on the history of parliaments, a fitter slogan than Bentham's Greatest Happiness is certainly Carlyle's "Love not pleasure, love God." The substance of Place's article may very well have contributed to the Greatest Happiness, but the act of reading it could scarcely have done so. Yet the reviewers' attempt at writing because they had something to say, not because they desired to say something, is by no means an unsuccessful literary experiment. Nothing in Lamb or De Quincey or Hazlitt is better than James Mill's paper on the *Edinburgh Review* or Southwood Smith's "The Use of the Dead to the Living," to mention only two of the more exciting Utilitarian reviews. Careful editorial revision by a man like Jeffrey would have improved the periodical appreciably. Yet the clear thinking, the sound knowledge, the genuine note of enthusiastic certainty in many of the *Westminster* articles would render them outstanding in any collection of early nineteenth-century essays. Bowring and Southern thought that its consistent heaviness, its deficiency in the graceful and the decorative, made the review monotonous and unsaleable; but if Lamb had written all its articles, it would have been as monotonous and perhaps as unsaleable.

The few attempts of the literary department to provide variety by means of articles of a light and humorous nature are almost invariably pitiful. A London dancing master named Wilson published in 1824 an absurd work called the *Danciad*, "being a descriptive sketch in verse on the different styles of dancing." It occurred to some waggishly minded Benthamite (perhaps "Southern, probably when drunk") to write a review of this book under the title of "Professor Wilson's Danciad," attributing it to the distinguished professor of moral philosophy at Edinburgh.[57] The idea itself reflects a sufficiently crude sense of humor, and the execution has no virtue to save the article from utter absurdity. Wilson's *Noctes Ambrosianae* treated it exactly as it deserved, with absolute disregard. One of Timothy Tickler's letters in *Blackwood's*, however, referred to it briefly as a dull joke and somewhat slanderous.[58] This is perhaps one of the articles referred to by J. S. Mill as "extremely offensive to us either in point of opinion, of taste, or by mere want of ability."[59] Another specimen of similar work is the review of *Letters to an Absent Brother*,[60] which, though it reflects sound literary judgment, contains far too much flat humor and too many pale puns to suit any intelligent critic. Instances of passing attempts at the humorous, sometimes successful, as in the review of *Debrett's Peerage*,[61] occurred at widely separate intervals; and Peacock's essay on Moore's *Epicurean* is a most amusing paper, a genuine relief from the typical *Westminster* seriousness. In general, however, it was not well for the literary department to try to be funny, even though the attempt may have been prompted by genuine humanitarianism. Relief was certainly needed, but the remedy was usually worse than the disease.

As we have seen, and as Bentham himself seems to have expected, the literary department of the review was the most frequent offender against the Utilitarian spirit. Even this department, in spite of several inconsistencies, did, however, produce a certain amount of work which combines excellent literary criticism with good Philosophic Radicalism. During the first four years, perhaps half the literary articles are of some real merit, or of importance in the development of the idea of utility. Add to these the better political and general articles, and you have a surprisingly high degree of usefulness, even of excellence in the broader sense. It is remarkable not that the review sometimes appears faithful to Bentham only in its fashion, but rather that it is as generally consistent as it is. It is true that it is not so consistent as Bowring meant it to be, or as Southern's *London,* by way of puffing, declared it to be. Considering the diverse interests of the reviewers, entire consistency was an impossible ideal. Bowring himself was a writer of hymns and album verse, Southern was an amateur antiquarian, Peacock a satirist, Crabb Robinson an omnipresent dilettante, Fox a Unitarian minister. Bingham, friend of Tom Moore, was a writer of verse and a singer of sentimental songs in drawing rooms. Roebuck, too, had his accomplishments, and John Stuart Mill during half these years was emotionally insecure, wondering in real anguish whether Utilitarianism was worth while. In his writing he still continued, however, to apply his father's rules to situations as they arose, as did the other young would-be *philosophes.*

His father himself, though often disgruntled at the conduct of the review and the thought that it was being edited by such a flabby Benthamite, never wavered from the belief that promoting the Greatest Happiness was the chief end of man. Malthusian father of nine children, democratic author of articles readable only to the learned, laissez-faire governmental reformer at the head of England's outstanding trade monopoly, uncompromising defender of the duty of the intellect to question, unsparing critic of those whose theory differed from their practice, he never questioned the dogma of utility or perceived that in his own life he was contradicting much of that dogma. He is the grand figure of the review, the most paradoxical and fanatic of them all. A Scot who had made up his mind and who wasted no energy in self-questioning, he was tireless in his unselfish efforts to promote the opinions in which he believed.

Mill owed his influence to Bentham, but the review owed its influence to Mill. He and his Philosophic Radicals, with all their weaknesses and crotchets, spoke out, in a review which under Bowring's editorship was not theirs and which had weaknesses and crotchets of its own, with an energy and conviction which we do not find in other respectable periodicals of that time. As their uncompromising but always chivalrous opponent, Christopher North, wrote of them in his *Noctes*, "In the ring they hit hard, and go right up to their man's head."[62] Their close and whole-hearted collaboration for those few years in furthering projects for increasing the amount of happiness in this world is the sort of thing which has reappeared too seldom since their time. In spite of "asperities of style," in spite of long and unreadable articles on the currency question, or absurd extracts from the popular poetry of Servians and Magyars, they created a notable thing. Whether they did more good than harm is a question that of course can never be answered. Fathers of Philistinism though they were, they uttered much truth and uttered it bravely and with dignity. One feels that when, in 1828, their school already breaking up, the Utilitarian intellectuals who followed Mill seceded definitely from the review which they had made great but which had never been their own, there passed away a glory from the earth.

VI

MORRISON'S PILL

The break-up which occurred in 1828 had been inevitable from the beginning. To the outside world the review had appeared the definite organ of a united group, but, as we have seen, it really never had been. From the outset, contributors had continually harassed poor Bowring, whom they disliked and who gave them some grounds for dissatisfaction.[1] In 1826, Bingham had begun editing the *Parliamentary History and Review,* exclusively political, and into this much of the energy of the Philosophic Radicals had been diverted. Southern's allegiance, too, was divided between the *Westminster* and the *London Magazine,* which was slowly dying under his editorship. He discontinued his connection with the *Westminster* in 1827. Circulation had fallen off considerably; the second edition of one thousand had soon become unnecessary. Advertising, which in early numbers had amounted to as many as twenty-eight pages (not counting notices of Baldwin's books, probably inserted gratis), had also gradually fallen off. By 1828 Bentham's four thousand pounds had been burned up, and clearly something had to be done. The Mills proposed taking over the review, provided the linguist-editor did not come with it; but Bowring busied himself and succeeded in gaining the support of Colonel T. Perronet Thompson, who became proprietor in 1828, leaving the editorship in Bowring's hands. This arrangement angered the Mills, who accused Bowring of duplicity, and they and their followers refused to have any further connection with the review.

The complete story of the mental anguish which the review in its first four years had caused those concerned would be long and pitiful, but in so far as it reflects the ways of editors and contributors it should be told. For the struggles raged loudest around the ever-burning question of editorial mutilations.

Unquestionably the most troublesome contributor was Francis Place. He would certainly have been difficult in any event. He was not a writer, as his contributions show, and yet he possessed as a self-made man considerable sensitiveness and no slight opinion of his own ability. He was the more difficult, however, because of his contempt for Bowring and his feeling that Bowring really did not wish him to have anything to do with the review which Place himself had planned with Mill and Bentham before Bowring was heard of.

At Bentham's suggestion, it developed later, Bowring asked him at the outset to write an article on Bentham's model prison, the Panopticon. Place replied,

One condition I have to make is this. That neither the editor nor any other person shall alter, abridge, or add to any article of mine. It will soon be known who it is that writes for the Review, and I am not willing to be the reputed father of any abortion or bastard. Mine must be *legitimate* children, however ugly or ungraceful they may be. . .[2]

Bowring replied that the condition was "inadmissable and impossible because incompatible with the unity of design and character which belongs or ought to belong to a periodical work," and Bentham declared, *"Ugly* or *ungraceful* children we cannot accept, nor can we traffic with pigs in a poke."[3]

This of course evoked a reply from Place, who throughout was consulting with James Mill. "No one but a mere mercenary can write on such terms, and I cannot write as a mere mercenary. These may be the usual terms for Reviews, may be the proper terms, but then I cannot write for Reviews."[4] As a matter of fact, they were the usual terms; it was the policy of both Gifford and Jeffrey to maintain absolute control in making alterations and corrections.[5] Bentham's reply, a six-page note, pointed out that the proprietors were under moral as well as legal responsibility, and noted that "Mill never made any such stipulation for himself on writing for the *Edinburgh*. Jeffrey cut and slashed him without mercy. He has not in regard to this one."[6]

At once Place wrote to Mill:

. . . if any person except himself or Bowring had projected the Review, he would have applauded me and would have said, "Jeffrey cut and slashed Mill without mercy. Well done, son Francis; go on; put a stop to that scandalous practice."[7]

In the course of negotiations Bentham made three separate pilgrimages from Queen's Square Place to Charing Cross to placate the resolute tailor, besides going into consultation with Mill. Bentham's conclusion was that they had better let him have his own way; but, as Bowring did not ask him to contribute on his own terms, Place retired from the combat (though, he said, he would have liked to participate in the review and would have welcomed the money), and did not actually contribute until 1826.

His later relations with the review were no happier. His first article, on the history of Egypt,[8] caused him considerable pain; Bowring did not send him the proofs, "and the consequence is," Place wrote, "the article has more than 100 errors in it, the names of places and persons are wrong spelt in many cases so absurdly lettered as to show an ignorance quite disgraceful to the editor. . . ."[9] Asking Francis Place of Charing Cross to write on the history of Egypt at all would appear to be another outstanding piece of editorial incompetence. At this same time his diary shows him, evidently still frightened at the thought of writing for a review, toiling a fortnight nine hours a day on his second article, "History of Parliament," not published until October, 1827. He feels it is a labor of love: "I know that some persons write in Reviews for money and that a few like myself write with a view to benefit others much more than for money." Yet obvious and justifiable bitterness is reflected in an N.B., inserted in an almost microscopic hand, obviously later: "I never received a shilling for anything written for the *Westminster Review.*"[10] Meanwhile Place and the Mills were enjoying frequent weighty conferences on the sad plight of the Utilitarian journal, "the conduct of the editors," and what was to be done about it.

Another prospective contributor whom Bowring drove away at the start was the veteran radical John Thelwall. Thelwall wrote to Place indignantly:

I have received a note from the Editors of the Westminster Review saying that they will be glad to *receive* an article from me on the subject proposed ("prosody and the utterance of the English language") but cannot pledge themselves to accept and insert it. If such be their mode of management with their contributors they must look for communications from those whose time has not yet become valuable, and whose capabilities are yet unknown. I cannot afford to put my time and labor into such a lottery. . ."[11]

Clearly, he considered himself insulted; he asserted that editors of other publications did not treat him in this way; indeed, that Southern had made no such suggestions while he was writing for the *Retrospective*.[12] It should be noted here, however, that Bowring's procedure in this respect was not at all unusual. For instance, Campbell, engaging Leigh Hunt in the same year to write for the *New Monthly*, reserved the right to reject articles unconditionally.[13]

Then there was trouble with John Neal, man of grievances, who had come over from the United States with his pen to defend his countrymen from all and sundry English libels and misconceptions. He wrote laudatory articles on America for *Blackwood's*, the *London Magazine*, the *New Monthly*, and several other periodicals, as well as for the *Westminster*, met the youngsters of the Utilitarian Society and made acid remarks about them in his autobiography; made even more acid remarks about Bowring; complained that Jeffrey kept articles submitted to him an unduly long time; and returned to America a confirmed Benthamite, and the prophet of Utilitarianism in Portland, Maine. There he established *The Yankee*, a weekly newspaper carrying as its motto "The Greatest Happiness of the Greatest Number—Bentham," and spreading the principle of utility in small doses. Neal himself thought very highly of his journal, stating that for a year and a half it "burst like a northern meteor upon our people. It was continued with triumphant success; entirely original; most of it— seven-eighths perhaps, written by myself. . . ."[14] Regarding one of his articles prepared for the *Westminster*, but not published, Bowring had to assert with some emphasis the principle of the unity of the review. Neal states that he sent a requested article with a note ordering its return unless it could be published "without material alterations and omissions." The proof which came to Neal showed that the article had been badly hacked and hewn, and that much had been interpolated. On his objecting, Bowring replied that "the Westminster Review must speak the opinions of the Westminster Reviewer, and not the opinions of any individual when those opinions differ from those of the Westminster Review."[15] So Neal, claiming that Bowring had inserted opinions directly the reverse of his, did not allow the article to appear, but sent it to Jeffrey, who kept it several weeks and then at Neal's request returned it. Neal also grew furious at the insertion, in his vindication of American writers in his article on the United States,[16] of remarks uncomplimentary to American oratory which he certainly did not write, and objected strongly to other revisions of this article by Bowring and John Mill. Though most of Neal's sound and fury appears to signify nothing, the insertion in his article of sentiments flatly contradictory to his does appear a trifle high-handed.

Neal reports[17] another instance of editorial ingenuity. It appears that Joseph Parkes, Birmingham liberal, wrote for the *Westminster* an article on Lingard's *History of England*. It was accepted by Southern, who later said that it was "a little too strong and would have to be *boned.*" Could the excised part, asked Southern, at this time also editor of the *London Magazine,* be printed in the *London?* Parkes replied no, whereupon most of the article appeared in the *London,* part in one place, part in another. The rest of the article was to appear in the *Westminster.* The tale is at least possible, and certainly articles answering the description appeared in both magazines.[18]

The woes of Crabb Robinson were also distinctly bitter. He finally broke his friendship with Southern because the latter, in a *Westminster* article attacking the Antiquarian Society, included uncomplimentary allusions to a member of its council, who happened to be Robinson's friend Ayrton.[19] It had been through Southern that Robinson had begun contributing to the review, and most of his articles were produced grudgingly at that editor's urgent solicitation. He did an article on Goethe,[20] showing that Colburn's 1824 translation of *Dichtung und Wahrheit* was made from a French translation and badly mutilated; and he ground out short notices of three other books. His diary shows that even in the first

year the review was chronically short of copy, particularly for the
so-called literary department. He had also lent Southern money,
which had not been returned. He had not been paid for his contributions. In fact, Robinson states that Southern generally did not
pay his contributors, though Bowring did.[21] The attack on Ayrton
after all this was too much.

This will lead to a breaking up of our acquaintance, no doubt [he
wrote in his diary] and I cannot help it. Southern is a fanatic of reform, as I have told him, and cares not whom he sacrifices—he is an
Iconoclast who enquires not in his zeal to break an idolatrous image
whether he may not slaughter or maim many a worshipper at the same
time.[22]

In short, Southern had not been quite a gentleman, only a gentleman of the press.

Bowring, furthermore, was only editor of the political department of the Utilitarian review, and rejected an article by Robinson
on Prussia, written with great effort at Southern's request. After
this rejection Robinson revised it somewhat and sent it to the
Quarterly, where it was accepted. The story is told in a letter from
Southern to Robinson,[23] on the back of which Robinson wrote: "To
be destroyed when properly referred to hereafter as illustrative of
the history of a published article written for one party and printed
by the other." The time for the reference appears to have come.
Wrote Southern:

About the article on Prussia—I must explain. . . Bowring came to me
full of lamentation (I write upon oath) speaking in the highest manner
of the talent of the article, and regretting that [what] would be considered a prize must go over to the enemy (as threatened by your note).
With every desire to insert a paper so well written and so full of information, he said [he] could not be instrumental in spreading notions
which he considered injurious to the cause which he had so deeply
at heart. He knew the Holy Alliance, its principles, its measures, and
its plans [too well] to publish anything which was likely to put them
in a favorable and as he thought an unjust light.

Southern concluded with abject apologies for his part in the affair.
It would have pleased the disgruntled Robinson to know of the
analogous incident of Hobhouse's laudatory article on Byron, sub-

mitted to the *Quarterly,* rejected for political reasons, and finally
published in the radical *Westminster.*

So with much suffering on the part of all concerned ended the
first dynasty of the review. In spite of internal dissension it had
accomplished much. In fact, it had accomplished about all that the
Westminster was destined to accomplish until 1836, when it was
absorbed by Mill's and Molesworth's *London Review* and became
the *London and Westminster.* From 1828 until the amalgamation
one observes in it little intellectual growth or vitality—only satisfaction that the middle-class millenium is at hand—a satisfaction
which contrasts strikingly with John Stuart Mill's own questionings
of democracy printed serially during the same period in Fonblanque's *Examiner* as *The Spirit of the Age;* which contrasts even
more strikingly with the new radicalism of Carlyle, likewise printed
serially during the same period in *Fraser's Magazine* as *Sartor
Resartus.* English thought stayed alive, but the *Westminster Review,* its task accomplished, relinquished its former place with the
leaders of English thought.

Little more though the *Westminster* had to say, it was still the
only review under Benthamite control, and as such continued to
exert whatever influence the peculiar prestige of the name could
lend. It continued to be undeniably Benthamite; it was no longer,
however, particularly philosophic, and its doctrine had already
suffered sufficient repetition to make it seem hardly radical. If anything, its preachments were rapidly becoming a trifle commonplace.
Enthusiastic partisans like Bowring and Thompson of course could
not see this. In 1828, the Reform Bill was still four years away,
and few of the measures that the *Westminster* proposed had actually been put into effect. Certainly the elder Mill could not see it,
either, for his later work is as fully charged with middle-class
dogmatism as his earlier. But one wonders what would have happened if the editorship of the review during the exciting Reform
Bill days had fallen to John Stuart Mill, whom the Utilitarian
ideal of thinking for one's self was already leading into something broader than Utilitarianism.

Bowring, however, hung on, much to the disgust of the Mill
group, who at once let it be known that they had withdrawn from

the *Westminster*. Naturally concerned about the effect of their withdrawal on circulation and prestige, Bowring throughout the first troubled year made frantic efforts to conciliate them, working through Place, whom he still dared approach, and the veteran liberal Joseph Hume. Meanwhile, he had to endure the usual labor involved in editing a new publication. Apparently he could not get a publishing house to undertake the venture; Baldwin, Mill's publisher, withdrew with Mill, and the review had to be jobbed out. Contributors obviously were scarce, with Mill and all his young disciples unavailable. Fortunately Thompson had boundless energy and a facile pen, and, reviewing his own and other people's books, usually accounted for not less than three articles for each number—about a quarter of the review. Bowring, of course, continued to write. James Mill finally relented slightly on the intervention of Place, and contributed his article on the ballot.[24] The aged Bentham began articles, most of which, of course, were never finished, but parts of which were utilized.[25] There are more able articles on medicine, at least one of them by Dr. Southwood Smith. Peacock did three articles, "Moore's *Byron*," "Thomas Jefferson," and "London Bridge,"[26] and Fonblanque contributed at least one more, the review of Peacock's *Crotchet Castle*. Most of the other reviewers during this period cannot be identified; probably they were insignificant people living as well as they could by writing. Carlyle, a man at this time almost in that class, sold the *Westminster* a leading article, his "Nibelungenlied,"[27] and on being reproved by Napier, then editing the *Edinburgh*, for going over to the enemy, replied that he had rather use the *Edinburgh* than any; "on the other hand, I am a person that, in all senses of the word, live by writing; and if one honest man seems to have no need of my produce, what can I do but travel on with it until I find another that does?"[28] Presumably there were many now unknown journalists who lived in this way whose work was accepted by the *Westminster*.

This was the best that the temperamentally optimistic Bowring could have hoped for, and his initial discouragement is reflected in an outcry in a letter to Place, still about the hostile Mills: "God knows the friends of the people might be better employed than in doing injury to one of the most important popular organs."[29] Yet the forthcoming number, he says, will be as good as any former number, "notwithstanding my difficulties." Perusal of the number does not substantiate his opinion. The new prospectus, of course, reflects no discouragement; and it patently seeks readers. The *Westminster,* it states, will continue to advocate the cause of the people, and

it will endeavor to relieve the grave and weighty discussions which agitate, or ought to agitate society, by a greater infusion of literary matter. While it seeks to instruct, as its higher and nobler calling—it will not forget to amuse.[30]

The number appeared in January, and on February 5 Bowring reported to Place that "the sale already promises a considerable increase—and this in spite of the *complete silence* of the London press," although he had sent out many advance copies. The silence, however, did not continue. There is some justification for Bowring's exultant note to Place of July 18, 1829,

The whole country is ringing with the Westminster Review—and with the marvelous improvement of the last three numbers. I have collected, I think, more than 100 criticisms, *all* agreeing on this point. You will rejoice at this—for you have behaved so kindly when so many were faithless.[31]

Knowing what Place thought of Bowring, one can fancy him reading this note with his tongue in his cheek; for all he had done up to this time was to listen. Place was too good a politician to discourage anyone from whom he could find out what was going on.

Journals carrying friendly notices of the revived *Westminster,* most of them under Benthamite or at least liberal management— the *Spectator,* the *Athenaeum,* the *Monthly Repository*—all took their cue from the prospectus and emphasized the fact that the articles had become lighter and more readable. It is true that these articles make less rigid demands on the intellect than many in earlier numbers, and most of them are considerably shorter. Whereas in the early days the review had carried about eleven articles, it now usually consisted of sixteen. But if it became easier reading, it grew also less penetrating and less exciting. It contained more purely literary articles, and these of considerably less value. The chorus of praise, often overdone, died out, incidentally, after the first year, and one seldom sees the *Westminster* mentioned in contemporary journals again. "The ringing of the whole country" was probably a case of concentrated puffing.[32]

But it soon became evident that no puffing could save the review, which was destined to receive its most serious blow from without just after it had suffered most from internal dissension. The *Edinburgh,* which for four years had suffered almost in silence while attacked by both liberals and Tories, now challenged its Benthamite tormentor, the *Westminster,* to debate, and won. The contest excited much public interest and many comments from the press, and at the end it was generally conceded that the *Westminster* was demolished and Utilitarianism itself philosophically discredited.

It did not take Francis Place long to find out that "the articles in the Edinburgh Review were written by young Mr. Macaulay for a purpose";[33] and as young Mr. Macaulay was at once recognized by Whig leaders as a promising politician and went into Parliament soon after, we may assume that the purpose was served.

What Macaulay did in the three *Edinburgh* articles[34] was really very simple. Otherwise he would not have been Macaulay, the Whig leaders would not have recognized him—and he would not have demolished the *Westminster Review.* By a penetrating attack on the purely theoretical approach to politics, and a defense of the Whig method of reform according to the dictates of practical experience and common sense, he demonstrated beyond all doubt that the Utilitarian philosophy of government was not infallible. He did not attempt much, but he attempted just enough; for one recognizes with something of a start that the Utilitarians had actually claimed infallibility. When faced with the simple proof that they had done so, and that they actually were not infallible, they were helpless.

It is possible, Macaulay pointed out in his review of Mill's *Essay on Government,* that under some circumstances monarchy might provide a better government than democracy, and that according to the self-interest principle a king might find it advantageous to rule well. Under some circumstances, the interest of the nation, and particularly of the lower class, might not be identical with that of the middle class. In short, "It is utterly impossible to deduce the science of government from the principles of human nature," because no general proposition except the self-interest principle, which Macaulay accepts, is universally true. Problems of government must be approached by the inductive method, not by a priori reasoning. Thus Mill's method in the *Essay on Government* is wrong, and an exact political science cannot be founded upon the general premises which Mill accepts or upon any general premises. The Whig method alone can be trusted. This is the substance of Macaulay's first article; his other two, in reply to the *Westminster's* defense of Utilitarianism, added little except a demonstration of his opponent's inadequacy in the debate. In this respect, however, they were so effective that it appears unfortunate for the *Westminster* that it ever defended its creed at all.

The defense, however, was undertaken. It occurred to someone, probably Bowring, that no less a person than Bentham himself should reply to the *Edinburgh's* formidable attack. At any rate, the old man set at work and accomplished an article, forty pages of copyist's manuscript in length, dated June 2, 1829.[35] Meanwhile the *Westminster* had spread the news that the forthcoming reply to the *Edinburgh* was to be by Bentham. Unfortunately, Bentham's article turned out to be purely a history of his own thought and no reply at all to the *Edinburgh;* so the faithful Thompson took it, wrote four pages of reply to the *Edinburgh,* and appended thereto the Bentham history of his own thought condensed to ten pages. He called this joint composition an article and printed it in the number for July, 1829.[36] The feebleness of the whole affair is well indicated by the treatment of Macaulay's main point, that Mill's method is deductive rather than inductive. "The pith of the charge against the author of the essays is, that he has written 'an elaborate treatise on government' and 'deduced the whole science from the assumption of certain propensities of human nature.' Now in the name of Sir Richard Birnie and all the saints, from what else *should* it be deduced?" asked Thompson. This is the incredibly stupid answer to an article which has maintained that it should not be deduced at all.

The incompetence of the *Westminster's* champion became increasingly apparent as the battle continued. Macaulay replied at once to Thompson's first article, attempting to be courteous to Bentham, the supposed author, who, he suggested, had not read the article to which he was attempting to reply. In this paper Macaulay showed that his position in the debate remained intact after the *Westminster* article, and attempted, not too successfully, to deal with the general philosophic question of the greatest happiness principle, pointing out that Christianity worked better than Utility because it supplied a very positive reward for contributing to the community's welfare. In the *Westminster* for October, 1829,[37] Thompson in replying to this article shifted his ground and declared that he wished only to expose the *Edinburgh's* sham democracy, "not to determine whether the Essay on Government was perfect." That being Macaulay's issue, he gave away the case then and there; and this article, Macaulay's reply to it, and Thompson's final word in the next number of the *Westminster*,[38] are all inconsequential, except in so far as they successively weakened the position of the Benthamite review.

Meanwhile the radicals were becoming very uneasy, as Place's collection of documents relating to the controversy shows. Place accumulated numerous clippings from contemporary journals, all most disheartening to a faithful Benthamite. The only favorable notices of the *Westminster's* part in the joint debate are four articles on the Utilitarian school in the *Western Times*,[39] signed B, and identified by Place as Bowring's. Since Bowring came to London from Exeter, the home of the *Western Times,* the identification is at least probable. The *Morning Chronicle*, the *Scotsman*, the *Examiner*,[40] and the *Oriental Herald*,[41] all Benthamite journals, did what they could in defense of the cause, but their efforts appeared inadequate; and like the equally friendly *Athenaeum*,[42] they could find nothing to say for the *Westminster's* handling of the contest. The *Caledonian Mercury*[42] quoted from the *New Monthly* to the effect that the *Edinburgh* was clearly winning, and itself ventured the opinion that ". . . it will be the death of the Utilitarians;

unless indeed they can provide themselves with an abler defender than the author of the reply to the Edinburgh Review in the last number of the *Westminster*," that reply being "in every respect a total failure." This clipping had been sent to Place by Joseph Hume, who was much exercised about the whole affair.

On September 16, 1829, after the second *Edinburgh* article, Hume wrote to Place urging him to intercede with Mill himself and persuade him to take over the defense of Utility. He had been talking with Bowring and wrote:

I think it a matter of great regret to the friends of liberal and good government that both the Mr. Mill's should have set themselves against the Westminster Review; and not only refuse to contribute to its pages, but actually say everything in their power against it. . . Mr. Mill has always said that the diffusion of good principles was his object, no matter how done; and, in support of his own principles, he certainly ought to give every aid in his power to the Westminster Review.

This, considering the fact that neither of the Mills was doing any journalistic work at this time, seems a not unreasonable statement. Hume pointed out of Bowring that

there is not a man in London more zealous and more desirous of the spread of everything that can support good government . . . and although in judgment he may not be up to the mark which Mr. Mill and his son think requisite to edit the Review, he certainly is deserving of their support.[43]

But the Mills sat silent. Hume was disappointed in Thompson's second article, and told Bowring so.

It is merely a critique in words and sentences [he wrote Bowring] and not easily understood unless by those who are fully masters of the whole of the preceding discussion. It takes a very limited and very confined view of the subject and does not, by any means, support the truth of the great principle which has been challenged by the Edinboro. . . There is a better article in the Oriental Herald on the subject. But something more than has yet appeared must be brought forward, or those who have hitherto styled themselves Utilitarians must hide themselves.[44]

Two weeks later he wrote once more to Place, inclosing the grim judgment of the *Caledonian Mercury,* and asking again, "Why does not Mr. Mill defend his own production?"[45] Place in a manuscript note supplied a reason:

I was with Mr. Mill at Dorking when the last [i.e., Macaulay's second article] was published. Mr. Bickersteth was there also. He and I were of the opinion that they were equally unfair and foolish, and not such as Mr. Mill should reply to.[46]

To those confirmed in the Utilitarian habit of thinking, the articles might appear so. It is indicative of the intelligence and increasing independence of John Stuart Mill that he considered his father's irrationally scornful attitude a sign of weakness, and was himself partially converted by Macaulay away from the doctrinaire approach to politics.[47] The *Edinburgh* attack aroused equally serious if not equally intelligent doubts in the minds of those outside the immediate Benthamite group. For instance, someone submitted to Hume, apropos of the discussion, a set of questions about Utilitarianism. They distressed Hume; he sent them on to Place; and they were shown to Thompson, the *Westminster's* spokesman. To Place they seemed important, involving as they did the impeccability of the Benthamite system. They had to do with the power of majorities over minorities. Did the Benthamites think that the majority should rule and direct the minority? Should the "greatest happiness" be secured at the sacrifice of the unfortunate minority? "If so, may not the majority of any community, who are the poorest," appropriate the property of the rich minority? Or "if 29 of a community, say of 30," decided to kill and eat the thirtieth, might they do so?

Place, not wishing to see the party thoroughly discredited, set at work on a reply. "Greatest happiness" is a relative, not an absolute term, and really means least evil, he said. The suffering of minorities, being the least evil, is inevitable. As for the poor plundering the rich, they evidently do not consider it conducive to the greatest happiness to do so, otherwise they would have done so long since. If "natural repugnance" to eating the thirtieth does not overcome considerations in favor of that procedure, then eat the thirtieth. But no "community sufficiently enlightened to understand the principle of utility" would indulge in this piece of cannibalism.[48]

This by-product of the controversy never saw the light in print, but one hopes that Place's reasoning satisfied Hume's inquirer. Even if it did, however, it seems probable that he agreed with the general verdict that the *Edinburgh* had at last demolished its hitherto dogmatically convincing opponent, and that Utilitarianism up to this time had been overrated.

So the Whigs locked the stable, but the horse had already been stolen. In politics and society generally Utilitarianism had done its work. It was only a question of time until the measures it had advocated and the culture it had proposed would become assimilated into English life. The Whig journals had helped in this movement, and now the Whigs were to get most of the credit from their contemporaries. Meanwhile the *Westminster* itself, though defeated, kept fighting for the middle class the political battle that was practically won, talking about the glories of that class, exulting in the political and cultural discomfiture of the aristocracy, beating over much old ground which we need not resurvey. It showed increased concern about the working class, that concern being generally for keeping them in their place. Frequently it was flippant or impudent rather than logical, as in the article entitled "Character of George IV,"[49] which lists many fascinating examples of the late monarch's habits, or in the first specific blow for the Reform Bill,[50] containing Thompson's exordium to the middle classes to assert themselves:

Noah was a prodigious radical, when, hearing the world was to be drowned, he went about such common-sense proceedings as making himself a ship to swim in. A Whig would have laid half a dozen sticks together for an ark, and called it virtual representation.

The procedure here is startlingly different from James Mill's, and this is the sort of thing which evoked press commendation for sprightliness.

Thompson's work in general is likely to be written in this light and flippant style. A particularly good example is the leading article of the first number under his proprietorship, his plea for removing Catholic political disabilities, of which thirty thousand reprints were distributed.[51] Beginning rather meretriciously with a yarn about fourteen black and six grey horses, it proceeds with some ability to state and answer in tabular form all known objections to Catholic Emancipation. The article appeared in January, 1829, while a bill to effect the reforms advocated was before Parliament; and in April of that year the major disabilities were removed. Thompson, not unnaturally, gave himself much credit for the measure. This article, James Mill's paper on the ballot, several articles on "Taxes on Knowledge,"[52] and sundry comments on the Reform Bill, are the only contributions of note in the political department after 1828.

The article on the ballot is vastly more able than Thompson's Catholic Emancipation propaganda, though not so attractive. This is the only identifiable contribution of the Mill faction after the split. It is so sound that today it appears thoroughly platitudinous, and one wonders how anyone could have hoped to carry on honest government under the system then existing as Mill describes it. Perhaps, as he intimates, no one did; and perhaps that is partly the reason why the obvious reform was so long in being effected. Certainly this article, given wider publicity by Fonblanque's quoting from it at length in the *Examiner*,[53] is a powerful blow for the right measure—machinery, no doubt, as Carlyle maintained, but machinery which Carlyle's perfected individual could have done without little better than the Utilitarians' own perfected individual.

Mention should be made of the part played by the review in the Reform Bill crisis—a relatively minor part. Thompson regularly ran brief prefaces of a page or two at the beginning of each number, and in these he vigorously advocated the measure, much in the tone of a professional agitator. In addition to these, the review contained one article of importance on the bill, and several small allusions to it. The one article,[54] of interest partly because it is not even nominally a book review, unless you count a bill as a book, throws much light on the radicalism of the review and incidentally of the bill itself. Writing on the passage of the First Bill by the Commons, the reviewer points out that the measure has been advocated because of a desire not so much for reform as for peace and quiet and commercial security. "The middle classes . . . knew that if a convulsion arose, victory to either party would be destructive to them." He attempts to intimidate the Lords with the threat that popular fury will demand their abolition, if by opposing the bill they should alienate the middle class, the assumption being that the Lords must choose between two alternatives, a battle of upper and middle classes against lower, which the reviewer evidently would prefer, or one of lower and middle against upper.

But once the bill is passed, the reviewer foresees a danger— that the Commons will be full of demagogues from the lower classes, that as a result "the reigning prejudices of the people will be fostered by being extolled and appealed to," that the aristocracy will see that it is to its advantage to appeal to the crowd and join these demagogues. Hence, in a moment of inspiration foreseeing Disraeli, the reviewer suggests that the third possibility in combinations may take place, upper and lower classes against middle. This would be fatal; throwing overboard as much of laissez faire as convenient, he declares that "a government ought to guide, not be guided by the people—they ought to guide them to good—but this should be the influence of superior understanding, not of superior power." He finds that need, as always, is to educate the people, now presumably in the principles of laissez faire in industry.

However, the article ends with a song of triumph, more enthusiastic than grammatical: though the times are perilous,

the strongholds of the aristocracy have been taken—the old system is broken up, and an opportunity is afforded, while confusion and despair are in the enemies camp, to make another inroad and utterly root them out.

In the immediate reform period, the review excels, as a matter of fact, in crowing, and after the bill was actually passed sang two more songs of triumph in the same vein. Rejoicing gradually gave place to disappointment, however, as the reformed Parliament did not at once bring into being a Utilitarian civilization, as it passed factory legislation and did not repeal the Corn Laws.

But at least the review could exert itself for the education of the people to prevent the dire catastrophe foreseen by the author of the "Parliamentary Reform" article. Here, as in the treatment of the bill itself, we see the incipient conservatism of one group of the erstwhile radicals. Thompson in an article on machine breaking[55] points out that the troubles of the laboring classes are all due to the Corn Laws. The machines are friends of the laborers, and if there were no Corn Laws plenty of food for everyone combined with increased production of goods would lead to unparalleled prosperity. The reviewer carefully avoids the burning question of bad factory conditions and of the inevitable unemployment resulting from the use of machinery. In general, the Corn Laws and free trade get much more attention from the review in the later period than they did in the earlier;[56] and to the system of tariffs all the misery of the working classes is attributed.

The Sadler factory bill, the review maintained, was a nefarious attempt on the part of the aristocracy to blind the nation to the abuses from which members of that class profited:

a fraud got up to distract attention from slavery abroad, and lay up a store of charges against the moral character of the manufacturing population, to be drawn upon whenever the question of the Corn Laws come on, in proof of the inadviseableness of permitting the extension of the manufacturing industry.[57]

It seems equally probable that the *Westminster* used the Corn Laws to detract attention from proposed factory legislation. An able article on the Sadler bill,[58] distinctly orthodox and conservative Benthamism, appears opposed to all factory legislation; later, when the Southwood Smith-Chadwick bill was brought in, the review neither supported it nor opposed it. For this bill, a Benthamite measure written by two former *Westminster* reviewers, was forward-looking. In fact, after the article on the Sadler bill the review does not mention factory reform at all.

The author of that article was not asleep to conditions; he based most of his conclusions on Dr. James Kay's penetrating study of the working class in Manchester. But he was so blinded by partisanship that he could not treat the material intelligently.

His survey of the existing situation deserves attention. There is overproduction; we cannot compete with other nations because the Corn Laws make the cost of labor and so of manufacturing too high. Furthermore,

Our poor laws stimulate the increase of an uneducated, toil-worn, and ignorant working class. We have a vindictive criminal code, which is so abhorrent to common sense that juries modify their verdicts to elude its vengeance. . . . In the provinces, there is no preventive police. . . . Our gaols, though improved, are still schools of vice, where the novice is initiated in the more subtle secrets of chicanery and fraud. . . Add to all this, that there is no system of national education for the people.

The reviewer quotes from Dr. Kay on extremely unsanitary living conditions among the workers—the story, that has become old, of unpaved streets filled with heaps of refuse; of unclean, ill-furnished houses, badly drained and damp; of discouraged and consequently debased and improvident workmen. He quotes him further to the effect that ill health among laborers is due not to long hours alone, but to these wretched living conditions in conjunction with long hours, and then arrives at the conclusion, not that something is wrong with the whole wage fund system, but that factory legislation is useless and that the Tories are brutes for introducing it. They should take measures to remedy the bad living conditions instead of interfering in the factories. Shorter hours will upset the whole balance of industry, more and improved machines will be installed, more people will be out of work, uprisings and all kinds of dire social disorders will ensue, and, worst of all, the Tories will have kept the Corn Laws. Here is clearcut devotion to the old laissez faire doctrine and to the manufacturing interests, obviously calculated to appeal to the *Westminster's* readers, as many as were left.

But even though laborers do live in unwholesome cellars because there are Corn Laws but no adequate poor laws and no ballot and because they cannot be taught "obstinate refusal to multiply,"[59] even though the radicals in the reformed Parliament accomplish nothing, yet the review during this period appears in general rather satisfied than dissatisfied with England as it is. It quotes with approval Dr. Thomas Chalmers's praise of wealth, to which "we stand indispensably indebted for our crowded cities, our thousand manufactories"[60]—and frequently points out that the wealth is passing from the drones (the aristocracy) to the worker bees (the middle class). Democracy is growing, not only in England, but on the Continent, especially in France. It has succeeded gloriously in America, which according to some reviewer's ecstatic statement was in 1832 already "ten millions of free men, earnestly engaged in adapting institutions of every kind to the only just end, 'the greatest happiness.' "[61] Peacock's article on Thomas Jefferson,[62] calling him "undoubtedly the greatest public benefactor that has yet appeared in the nineteenth century," and eulogizing him for his part in the American Revolution and for preserving democracy from panic during the horrors of revolution in France, harmonizes excellently with the triumphant tone of the review during this period.

Even the English working classes are improving, are learning the futility of rioting and violence, may in time learn that they cannot hope to accomplish anything through trades unions,[63] because "supply and demand regulate the value of everything."[64] The review becomes curiously paternalistic toward these laborers in its latest and least-read years, and in its number for April, 1834,[65] goes so far as to advocate government-owned public parks for them. Such a measure would of course touch the purses of the manufacturing capitalists only indirectly; and it has the merit of humanitarianism, which the *Westminster* never repudiated, and which Bowring and Thompson certainly thought they possessed. The peroration on how free the foot and buoyant the spirits of factory workers treading the turf rather than the harsh gravel contains much unconscious pathos and probably little or no conscious hypocrisy.

Another telltale straw is Thompson's leading article on Saint-Simonism,[66] the creed from which John Stuart Mill at this very time was deriving breadth and stimulation. This article had the chance to do one of three things—to point out what radicals could learn from Saint-Simonism, as the young Mill might have done, to demonstrate its fallacies, as the elder Mill certainly would have done, or to ridicule it. Thompson chose the last and easiest approach, that of the confirmed partisan conservative, asking his anti-individualist opponents such questions as why hen-sparrows do not sit on each others' eggs[67] and accusing the Saint-Simonians of being impractical visionaries—the same tactics so severely condemned by the *Westminster* itself in its attacks on the Whigs and Tories in its first years. And perhaps unconsciously following the practice of earlier reviewers, he declares that the Saint-Simonians talk about sex, and insinuates unmistakably and not too delicately that their system is immoral and a menace to the sanctity of the English home.[68] Such a charge would be enough to frighten readers of the review away from the entire program of the new cult, as it had frightened earlier conservatives away from the poetry of Shelley and Byron and from the work of that important figure in the Utilitarians' own hagiology, Malthus. A parting sneer at Owen and the Coöperatives concludes the thoroughly smart-aleck condescension of the forty-two-page review.

Thus members of this branch of the Benthamite party, the least intellectual branch, were rapidly becoming vigilantly conservative, utilizing the alert thought of the past only to justify measures leading to their own advancement, applying this once alert thought to new conditions possibly quite different from those to which it was originally intended to apply, contributing nothing themselves. The age of Philistinism was approaching, and its harbinger was the *Westminster*, under the Thompson régime no longer animated by the benevolence and intellectualism of its first four years. It represents what Carlyle and Arnold and all who fought for sweetness and light and humanitarianism opposed throughout their lives. Thompson's strikingly malapropos deification of Bentham, in the *Westminster's* notice of his death, may mean much: "the second teacher of The Greatest Happiness . . . is gone to joint the First."[69] Benthamism was becoming a respectable institution, and, considering Bentham's religious views, it is ironic enough that it should be combined with Christianity as part of the middle-class dogma not to be doubted, that the cult of competition and increase of wealth should be set up alongside the injunction, "Lay not up for yourselves treasures upon earth." Here are the two banks of Butler's *Erewhon*.

It must have been a great relief to Bowring, a writer of hymns, and Thompson, the son of devoted Methodists, thus to declare Benthamism Christian. Perhaps they would not have dared to do so if Bentham had been still alive. But before his death they had annexed literature, in which Bowring was already interested and which has been generally adorned with a halo of politeness and respectability. Moreover the *Westminster's* early opposition to literature had attracted much adverse comment, and it may have appeared to the new proprietors that a reversal of the old position would help sales. For the first few years of their control the journal contained a greater proportion of non-political reviews than had appeared in it during the days of the Mills, though the contributions of the later dynasty were generally less valuable. And in 1830, in a leading article on Coleridge's poems,[70] the *Westminster* explicitly retracted its contention that poets are not reasoners.

The article is interesting for other reasons also. Though Coleridge's politics were far from Benthamite, it contains extremely favorable criticism—the most favorable bestowed on a writer by a political opponent since the founding of reviews, and the most favorable Coleridge had yet received. This does not, however, prove political apostasy on the part of the *Westminster*. More unusual still, the article ends with a tribute in the first person to Coleridge's poems, an unheard-of breach of review etiquette, particularly for Bowring with his more than usual insistence that there were to be no reviewers, only a review. The poetry of Coleridge, the reviewer says, "has soothed my afflictions; it has multiplied and refined my enjoyments; it has endeared solitude; and it has given me (or at least strengthened in me) the habit of wishing to discover the good and beautiful in all that meets and surrounds me." That Bowring should have permitted this to stand appears possible only under one condition, that he wrote the article himself. For this reason along with others* I am confident in assigning the authorship of

* (1) The method is the same as that in reviews known to be by Bowring: (*a*) General philosophizing on the functions of poetry. (*b*) A general estimate of the poet. (*c*) Particular examination of his work, with numerous "specimens." (*d*) Repetition of the general estimate. Cf. particularly "Tennyson's Poems" (XIV, 210ff.); "Popular Poetry of the Servians" (VI, 23ff.). (2) Notable stylistic and content similarity between this article and Bowring's "Tennyson." Both were written by an oratorical and ornate stylist. The generalizations on poetry are strikingly similar, and there is a similar parade of learning in both. Note particularly the common contention that good poets are good thinkers and should interest themselves in psychology, and the comments on Shakespeare, Wordsworth, and Coleridge himself. Professor Graham (*English Literary Periodicals*, p. 253) assigns the review to John Stuart Mill, but I am unable to find

this very curious paper to him, in spite of my inability to discover direct evidence.

We are most interested in the adoption of literature—and Coleridge's poems—by the Benthamites. Bowring, of course, does not desert the faith; he merely states that the Benthamites are poets, and that Coleridge, being a poet, is a Benthamite. Which would seem to be a rather large mouthful.

In more detail, here is the case: People think that Benthamites because they are logical cannot be poetical. But

so far from there being any natural incongruity between the reasoning and imaginative faculties, as dunces have always been delighted to believe, it may rather be affirmed that they have a mutual affinity, and rarely attain their full development but when they exist in union.— Produce who can the name of a first-rate poet who was not a sound reasoner.

Milton, defender of free speech; Shakespeare, who could create thoroughly logical senators, lawyers, or cardinals; Jeremy Taylor, "a poet whose name indeed may be transplanted among the logicians;" Wordsworth, who "makes syllogisms of odes and odes of syllogisms" and who teaches "the truth of humanity's essence" —all are sound reasoners. Likewise, as one perceives by reading his essays, Lord Bacon was a poet, though better known as a reasoner; Hobbes was a poet, his *Leviathan* being "but the amplification of a poetical conception." Burke was a poet because he had an intellect notable for "the vivacity, variety, and power of its pictorial delineations." The climax comes with Bentham, who, it turns out, is also a poet. His mind "is far more free from failure, when directed to the purpose of conveying the truth he would reach by means of material illustration, than the most fanciful of the carping critics." So "a philosopher must always have something of poetry in him, and a poet of philosophy; . . . there is no dissociating the true and beautiful." And so "Mr. Coleridge is a Benthamite in his poetry; a Utilitarian; a 'greatest happiness' man; for, as a poet, he writes

---

evidence for Mill's authorship in the face of his own emphatic statement (*Autobiography*, p. 91) that he refused to contribute to the review under the Thompson régime.

under the controlling and dictating power of truth and nature, under the inspiration of his own profound convictions and emotions." Moreover, good poetry makes a distinct contribution to the greatest happiness of the greatest number, being "one of the most effective agencies of human enjoyment." Poetry which may be admitted to the best Utilitarian circles must have many noble qualities, which are listed; especially "there should be the charm of 'divine philosophy,' . . . the whole should be based upon a profound knowledge of human nature, its constitution and history, its capabilities and its destiny. . . ."

By this reasoning, faintly reminiscent of Shelley's *Defense of Poetry*, Bowring proves that Coleridge qualifies as a Benthamite. For in his poems he sympathizes with revolution and excels in "the exposition or investigation of the workings of the human mind," as seen in the Ancient Mariner's shrinking from the confession of his crime. This, one might suggest, partially proves Coleridge a poet and a philosopher, but certainly does not convincingly convict him of Benthamism, the Benthamites obviously believing many things not included in Coleridge's poetry. The case is a clear attempt to corner for Bowring's creed all virtue extant, to broaden the words Utilitarian and Benthamite to mean little or nothing specifically, but to carry a fine, vague, agreeable connotation. We have seen how by the same deplorable fallacy the same group of Bentham's disciples were to appropriate Christianity. Poets contribute to the greatest happiness, therefore poets are Benthamites. Christ taught the greatest happiness, therefore Christ was a Benthamite. Rotary Clubs of our own day have by precisely the same fallacy declared Christ a Rotarian. The rank and file do not detect the fallacy, most of them not wishing to; and their feeling of respectability is increased as the name under which they march becomes connected with more and more of the respectable virtues and institutions.

Considering the unalloyed partisanship of the method, then, we cannot find in this article much evidence that the group at this time directing the review were blazing new trails, either by adopting poetry or by printing a favorable review of a political opponent. We can, however, find here further evidence that what in 1824 appeared a sound intellectual party seeking truth at all costs was by 1830 obviously breaking down, disintegrating elements having existed in it, as we have seen, from the start.

The old cry that literature is a seducer was seldom raised after this. Poets of Holland, Hungary, Illyria received all the attention that the linguistic Dr. Bowring could desire. Ancient Bohemian ballads appeared both in translation and in what may be presumed to be ancient Bohemian. Severity toward Scott, much lessened in the review of *Tales of A Grandfather*,[71] entirely disappeared—six months before the Coleridge review—on the publication of *Anne of Geierstein*.[72] In Scott's novels, the reviewer declared, "there is a stirring life, a truth of conception, a brilliancy of painting, and a vigour of expression . . . which will amply reward the labour bestowed on their perusal." In 1832 a review of Moore's *The Life and Death of Edward Fitzgerald* makes at least partial amends for ancient wrongs: it is largely summary, commending the author's style, and accusing him of no major crimes. On the appearance of *The Alhambra,* the *Westminster* directly reversed its earlier position on Irving, and joined the chorus of praise which regularly greeted his books in England.[73] The Utilitarians evidently were now wealthy enough to delight in the romantic charm of ruined castles.

They are greatly mistaken [the reviewer of *The Alhambra* pointed out], who imagine that the luxuries of sentimentalism—when they can be afforded, as in advanced stages of civilization, and when they are not of a kind to enervate—may not be reconciled with an enlightened view of the doctrine of utility.

There is one distinct exception to the rule that penetration in book reviewing is generally lacking during this period. That is the paper on Fenimore Cooper,[74] in which it is stated that his gentlemen and young ladies are "in sad want of oil, moving rustily and with creaking," that his plots are always commonplace, his conversations "needlessly spun out and trivial." He excels in depicting "nature in sublime and unadorned simplicity," and in presenting "artless, energetic characters, which are his peculiar province." Other reviews contribute but slightly to the greatest happiness. Of the writers of fashionable novels, "stories of grown children," the *Westminster* called them, the reviewers liked Lady Morgan little,[75] Disraeli not at all. "To parasites, sycophants, toad-eaters, tuft-hunters and humble companions it will be a book full of comfort and instruction in their callings," the Benthamites declared of *The Young Duke*. Reviewing it under the title "The Lackey School of Authors,"[76] they attacked it for its silly emphasis on feeding and dressing, its adulation of rank, its acceptance of all the ways, however evil, of high life. Mrs. Gore they approved, because she made the peerage ridiculous.[77] Bulwer also they approved, *Pelham* almost without qualification, detecting satire in it;[78] *Devereux* with considerable qualification, suggesting that Bulwer ought to try something besides fashionable novels.[79] Nevertheless they found that he, unlike Disraeli, actually knew what he was talking about, and by presenting a true picture of what Carlyle was to call the Dandiacal Body contributed to the refinement of public taste. Apparently even a fashionable novel might have its merits if written by a gentleman with Utilitarian leanings.

For the rest, it may be said that the reviewers rather liked Trelawney's Byronic *Adventures,* disliked Leitch Ritchie's *The Game of Life,* a novel depicting the sordid conditions of the slums, declaring that he should have emphasized "the robbery of the laborious classes by the privileged." They thoroughly scorned Mrs. Trollope's *The Refugee in America*[80] for ridiculing the people of a middle-class republic. These opinions may all be accounted for by the old Utilitarian bias. Except for several articles which illustrate the growing political complacency of the review, the other book notices do not matter. Incidentally, the *Westminster* in its last three years under Bowring contained relatively few literary articles—a commentary on the depth of the newly announced Benthamite devotion to literature.

Perhaps the most amusing phase of the *Westminster's* activities during this period is the attempt to show that under the democratic order, following the new Utilitarian enlightenment, literature and all the arts will be much finer than ever before. In the early thirties the improvement in literature as in politics, according to the *Westminster,* was already discernible. At times one would think the millenium actually come. In 1831 Harriet Martineau's *Traditions of Palestine* evoked this ecstatic comment:

What a country is England! where a young lady may put forth a book like this—quietly, modestly, and without the apparent consciousness of doing any extraordinary act, and what is more, where talent and knowledge are so universal and so generally reckoned upon that others see as little to be surprised at in the circumstance, and receive the boon with the indifference of an ordinary courtesy.[81]

So with music. Here the millenium has not come, but it is inevitably coming. A certain Dr. Crotch, it appears, wrote a book in which he stated that this art was on the decline. The reviewer found the author's name a godsend, and replied,[82]

We take the notion to be a mere crotchet. . . Progress is the law of humanity . . . and all the Fine Arts have before them a long and glorious career, if not an interminable one. They are the ornament and the light of life to men of highly cultivated minds. The universality of a state of high mental cultivation will be one of the results of that great reorganization of society which must take place—which has actually commenced. The march of improvement will have its music

—presumably a much improved music. "The public taste improving, and the art declining, are, for any length of time, totally incompatible phenomena." Fortunately it is not necessary to wait, for the new genius has already been evoked by the new public—and who should this genius be but Miss Eliza Flower! She would be a logical choice, having picked up at least a modified Benthamism from W. J. Fox while living in his home and acting as his secretary. She did *Musical Illustrations of the Waverley Novels,* and it is in these that, according to the reviewer, "there are not only indications of a genius as indisputable as could have been displayed in the highest walks of the art, but there is also a new ascent gained, a new prospect opened, in the art itself." The ten pages of praise that follow this mighty utterance are unbelievably absurd. There is comparison with Purcell, Handel, and Mozart. Miss Flower's work is apparently immaculate: "she never oversteps those boundaries which the greatest masters have sometimes transgressed, and exposed themselves thereby deservedly to ridicule." The songs are said to possess mental philosophy, which makes them belong as much to science and literature, as to art, and entitles them to analysis among the best intellectual productions of the day. They are a specimen of the songs of the world to come, when the human race shall have won the world from monopolists, and learned to enjoy it.

The miraculous transformation of which this work is an example will, says the reviewer, affect painting, statuary, architecture as well as music:

All are susceptible to indefinite improvement . . . all are destined to act, and in turn be acted upon, by the spread of information, acquirement, education in the best sense of the word, amongst the great body of the people. To each and all a mightier stimulus will be applied than has yet been felt, in the power of popular applause and enjoyment, which will be as Moses striking the rock. . .

Six articles on music, all by Thompson, appeared in the review after this, but the Moses of popular applause could have had little to do with them. The object of one, it is true, was "to promote the greatest happiness in the department of sweet sounds." Another begins by postulating an appallingly dynamic universe, in which "music, the poetry of geometry, is on the march like everything else." It is not surprising to discover that this was written by a Fellow of the Royal Society and Colonel of Dragoons, author of a work on music and one on mathematics. Fortunately, anonymous reviewing was still the mode, for Thompson himself, following the excellent precedent of Sir Walter Scott, reviewed each of these books of his, treating his work without undue enthusiasm but reflecting his own conviction of its value. To his *Instructions to My Daughter, for playing on the Enharmonic Guitar* he devoted some fifty pages,[83] declaring it "a piece of musical radicalism," and summarizing and explaining it. The review, largely synopsis, is so technical as to be almost incomprehensible except to the expert in music. Thompson, being a theoretical mathematician, appears to have had the now defunct cause of just intonation very much at heart, and in this article and all his others he insists on "scientific" mathematical accuracy in the division of the scale. He brands equal temperament with the most violent terms of Utilitarian abuse: Gothic, Tory, unprogressive, and illogical. His "enharmonic guitar," however, devised with extra frets, and an "enharmonic organ" with a most elaborate keyboard built a few years later on the principles he advocated, partially served to redeem the age and demonstrate that music was on the march along with the times. Curiously enough, his position was not radical except in so far as he was defending a practically lost cause, for there had been many champions of just intonation, particularly in the eighteenth century; nor could Thompson have expected any overwhelming popular applause for his critical efforts. Eliza Flower's simple settings for Scott's songs and enharmonic guitars and organs are indeed strange bedfellows. They share, however, the honor of having marked the Utilitarian excursion into music and of having been used to demonstrate the sovereign virtue of the new age in all respects whatsoever.

The efforts of the mentally ubiquitous Thompson to carry radicalism into mathematics are less futile and more easily comprehensible to possible readers of the review than his campaign for just intonation. Reviewing his own book declaring war on axioms in geometry,[84] he attacks the Toryism which accepts short cuts and takes things for granted, and proposes to prove all axioms if provable and not identical propositions. Declaring his own efforts in the book he is reviewing "laudable, if successful," he goes ahead with entire confidence to establish his success. "No good ever yet came of axioms. Legitimacy is an axiom; persecution is an axiom." Apparently the assumption was that if the reader agreed with the review politically he must agree mathematically, or vice versa.

This did no harm, and, like the articles on just intonation, gave Thompson a chance to connect one of his numerous hobbies with the greatest happiness. Miss Eliza Flower's music died a quiet death, and so did Harriet Martineau's *Traditions of Palestine*. But when, by lucky or unlucky accident. the Benthamites adopted the future Victorian laureate to demonstrate the great advantages of the March of Mind in poetry, they really did something. They altered slightly the course of English literary history, and innocently helped to make one man very unhappy.

Their party, to be thoroughly respectable and as good as the Whigs and the Tories, sadly needed a poet. We have remarked on the distinct shortage of literary men with Utilitarian bias and the resulting inability of the *Westminster* to participate in the usual practice of puffing the novels and verses of men of one's own party. Their best candidate, Peacock, had gone and written *Crotchet Castle*, and what could one do with a man like that? But Tennyson looked promising. At Cambridge, Thompson's university, he had been a member of a group of liberals with a mission, and he had given clear proof of his liberalism by his interest in the contemplated Torrijos revolution in Spain. There is no evidence in the *Westminster's* review of his 1830 volume, *Poems, Chiefly Lyrical*,[85] to indicate that Bowring, the author, detected any traces of Utilitarian dogma in his verse, but neither did the reviewer in Eliza Flower's music. He had found radicalism in the early poetry of Coleridge, but of course Coleridge was by now a confirmed Tory and could not well represent the beneficent effects of the new era. The young Tennyson, however, a liberal product of that era, would serve. Besides, Bowring would have genuinely liked his sentimentality.

"It would be a pity that poetry should be an exception to the great law of progression that obtains in human affairs; and it is not." So begins the fatal review. It proceeds to proof. Great poetry, as was pointed out in the paper on Coleridge, is the result of great thought. Shakespeare is the greatest of poets "because he was one of the greatest of philosophers." Poetry depends especially on "our ever-growing acquaintance with the philosophy of the mind and of man," and "the real science of mind advances with the progress of society like all other sciences." Poetry therefore must keep getting better and better with the progress of society; and the poetry of Coleridge and of Wordsworth shows that it has actually done so. The Tennyson volume, too, Bowring thinks, is "the precursor of a series of productions which shall beautifully illustrate our speculations, and convincingly prove their soundness." Logically, of course, this means that Coleridge and Wordsworth were better poets than Shakespeare and that Tennyson should be better than any of them. But it is not likely that Bowring extended his logic that far.

Not likely, but possible. For the new age with its advances has made possible the writing of psychological poetry, "the analysis

of particular states of mind," and it is in this, the review would
have us believe, that Tennyson excels. In *Supposed Confessions of
a Second-rate Sensitive Mind,* "the author personates (he can per-
sonate anything he pleases, from an angel to a grasshopper) a
timid sceptic, but who must evidently always remain such, and
yet be miserable in his scepticism." Bowring finds this "as good a
subject for poetical description as even the shield of Achilles
itself," and defends his position thus:

Such topics are more in accordance with the spirit and intellect of the
age than those about which poetry has been accustomed to be conversant;
their adoption will effectually redeem it from the reproach of being
frivolous and enervating. . .

The Lilians, Madelines, Isabels are of course not frivolous or
enervating. These too are jewels of realistic portraiture and psychological acuteness. "There is an appropriate object for every
shade of feeling, from the light touch of a passing admiration to
the triumphant madness of soul and sense, or the deep and ever-
lasting anguish of survivorship." In short, Tennyson "has the secret
of the transmigration of the soul" and by becoming what he cre-
ates can write very, very convincing poetry. He impersonates mer-
men and mermaidens as well as angels and grasshoppers, "takes
their senses, feelings, nerves, and brain, along with their names and
local habitations." There is said to be excellent analysis of states of
mind, too, in *Nothing Will Die* and *All Things Will Die,* which
are compared in this respect with *L'Allegro* and *Il Penseroso,* and it
is found that the former contain "not less truth, perhaps a more
refined observation." It appears that Tennyson is a rather considerable genius; and Bowring urges him to live up to the specifi-
cations that he himself has drawn up in *The Poet* and "shake the
world." Real poets should do more than amuse.

They can influence the associations of unnumbered minds; they can command the sympathies of unnumbered hearts; they can disseminate principles; they can excite in a good cause the sustained enthusiasm that
is sure to conquer; they can blast the laurels of tyrants; and hallow
the memories of the martyrs of patriotism; they can act with a force,
the extent of which it is difficult to estimate, upon national feelings and
character, and consequently upon national happiness.

Bowring's obviously absurd praise, combined with eulogies from Leigh Hunt's *Tatler* and from *The Englishman's Magazine,* organ of Tennyson's Cambridge coterie, the Apostles, was bound to anger the more conservative reviewers. Here *Blackwood's* came into its own. Abounding in Toryism and common sense, Maga saw a young man of some gifts being adopted by Benthamites and other radicals and lauded with ridiculous hyperbole. So out came the Cockney label again from the files of the Keats controversy, and Christopher himself insisted that the 1830 volume proved Tennyson not a Phoenix, but merely a Swan.[86] Turning his customary handsprings as he went, he annihilated the reviewers very thoroughly, praised Tennyson moderately, gave him much paternal advice in his usual bantering manner, and closed his masterly article in triumph.

First he paid his respects to the eulogies from Hampstead, then to the pompous critique in the *Englishman's Magazine,* then to "the narcotic dose administered to him [Tennyson] by a crazy charlatan in the *Westminster.*"

The last mentioned received the lion's share of attention, it being probably the most absurd. Calling the reviewer a quack, Wilson quoted at length the remarks on the secret of the transmigration of the soul as "a perfect specimen of the super-hyperbolical ultra-extravagance of outrageous Cockney eulogistic foolishness, . . . the purest mere matter of moonshine ever mouthed by an idiot-lunatic. . . ." *The Merman* and *The Mermaid,* cited by Bowring to illustrate Tennyson's metaphysical acumen, Wilson then proceeded to quote as examples of "distinguished silliness," pointing out maliciously that the mermaid of Tennyson's poem was "a strong anti-Malthusian." He concluded the attack on the *Westminster* by exhibiting Tennyson to great disadvantage exercising his transmigratory power on the swan, the grasshopper, and the owl. "But Alfred is greatest as an owl. . . . All that he wants is to be shot, stuffed, and stuck in a glass-case, to be made immortal in a museum." The remaining nine pages of the review are in the main complimentary to Tennyson. Wilson approved of his "delicate perception of the purity of female character" as seen in the Adelines, Lilians, and Isabels, and he liked *Mariana,* the *Ode to Memory,* and *Recollections of the Arabian Nights.* It appears that in general he liked Tennyson but disliked his friends. In annihilating the friends, however, he had annihilated something of Tennyson. And we know how Tennyson did not like it, and wrote a saucy squib about Wilson, and how the *Quarterly Review* blasted Tennyson's reputation and sales by its attack on the 1832 volume which made Tennyson very unhappy indeed, so unhappy that he published nothing more for ten years. This was the last major calamity to befall a poet as the result of reviewing with political bias.

We have noted the *Westminster's* increasing satisfaction with the progress of the arts under democratic auspices. The condition of the drama alone gave the reviewers scant cause for rejoicing. Reviewing the report of the parliamentary investigating committee on the state of the theater,[87] they declared that in this department Utilitarianism still had progress to make. With the vastly improved public and all the consequent increase in potential popular applause, the drama might be expected to be better than ever. But because of the continuance of the licensing acts whereby two theaters were given a legal monopoly, free competition was impossible. Hence the drama could not develop. The trouble with the theater was not enough laissez faire. But Benthamism was already solving all other problems of English culture, and if it were allowed free jurisdiction in the theater it would speedily solve that difficult problem also. It may be remembered that the licensing acts were repealed in 1837, and that the revival of the theater did not begin until fifty years after that date.

Glancing back through the files of the *Westminster* from 1828 to 1836, one finds that Benthamism under one group of its disciples has indeed grown into a very huge Morrison's Pill, advertised as a sovereign cure for all the ills that society is heir to. Such development, clearly demonstrable in the official organ of the creed, is not inconsistent with the early tendencies of the organ. The *Westminster,* like the society of which it was the forerunner, could have been saved from smug complacency only by the clear, constant, and disinterested thinking which it had advocated in its first years. Such thought alone, recognizing the diversity of elements that cause the growth of excellence in human activity, could have dictated the abandonment of the fatal a priori method. At the same time it could have tempered the blind partisanship which is the outstanding characteristic of the review in the early thirties.

It is not surprising that John Stuart Mill, now almost ready to assume the leadership of a new and vital radicalism, complained bitterly of the narrowness of Thompson and his reviewers.[88] By 1834 he considered the time ripe for founding a new radical review, to be called the *London Review* and to serve as the organ of all advanced opinion whether of the old Benthamite school or not, the articles to represent the views of individual contributors and to be indicated as such by distinctive signatures. The new *London,* backed by the wealthy young liberal, Sir William Molesworth, proved to be better than the *Westminster* had ever been, obviously a distinguished organ of English radicalism; and one sighs with relief to read of the decision of Mill and Molesworth to do away with the unintelligent and wretchedly written *Westminster* by buying it up. Molesworth gave Thompson a thousand pounds for it, much more than it was worth, and in 1836 the combined journal appeared as the *London and Westminster Review.*

VII

BENTHAMISM IN THE VICTORIAN ERA

The amalgamation of the *Westminster* with Mill's *London Review* in 1836 brought to an end the partisan propagandist activities of the Benthamites, who themselves as a party were also disappearing at the same time. Bentham died in 1832, and James Mill in 1836. But the *Westminster Review*, though undergoing several transformations, continued until 1914; the belligerent contributors to the old journal carried on their warfare in other fields; and the influence of their early propaganda still to some imponderable extent survives and is active even in our own day. Loyalty to the best traditions of Victorian story-telling dictates, therefore, a brief epilogue summarizing what happened after 1835.

We have observed in detail the devastating effect of large doses of Benthamism upon the relatively inferior thinkers who believed, as the sage himself too often gave them reason for doing, that their creed provided a complete and all-inclusive solution to every problem of living. Equipped with such a Morrison's Pill, they rapidly became quite unsusceptible to the genuine intellectual stimulus of Bentham's critical method, and stopped asking why, though they still preached skepticism as part of their dogma. Many persons who never had any connection with the *Westminster,* but who, through it, received Benthamism at third or fourth hand, must have been similarly affected. Unfortunate, of course; but men who remain disciples are obviously unlikely to become leaders. The only member of the original group of *Westminster* reviewers who did become an intellectual leader, John Stuart Mill, discontinued his discipleship, though for much of his thought he continued to be indebted to Bentham.

The others, almost without exception, although lacking Mill's intellectual originality, nevertheless did enjoy distinguished careers in practical life; nor is there evidence that they all became mentally fossilized. Many of them aided materially in effecting reforms advocated in the old *Westminster*. Roebuck, Grote, Buller, Thompson, and Bowring himself served in Parliament during the thirties, vigorously if not too sucessfully continuing there their fight for the enactment of Benthamite measures. Grote, more famous now as the historian of Greece, distinguished himself then by moving at every session the introduction of the ballot Roebuck as regularly demanded state education, the reform which he supported with greatest vigor in the series of popular tracts that he published during the same period.

Perhaps the finest achievements of the Benthamites toward the greatest happiness were accomplished by men outside the House. William Ellis became infected with the faith in popular education, and, though immersed in his own business affairs, took time to sponsor experiments in teaching political economy to children, a project which culminated in 1848 in the founding of the Birkbeck Schools. Eventually Ellis, an admirable illustration of Benthamite earnestness, material success, and philanthropy, was cheerfully supporting out of his own pocket as many as ten of these schools for educating the lower classes in useful knowledge.

The later careers of Southwood Smith and Edwin Chadwick, active as these men were on important government commissions and in projects for social welfare, are perhaps even better examples of the practical application of Benthamite teachings. The combined efforts of these two men dictated the provisions of the Factory Bill of 1833, which limited the working day for children employed in factories and contained a clause directing employers to provide for educating them outside working hours. For the final form of the Poor Law Act of 1834, a distinctly Benthamite measure stimulating individual effort on the part of laborers by denying outdoor relief to able-bodied paupers, Chadwick was almost alone responsible. The theory of its sponsors that the lot of self-supporting laborers should be more pleasant than that of the indigent in workhouses led to evils such as Dickens attacked in *Oliver Twist,* but this fact should not blind us to the importance of the measure in correcting obvious abuses of outdoor aid. Chadwick's interest in social welfare is further reflected in his important work as champion of the Public Health Act of 1848, under which he served as commissioner. It is pleasant to note that Dr. Smith under the same act became a member of the first Board of Health, having been previously occupied in establishing and directing his "Sanitarium," an institution operating as a health insurance project whereby the poor who while in good health had contributed a small fee received treatment free of charge during illness. Such public usefulness characterized Smith and Chadwick throughout their lives.

Benthamite principles and disciples likewise had certain immediate effects on the British colonial possessions. John Austin in 1836 was appointed commissioner to reform the government of the island of Malta. Charles Buller, who in 1838 accompanied Lord Durham to Canada, collaborated on the report of 1839 resulting in "the concession to the legislative assembly of Canada of full control over the administration of the colony."[1] Such action is clearly reminiscent of the old *Westminster's* attitude on the same subject, and the *London and Westminster,* defending Lord Durham's position,[2] in Mill's own opinion turned the tide of popular favor in a bitterly contested dispute. Mill with his usual clear vision considered this championship of Lord Durham one of his two great achievements as editor of the review, pointing out that the report "began a new era; its recommendations, extending to complete internal self-government, . . . have since been extended to nearly all the other colonies, of European race, which have any claim to the character of important communities."[3] In other words, the present form of government of the British colonial possessions is largely due to the efforts of the men who once were *Westminster* reviewers.

In the thirties Benthamite principles of government spread to India as well as to Canada, largely, paradoxically enough, through the medium of the man who in 1829 had been the means of bringing the school into general disrepute. When Macaulay went to India as legal adviser to the commission for reorganizing that dependency, he took with him and put into effect much Benthamism in the form of advice from his erstwhile victim, James Mill, and he was accompanied by a former *Westminster* reviewer,

Charles Hay Cameron. It is not surprising to find that Cameron successfully interested himself in the founding and administration of schools and became president of the Council of Education in Bengal. Returning to England in 1848 after having enjoyed high praise from the citizens of Calcutta at a public meeting in his honor, he gave further evidence of his Benthamism by becoming relatively obscured in the shadow of his more famous wife, the amateur photographer and friend of the laureate.

Even the bibulous antiquarian literary editor, Henry Southern, enjoyed a career. After several gloomy years which followed the death of the *London Magazine* and his withdrawal from the *Westminster*, he emerged into the friendly light of the diplomatic service, first as secretary to the English liberal ambassador to Spain, George Villiers, and later, appropriately enough, as minister to two republics, first the Argentine and then Brazil. As for the editor-in-chief, Bowring, a complete account of his later exploits is material for a volume by itself.[4]

Sometimes as a member of government commissions, sometimes on his own initiative, he worked for British commercial interests in France, Italy, Switzerland, Prussia, Egypt, Syria, and Turkey. While in Parliament he fought for the introduction of the decimal system in coins, on which he wrote a book, and secured the introduction of the florin as the first step toward the full accomplishment of that enterprise. He also exercised himself in behalf of the oppressed Manxmen and secured them relief by act of Parliament. A faithful adherent of free trade at home as well as abroad, he was instrumental in the establishment of the Manchester Anti-Corn-Law League, and coöperated with Cobden in the propagandist activities of that organization. Later he served as consul at Canton, and in 1854 was appointed plenipotentiary to China and governor of Hong Kong. The same year he was knighted by the Queen—besides Chadwick the only Benthamite so honored. While in the Orient he stirred up a minor war with China, established commercial relations with Siam, and investigated and wrote a book on the Philippines. During his lifetime he received Belgian, Portuguese, Spanish, Austrian, Swedish, and Italian decorations, and became "a noble of the first class of Siam, with the insignia of the White Elephant." At such achievements let no dog bark: Bowring in spite of the rumors circulated against him in his early years is in a sense the hero of this book, for he best represents the efficacy of the Greatest Happiness principle in promoting the welfare of the individual.

But he, like most of the other *Westminster* reviewers, is now forgotten by the rank and file of the cultured, though one encounters them all frequently when one penetrates ever so little below the surface of the Victorian whirlpool. One name alone we need not dive to reach: John Stuart Mill, whose work is of particular importance for this study. For he it was who continued the *Westminster Review,* the organ no longer of Benthamites alone, but of all sincere liberals; and he it was, too, who kept alive the best in Utilitarian thought and passed it on to liberals of the latter part of the century. Thanks largely to him, the labors of the Benthamite propagandists did not result in Philistinism alone.

Mill states that he had two main objectives in his conduct of the *London and Westminster.*

One was to free philosophic radicalism from the reproach of sectarian Benthamism; . . . to show that there was a Radical philosophy, better and more complete than Bentham's, while recognizing and incorporating all of Bentham's which is permanently valuable.

The other was to inspire and strengthen the English radical party, particularly in Parliament.[5] Though he considered himself unsuccessful in this definitely political venture, he did recognize that through the review he contributed breadth to radical thought.

It is the successful rather than the unsuccessful phase of his enterprise that interests us here. Conceived partly in reaction against the bigotry which the *Westminster* under Thompson had represented, Mill's new radicalism resulted in the publication of perhaps the soundest and most brilliant English periodical of the century. All shades and types of advanced opinion are included in the *London and Westminster,* from James Mill's acutely analytical rationalism, applied in the old way to the destruction of current abuses and invention of machinery for carrying on the activities of society more effectively,[6] to Carlyle's deep mystical insight, impatient of all measures, interested largely in the serious leadership of men who recognized what he considered the eternal verities.[7] Carlyle, needing money, tempered the wind to the shorn lamb and omitted from his articles all the violent diatribe against the Utilitarians that he might have been tempted to include. Nevertheless, the striking contrast of his work with the rationalism of the old *Westminster* is self-evident. Life to the Benthamite reviewers was never an "incongruous whirlpool," nor did those theorists teach that "the world's wealth is its original men."[8] Carlyle's condemnation of Walter Scott's triviality would not have been out of place in the *Westminster,* but that journal would scarcely have criticized his love of material success as Carlyle did. Mill, wishing to free philosophic radicalism from bigotry and narrowness, advisedly included among his reviewers the Scottish mystic, whose financial worries the friendly editor was glad to lighten.

Mill's own articles, which in spite of his ill health were many,[9] contributed perhaps even more than Carlyle's toward the broadening of radical thought. Before he secured control of the *Westminster,* he had expressed in the *London* grave doubts as to the perfection of democracy as a form of government, quoting the blackest statements of de Tocqueville, and pointing out the dangerous power of majorities over minorities.[10] He had also suggested that defects might exist in the middle class, which he accused of "a general indifference to those kinds of knowledge and mental culture which cannot be converted into pounds, shillings, and pence."[11]

Probing deeper into the tendencies of the new age of democracy for which the Benthamites had helped prepare the way, he produced as the leading article of the first number of the *London and Westminster* his brilliant "Civilization."[12] Declaring that "the energies of the middle classes are almost confined to money getting, and those of the higher classes are nearly extinct," he outlines in this article the social ills that may result from the inevitable democratic régime unless they are counteracted in time. Chief among the tendencies that he deplores is the increasing impotence of individual effort, the increasing enervation of individual character. Reversing the position of Thompson's *Westminster,* he states that with the diffusion of knowledge and the growth of democracy there has come "no increase of shining abil‐ ity, and a very marked decrease of vigor and energy." For this condition he proposes two remedies. The first, again reversing the position of the old *Westminster,* is coöperation among individuals rather than competition. The second is education.

He devotes fully a fourth of his article to this second remedy, which, like the orthodox Benthamites, he views with respect, but for which he proposes ideals differing from theirs so radically as to foreshadow the position of Matthew Arnold in the debate with Huxley. He would not cure the vices of the universities "by bringing their studies into a closer connection with what it is the fashion to term 'the business of the world,' " by removing logic and the classics from their curriculum. Rather he would have these subjects

taught far more really and deeply than at present, and . . . would add to them other studies more alien than any which yet exist to "the busi‐ ness of the world" but more germane to the business of every rational being, the strengthening and enlarging of his own mind and character.

Assuredly reform agitation of this sort possesses a breadth conspicuously lacking in the old *Westminster.* Mill's two articles, "Bentham"[13] and "Coleridge,"[14] also represent superbly this new characteristic of philosophic radicalism. In the former, Mill care‐ fully points out not only the merits but the defects of Bentham's thought. The latter, a study of Coleridge's philosophy, is a bril‐ liant analysis of the possible contribution of intelligent conserva‐ tism toward the improvement of social conditions. Unlike Bow‐ ring in his review of Coleridge's poetry, Mill has no interest in proving the Highgate prophet a Benthamite; he tries honestly to see him as he was and to show radicals what they may learn from him. The article, distinguished for intelligent understanding and appreciation of a political opponent, might well be considered Mill's valedictory to partisan agitation, for it is his last contribu‐ tion as editor of the radical review, certainly the finest example of true magnanimity ever to appear in that journal.

The impression that the *London and Westminster* is a bona fide magazine and not a propaganda sheet is further strengthened by the variety of topics treated in it. Works of purely literary interest are reviewed frequently as such, never with marked political bias, usually with none at all. Leigh Hunt's article on Lady Mary Wortley Montagu,[15] mildly amusing and pleasantly interesting, contains not a word of politics, nor does his sketch of the Tower of London.[16] Bulwer-Lytton's papers on Gray[17] and Lamb,[18] and Mill's own judiciously favorable review of Tennyson,[19] which somewhat counteracted the harm innocently done the poet by the *Westminster,* are all equally devoid of political interest. Mill's laudatory essay on Carlyle's *French Revolution,*[20] an article which in its modest author's opinion helped much to secure a favorable reception for that work and to make Carlyle famous,[21] is tinged but slightly with politics.

Mill, predecessor of Matthew Arnold in attempting to dispel somewhat the provincialism which he found characteristic of the English,[22] devoted much of the review's space to foreign literature, securing from the brilliant French classicist, Nisard, articles on two romanticists, Lamartine[23] and Hugo,[24] from de Tocqueville an article on the political and social condition of France,[25] and from Mazzini papers on modern Italian literature[26] and on Fra Paolo Sarpi.[27] Mill himself contributed his eminently wise paper on Alfred de Vigny[28] and his analysis of the work of Armand Carrel.[29]

Other members of the versatile band of contributors to the liberal journal were Molesworth, for a time the owner of the review, Roebuck, W. E. Hickson, Henry Cole, and Mill's subeditor, John Robertson, all of whom wrote on political topics. Among the authors of more general works were W. J. Fox, John Sterling, whose most important contribution is a leading article on Carlyle,[30] the ubiquitous Harriet Martineau and her brother James, Blanco White, and Richard Monckton Milnes, who wrote for the *London and Westminster* an article on Emerson.[31] Peacock wrote for the *London* but not for the *London and Westminster.* It is indicative of literary discrimination on the part of the editorial staff that the review of the great Dickens[32] was by a then obscure free lance journalist whose signature was a diminutive theta* and whose name was W. M. Thackeray.

Yet for all its excellence the review lost its proprietors money. Circulation averaged about twelve hundred a number,[33] considerably below the mark set by the old *Westminster*. Molesworth eventually gave up the enterprise, transferring the ownership of the review to Mill, who in turn relinquished it in 1840. Occupied with his *Logic*, weakened in health, and discouraged in his hopes for an independent radical party, he decided that his energies should be used elsewhere. Stipulating that the review should resume the name of the *Westminster*, he turned it over to Hickson, a younger contributor, who continued it until the early fifties, finally selling it to John Chapman, in whose family it remained until its discontinuance in 1914.[34]

It persisted as a sound, respectable journal with liberal and intellectualist tendencies, and in the early days of Chapman showed promise of again assuming the leadership of advanced English thought. Appropriately enough, it attained at the same time the added distinction of being the first English review to have a woman as assistant editor. Though during this brief period (1851-53) the review contained articles by such men as J. A. Froude, George Henry Lewes, and Herbert Spencer, perhaps its greatest service was to act as a medium through which the woman editor came into contact with mid-century intellectualism. Without such contact it is very unlikely that Mary Ann Evans would ever have become George Eliot. Such was the last major contribution of the journal instituted by the Benthamites, for the *Fortnightly Review*, founded in 1865 and edited first by George Henry Lewes, later by John Morley, soon occupied the place which had never been adequately filled since Mill's withdrawal from the *London and Westminster*.

* Other signatures are as follows: Carlyle, C. or S. P.; Cole, H. C.; de Tocqueville, Δ; Fox, W. J. F.; Hickson, W. E. H.; Hunt, hand and index finger; Bulwer-Lytton, E. B.; H. Martineau, H. M.; J. Martineau, J. M.; James Mill, P. Q.; J. S. Mill, A or A. B.; Milnes, R. M. M.; Molesworth, W. M.; Nisard, D. N.; Peacock, M. S. O.; Robertson, R.; Sterling, £; White, W.

In that review Mill had indeed admirably illustrated the better of the two main tendencies which developed from Benthamism and the old *Westminster*. Distressing and incomprehensible the new radical journal must have appeared to faithful partisans of the orthodox school. Bowring, whole-heartedly engaged in encouraging Manchester's free trade sentiment, certainly could not understand. "Dr. Bowring spoke of Mill with evident contempt as a renegade in philosophy, Anglicé—a renouncer of Bentham's creed and an expounder of Coleridge's," Caroline Fox recorded. "The further men wander from simplicity," the loyal member of the Manchester school continued, "the further are they from truth."[35]

So Bowring and the orthodox went on in their way, and Mill went on in his, and the *Westminster Review* itself continued likewise, all mingling with and becoming part of Victorian life, all owing something, like Victorian life itself, to the old enterprise whereby the Benthamites had hoped to convert England to their creed. Broadly speaking, Bowring's way, the way of the original *Westminster,* charted according to what he called simplicity, represents the path of the ordinary middle-class individual during the rest of the century, and Mill's represents the path of the leading intellectuals during the same period. For the most part the precise windings of both paths are concealed in the very complex forest of the Victorian period, but from time to time we can see clear evidences of one or the other. For example, we catch a glimpse of J. A. Roebuck, an erstwhile *Westminster* reviewer following the path of simplicity, as he emerges from the forest with characteristic shouts in praise of the "unrivalled happiness" of middle-class England. He remains visible long enough to be shot at by Matthew Arnold with the famous "Wragg is in custody," and then disappears again into the forest.[36] If we may believe Arnold and other contemporary observers, we must conclude that Roebuck's path of simplicity, of Philistinism complacently satisfied with the enjoyment of material prosperity, was in the Victorian age a very broad path which many followed.

The other path, that of altruistic intellectualism, can be traced by the observer of today with somewhat greater definiteness. Leaders of English thought in the latter half of the century were almost unanimous in owning their intellectual debt to John Stuart Mill, whose writings and personal example left a marked imprint on his age. "For twenty years no one at all open to serious intellectual impressions has left Oxford without having undergone the influence of Mr. Mill's teachings," wrote his leading disciple, the late Viscount Morley, on the death of the great leader in 1873.[37] "The better sort of journalists," he continued, "educated themselves on his books."[38] Years later, on the centenary of Mill's birth, Morley called him "the first guide and inspirer of a generation that has now all but passed away,"[39] proving the appropriateness of that title by quotations from Gladstone, Henry Sidgwick, and Herbert Spencer. The deep influence of this lifelong champion of womanhood makes it appear perhaps not a pure coincidence that a leading contributor to Morley's intellectual *Fortnightly Review,* George Meredith, devoted his novels more and more to the amelioration of woman's position. Perusal of the *Fortnightly* itself leaves the indelible impression that fundamentally the journal is a Mill periodical. Thus it is that the efforts of Bentham's materialist middle-class followers contributed to the finer as well as to the meaner phases of Victorian life.

For more than a hundred years the sage himself, in accordance with his will, has sat patiently in University College, London, which he and his reviewers helped to found, smiling as though conscious of his continued influence. An increasingly dominant empiricism, leading men to base their thinking on experiential facts and to live for this world rather than the next, was the principal legacy that he and the *Westminster* reviewers passed on to posterity. Applying this mode of thought, Victorian man brought about the dominance of the middle class and made individualism and high pressure competition in business a commonplace. Even the questioning of the individualist competitive spirit in England and of late in the United States has been on the principle of the greatest happiness of the greatest number. Laws have grown more humane, and sanitation is now in some quarters almost a fetish. Universal suffrage has come, and the ballot, and compulsory education—institutions now regarded as commonplaces of existence. Women, having secured the right to hold property and to vote, now engage in activities a century ago assumed to be peculiarly man's province, and there are few left to mourn the passing of chivalry. Even literature has to an increasing extent devoted itself to social ends. Tennyson, the New Man's official bard, to cite only one of many examples, adopted the cult of progress and engrafted it in his religion, even contributing an early and somewhat ill-fated attempt to catch the poetry of the age of steam:

Let the great wheels spin forever down the ringing grooves of change!

It has indeed been an age of steam, of invention, of progress and march of mind. Change, reform, we take for granted now. Only the least discriminating of the old *Westminster* reviewers would attempt to arrogate to the prophet and his disciples the sole credit for such a consummation. Yet it is significant that Bentham sits today in University College, though few know that he is there, his face still cheerful with the old smile.

APPENDIX: IDENTIFICATION OF AUTHORSHIP

The following list consists principally of articles identified by reliable biographers or other good evidence. The best evidence is in each case indicated in parentheses. Where the assignment is dubious, I have enclosed the title of the article in square brackets. Numbers following titles indicate appropriate volume and page in the *Westminster*.

I have failed to discover the editorial files for this period of the review. The journal changed publishers and editors too frequently for the proper preservation of records. But of particular value as sources for identification have been the manuscript diary of Francis Place in the British Museum, the complete typescript of the diary of Crabb Robinson in Dr. Williams's Library, London, and the Bentham manuscripts in University College, London, and in the British Museum. These sources are indicated below respectively as Place, Robinson, Bentham U. C., and Bentham B. M. Other notations indicate books listed in the Bibliography.

Contributors who certainly wrote for the review more articles than I have been able to identify are noted as "incomplete," and those whose lists are not known to be complete are noted as "possibly incomplete." I am unable to identify with certainty any articles by the following persons who were contributors: Charles Barker, probable author of many of the important literary articles; Walter Coulson; "a German named Garnier" identified as a contributor by Neal; Thomas Jefferson Hogg; J. A. Roebuck; and J. A. St. John.

AUSTIN, JOHN
 Edinburgh Review. Primogeniture, II, 505 (Mill, *Autobiography*)
AUSTIN, CHARLES (possibly incomplete)
 Greek Courts of Justice, VII, 227 (Bain, *John Stuart Mill*)
BENTHAM, JEREMY (possibly incomplete)
 Humphrey's Property Code, VI, 446 (Bentham, "Works")

BENTHAM, JEREMY—*Continued*

Anatomy, X, 116, with Southwood Smith. Page 138, from "recommending in the most impressive manner" through "no small degree objectionable" is by Bentham, and the article from this point incorporates his written suggestions. (Bentham B. M. Addl. 36652, D, f. 11, 12, 13)

Bentham, Brougham, and Law Reform, XI, 447. The substance of the article, and much of the phraseology, is Bentham's. (Bentham U. C. Portfolio 11-A)

Greatest Happiness Principle, XI, 526, with Perronet Thompson. Much of the early part of the article is by Bentham. (Bentham U. C. Portfolio 14)

Mr. Brougham and Local Judicatories, XIII, 420. Parts are by Bentham. (Bentham U. C. Portfolio 11-A)

Note, XIV, 454, with additions by another reviewer. (Bentham U. C. Portfolio 107)

BINGHAM, PEREGRINE (incomplete)

Moore's Fables for the Holy Alliance, I, 18 (Mill, *Autobiography*)

Vocal Music, I, 120 (Moore, *Journal*)

[Moore's Irish Melodies, III, 125] (internal evidence)

BOWRING, JOHN (incomplete)

[Politics and Literature of Russia, I, 80] (internal evidence)

The Greek Committee, VI, 113 (Place)

Runes of Finland, VII, 317 (L. B. Bowring)

Living Poets of Holland, X, 36 (*ibid.*)

Living Poets of the Magyars, XI, 29 (*ibid.*)

Poetry of Coleridge, XII, 1 (internal evidence)

Frisian Literature, XII, 186 (L. B. Bowring)

Tennyson's Poems, XIV, 210 (Hallam Tennyson)

[At least a half dozen other articles, all dealing with foreign literature—Frisian, Bohemian, Servian, Illyrian—are almost certainly by Bowring.]

CAMERON, CHARLES HAY (possibly incomplete)

British Code of Duel, IV, 20 (reprinted as his)

CARLYLE, THOMAS

The Nibelungenlied, XV, 1 (Carlyle's "Works")

CHADWICK, EDWIN (possibly incomplete)
Life Assurances, IX, 384 (Marston)
ELLIS, WILLIAM
West India Slavery, I, 337 (Blyth)
Charitable Institutions, II, 97 (*ibid.*)
Exportation of Machinery, III, 386 (*ibid.*)
McCulloch on Political Economy, with J. S. Mill, IV, 88 (*ibid.*)
Machinery, V, 101 (*ibid.*)
FONBLANQUE, ALBANY (incomplete)
Moore's Life of Sheridan, IV, 371 (E. B. de Fonblanque)
Montgomery's Satan, XII, 355 (L. B. Bowring)
Peacock's Crotchet Castle, XV, 208 (Van Doren)
FOSCOLO, UGO
Wiffen's Tasso, VI, 404 (*opere*)
Memoirs of Casanova, VII, 400 (*ibid.*)
FOX, WILLIAM JOHNSON
Men and Things in 1823, I, 1 (Garnett)
GRAHAM, GEORGE J. (incomplete)
Law Abuses: Pleading—Practice, VI, 39 (Place)
GROTE, GEORGE
Institutions of Ancient Greece, V, 269 (Mill, *Autobiography*)
GROTE, HARRIET (incomplete)
Memoirs of the Countess of Genlis, VI, 134 (Place)
HOBHOUSE, JOHN CAM (possibly incomplete)
Dallas' *Recollections* and Medwin's *Conversations*, III, 12 (Hobhouse)
KENRICK, JOHN (possibly incomplete)
Niebuhr's History of Rome, XI, 353 (Ms. letter, B. M. Addl. 34614, f. 189)
MERLE, GIBBONS (possibly incomplete)
The Newspaper Press, X, 216 (Fox Bourne)
MILL, JAMES
Edinburgh Review, I, 206 (J. S. Mill, *Autobiography*)
Quarterly Review, II, 463 (*ibid.*)
Southey's Book of the Church, III, 167 (*ibid.*)
Ecclesiastical Establishments, V, 504 (Bain, *James Mill*)

MILL, JAMES—*Continued*
  Formation and Publication of Opinions, VI, 1 (*ibid.*)
  State of the Nation, VI, 249 (*ibid.*)
  The Ballot, XIII, 1 (*ibid.* and Place)
MILL, JOHN STUART
  Edinburgh Review, I, 505 (Mill, *Autobiography*)
  Religious Prosecutions, II, 1 (Bain, *John Stuart Mill*)
  War Expenditure, II, 27 (*ibid.*)
  Brodie's History of the British Empire, II, 346 (*ibid.*)
  Quarterly Review—Political Economy, III, 213 (*ibid.*)
  Law of Libel and Liberty of the Press, III, 285 (*ibid.*)
  [Game Laws, V, 17] (*ibid.*)
  Mignet's History of the French Revolution, V, 385 (*ibid.*)
  Age of Chivalry, VI, 62 (Place)
  [Corn Laws, VI, 169] (Bain, *John Stuart Mill*)
  [Corn Laws, VII, 169] (*ibid.*)
  [Godwin's History of the Commonwealth, VIII, 325] (*ibid.*)
  Whately's Elements of Logic, IX, 137 (*ibid.*)
  Scott's Life of Napoleon, IX, 251 (Mill, *Autobiography*)
NEAL, JOHN
  United States, V, 173 (Neal)
PARKES, JOSEPH (possibly incomplete)
  [Dr. Lingard's Vindication, VII, 187] (Neal)
PEACOCK, THOMAS LOVE
  Moore's Epicurean, VIII, 351 ("Works")
  Moore's Byron, XII, 269 ("Works")
  Thomas Jefferson, XIII, 312 ("Works")
  London Bridge, XIII, 401 ("Works")
PLACE, FRANCIS
  History of Egypt, VI, 158 (Place)
  History of Parliaments, VIII, 253 (Place)
ROBINSON, HENRY CRABB
  Goethe's Memoirs, I, 370 (Robinson)
  A Grammar of Infinite Forms, I, 546 (*ibid.*)
  A Tour in Germany, II, 271 (*ibid.*)
  Rosaline de Vere, II, 283 (*ibid.*)

SMITH, THOMAS SOUTHWOOD (incomplete)
Education, I, 43 (Mrs. Lewes)
The Use of the Dead to the Living, II, 59 (reprinted as his)
Contagion and Sanitary Laws, III, 134 (Mrs. Lewes)
Plague—Typhus Fever—Quarantine, III, 499 (Mrs. Lewes)
Nervous System, IX, 172 (Bentham B. M. Addl.. 36652, D, f.
11)
Nervous System, IX, 451 (*ibid.*)
Anatomy, X, 116, with Jeremy Bentham, q.v. (*ibid.*)
(Several other articles on medicine are almost certainly by Dr.
Smith.)
SOUTHERN, HENRY (incomplete)
Chile and La Plata, VI, 202 (Place)
De Potter's Trial, and the Belgian Insurrection, XIII, 378 (Ms.
letter to Napier, B. M. Addl. 34614, f. 458)
THOMPSON, THOMAS PERRONET (Colonel Thompson's contribu-
tions to the *Westminster* are collected in his *Exercises, Political
and Others,* 6 vols., London, 1842. Many of them are brief
notices of minor works. Only the more important articles are
listed below.)
Instrument of Exchange, I, 171
Arabs and Persians, V, 202
Catholic Question, X, 1
Beranger's Songs, X, 198
Absenteeism, X, 237
System of Fagging, X, 234
Banking, X, 360
Disabilities of the Jews, X, 435
Corn Laws, XI, 1
Greatest Happiness Principle, XI, 526 (with Jeremy Bentham)
Slavery in the West Indies, XI, 275
Change of Ministry in France, XI, 494
Edinburgh Review and the Greatest Happiness Principle, XI,
254
Free Trade, XII, 138
Radical Reform, XII, 222

THOMPSON, THOMAS PERRONET—*Continued*

Edinburgh Review and the Greatest Happiness Principle, XII, 246

Taxes on Literature, XII, 416

Religious Disabilities, XIII, 188

Distress of the Country, XIII, 218

Great Britain and France, XIII, 240

Geometry without Axioms, XIII, 503

Revolution of 1830, XIII, 509

Defensive Force, XIV, 1

East India Trade, XIV, 93

Machine Breaking, XIV, 191

European Revolution, XIV, 245

Parliamentary Reform, XIV, 440

Military System of Napoleon, XV, 225

Belgium and the Holy Alliance, XV, 267

Prospects from Tory Reaction, XV, 526

Political Economy, XVI, 1

House of Peers, XVI, 121

St. Simonianism, XVI, 279

Silk and Glove Trades, XVI, 425, and all subsequent articles under this title

Enharmonic of the Ancients, XVI, 429

Dr. Chalmers on Political Economy, XVII, 1

Prospects of Reform, XVII, 248

McCulloch's Edition of the Wealth of Nations, XVII, 267

The Fall of the Constitution, XVII, 514

Tithes, XVIII, 162

Dutch War, XVIII, 249

Equitable Adjustment, XVIII, 263

Tithes, XVIII, 365

Property Tax, XIX, 1

The Mercantile System, XIX, 269

Dr. Chalmers's Bridgewater Treatises, XX, 1

Jews' Harps, XX, 74

Belgian Independence, XX, 125

Importance of Paying Twice Over, XX, 238

THOMPSON, THOMAS PERRONET—*Continued*
   The Suffering Rich, XX, 265
   Impressment and Flogging, XX, 489
   Deontology, XXI, 1
   Outpost Cavalry, XXI, 204
   First Report of Messrs. Villiers and Bowring, XXI, 257
   Cab and Omnibus Nuisance, XXI, 395
   John Hopkins on Political Economy, XXII, 1
   Enharmonic Organ, XXII, 56
   Lady Morgan's Princess, XXII, 281
   Mrs. Loudon's Philanthropic Economy, XXIII, 1
   Colonel Thompson also wrote each "Program" printed in the
     review
TOOKE, W. EYTON (incomplete)
   State of Ireland, VII, 1 (Place)

NOTES

CHAPTER I

1. E. Copleston, *Advice to a Young Reviewer*, p. 1.
2. Jeffrey to Thomas Moore. Moore, *Memoirs, Journal, and Correspondence*, II, 40.
3. G. M. Harper, *William Wordsworth*, II, 208.
4. *Edinburgh Review*, I, 71.
5. *Ibid.* XXII, 448.
6. *Ibid.*, XXVIII, 151ff.
7. *Ibid.*, XI, 215.
8. *Ibid.*, II, 90ff.
9. *Ibid.*, II, 462ff.
10. *Ibid.*, VIII, 456ff.
11. *Ibid.*, XXIX, 1ff.
12. *Ibid.*, XLV, 18.
13. *Quarterly Review*, XV, 473ff.
14. *Edinburgh Review*, XXVI, 476ff.
15. *Ibid.*, XXXIV, 203ff.
16. *Ibid.*, XXXVIII, 349ff.
17. *Quarterly Review*, XXI, 460ff.
18. *Ibid.*, XVI (Jan., 1817), 430ff.
19. *Ibid.*, XXVII (July, 1822), 476ff.
20. *Edinburgh Review*, XXXVI (Feb., 1822), 413ff.
21. *Blackwood's Magazine*, III (Aug., 1818), 524.
22. Thomas Carlyle, *Characteristics*, in "Works," XXVIII, 25.
23. *Revue encyclopédique*, XXXII, 670.
24. "Mr. Robert Montgomery's Poems, and the Modern Practice of Puffing," *Edinburgh Review*, LI (April, 1830), 193ff.
25. B. M. Addl. 34614, f. 412.
26. *Monthly Magazine*, LV, 501.
27. T. L. Peacock, "An Essay on Fashionable Literature," *Notes and Queries*, Series XI, II, 62.

CHAPTER II

1. April 26, 1817, p. 58.
2. John Morley, *Diderot and the Encyclopaedists*, in "Works" (London, 1921), II, 105.
3. Carlyle, *Sartor Resartus*, in "Works," I, 168.

4. John Neal, *Wandering Recollections of a Somewhat Busy Life*, p. 54.
5. J. A. Roebuck, *Life and Letters*, p. 27.
6. "Wiffen's Tasso," VI, (October, 1826), 404ff.; "Memoirs of Casanova," VII (April, 1827), 400ff.
7. B. M. Addl. 34614, f. 189.
8. *Ibid.*, ff. 181-183.
9. J. B. Priestly, *Thomas Love Peacock*, p. 52.
10. William Allen, *Life*, II, 377.
11. John Bowring, *The Works of Jeremy Bentham*, X, 516.
12. B. M. Addl. 35146, f. 584.
13. L. B. Bowring, *Autobiographical Recollections of Sir John Bowring*, p. 61.
14. Moore, *Journal*, I, 348.
15. Samuel Smiles, *A Publisher and his Friends*, II, 199.
16. Caroline Fox, *Memories of Old Friends*, pp. 32ff.
17. Neal, *Wandering Recollections*, p. 273.
18. *Ibid.*, p. 275.
19. *Ibid.*, p. 273.
20. *Ibid.*, p. 281.
21. Harriet Martineau, *Autobiography*, I, 311.
22. B. M. Addl. 37949, f. 177v.
23. H. C. Robinson, *Diary* (typescript, Dr. Williams's Library), pp. 168, 186.
24. *Ibid.*, p. 391.
25. B. M. Addl. 35146, f. 46.
26. J. S. Mill, *Autobiography*, p. 64.
27. John Bowring, *The Works of Jeremy Bentham*, X, 540.
28. *Ibid.*
29. L. B. Bowring, *Autobiographical Recollections of Sir John Bowring*, p. 7.
30. Liverpool Papers, B. M. Addl. 38298, a and b.
31. B. M. Addl. 35146, f. 66v.
32. John Bowring, *The Works of Jeremy Bentham*, X, 540.
33. Place recorded in his diary, 1826, " . . . Mr. McCulloch for a gossip—he told me that on an average of the last three years the Edinburgh Review had sold 11,000." B. M. Addl. 35146, f. 11.
34. Smiles, *A Publisher and his Friends*, II, 160.
35. *Ibid.*, p. 158.
36. Mill, *Autobiography*, p. 67.
37. *Westminster Review*, I (January, 1824), 206ff.

CHAPTER III

1. *Westminster Review*, II (Oct., 1824), 463ff.
2. *Ibid.*, I (April, 1824), 505ff.

3. *Ibid.,* I, (Jan., 1824), 1ff.
4. *Monthly Magazine,* LVII (March, 1824), 130.
5. *Blackwood's Magazine,* XV (Feb., 1824), 144ff.
6. *Westminster Review,* I (April, 1824), 529.
7. *Ibid.,* I (April, 1824), 530.
8. *Ibid.,* I (Jan., 1824), 101ff.
9. Important articles, and articles containing important allusions, are as
    follows: I (Jan., 1824), "Moore's Fables for the Holy Alliance,"
    20f.; "Travels in the United States and Canada," 101ff.; "Quar-
    terly Review," 250ff. II (July, 1824), "Use of the Dead to the
    Living," 88f.; "Travels in the United States and Canada," 170ff.;
    "Newspapers," 210; (Oct., 1824), "Influence of America on the
    Mind," 554ff.; "Quarterly Review," 484ff.; "Tales of a Travel-
    ler," 334ff. III (Jan., 1825), "Project of a New Penal Code for
    the State of Louisiana," 58ff.; "A Summary View of America,"
    283f.; (April, 1825), "On Emigration," 448ff. V (Jan., 1826),
    "United States," 173ff.
10. *Westminster Review,* II, 178.
11. *Ibid.* I (Jan., 1824), 105.
12. *Ibid.,* I, 120.
13. *Ibid.,* I, 250ff.
14. *Ibid.,* V (April, 1826), 269ff.
15. *Ibid.,* II (July, 1824), 121ff.
16. *Ibid.,* V (Jan., 1826), 249ff.
17. *Ibid.,* VI (July, 1826), 134ff.
18. *Ibid.,* V (April, 1826), 385ff.
19. "Biography of French Ministers," V (April, 1826), 457ff.; "Mont-
    loisier's French Monarchy," III (Jan., 1825), 35ff.
20. *Westminster Review,* IV (Oct., 1825), 408ff.
21. *Ibid.,* VIII (Oct., 1827), 328ff.
22. *Ibid.,* II (Oct., 1824), 346ff.
23. *Ibid.,* VI (July, 1826), 62ff.
24. "Mills' History of Chivalry," V, (Jan., 1826), 59ff.
25. *Westminster Review,* IV (July, 1825), 252.
26. *Ibid.,* V (April, 1826), 513.
27. *Ibid.,* V (Jan., 1826), 1ff.
28. *Ibid.,* VI, 249ff.
29. *Ibid.,* II (July, 1824), 27ff.
30. *Ibid.,* II (Oct., 1824), 306.
31. *Ibid.,* VII (April, 1827), 484ff.
32. *Ibid.,* III (April, 1825), 349ff.; VI (Oct., 1826), 373ff.; VII (Jan.,
    1827), 169ff.; IX (April, 1828), 313ff.
33. *Ibid.,* III (April, 1825), 386ff.; V (Jan., 1826), 136ff.; VII (Jan.,
    1827), 126ff.
34. For example, IV, 213.

35. *Westminster Review,* IV (July, 1825), 88ff.
36. *Ibid.,* II (Oct., 1824), 289ff.
37. *Ibid.,* XIII (Oct., 1830), 312ff.
38. *Ibid.,* VI (Jan., 1826), 101ff.
39. *Ibid.,* II (July, 1824), 97ff., "Charitable Institutions."
40. Oct. 14, 1824; B. M. Addl. 38103, f. 333v.
41. *Westminster Review,* III (April, 1825), 42ff.
42. *Ibid.,* III (April, 1825), 420ff.
43. *Ibid.,* IX (Jan., 1828), 41ff.
44. *Ibid.,* IV (Oct., 1825), 315ff.; VI (July, 1826), 231ff.
45. *Ibid.,* VII (Jan., 1827), 91ff.
46. *Ibid.,* I (Jan., 1824), 141ff.
47. *Ibid.,* IV (July, 1825), 60ff.; VI (July, 1826), 39ff.
48. *Ibid.,* VI, 446ff.; Bowring, "Works," V, 387ff.
49. Bentham MSS, University College, Portfolio 78.
50. *Westminster Review,* II (Oct., 1824), 403.
51. *Ibid.,* V (Jan., 1826), 23ff.
52. *Ibid.,* IX (Jan., 1828), 99ff.
53. *Ibid.,* I (Jan., 1824), 146ff.
54. *Ibid.,* II (July, 1824), 598.
55. *Ibid.,* III (Jan. and July, 1825), 134ff., 499ff.
56. *Ibid.,* III (Jan., 1825), 154.
57. *Ibid.,* V (Jan., 1826), 149ff.; VI (Oct. 1826), 303ff.; VII (Jan., 1827), 208ff.; VII (April, 1827), 416ff.; IX (Jan., 1828), 172ff.; IX (April, 1828), 451ff.
58. *Ibid.,* IX, 460.
59. *Ibid.,* IX, 463.
60. *Ibid.,* I (April, 1824), 336ff.
61. *Ibid.,* IV (July, 1825), 20ff.
62. *Ibid.,* IX (April, 1828), 384ff.
63. *Ibid.,* VIII, 105ff.
64. *Ibid.,* VIII (July, 1827), 1ff.
65. *Ibid.,* VIII (July, 1827), 70ff.; IX (Jan., 1828), 71ff.
66. *Ibid.,* VII (Jan., 1827), 1ff.
67. *Ibid.,* IV (Oct., 1825), 261ff.
68. *Ibid.,* I (April, 1824), 289ff.
69. *Ibid.,* V, (April, 1826), 457ff.
70. *Ibid.,* I (April, 1824), 453ff.; II (July, 1824), 149ff.
71. *Ibid.,* VI (July, 1826), 113ff.
72. *Ibid.,* I (April, 1824), 453ff.
73. *Ibid.,* II (Oct., 1824), 410ff.
74. *Edinburgh Review,* XLII (Aug., 1825), 367ff.
75. *London Magazine,* New Series VII (Feb., 1827), 283.

CHAPTER IV

1. Mill, *Autobiography*, p. 93.
2. *Westminster Review* IV (July, 1825), 147ff.
3. David Hartley, *Observations on Man* (2 vols., London, 1810), I, 5ff.
4. *Westminster Review*, III (Jan., 1825), 167ff.
5. B. M. Addl. 33546, f. 69.
6. *Westminster Review*, IV (Oct., 1825), 457ff.
7. *Ibid.*, V, 504ff.
8. *Ibid.*, II, 210f.
9. *Ibid.*, II (July, 1824), 1-27.
10. *Ibid.*, III (April, 1825), 285ff.
11. *Ibid.*, II, 20.
12. Samuel Warren, *Ten Thousand a Year* (New York, Routledge, n.d.), 450ff.
13. *Westminster Review*, I (Jan., 1824), 43ff.; IV (July, 1825), 147ff.; VII (April, 1827), 269ff.
14. *Ibid.*, IV, 149.
15. *Ibid.*, IV, 150.
16. *Ibid.*
17. *Ibid.*, IV, 154.
18. T. H. Huxley, "A Liberal Education, and Where to Find It," in *Collected Essays*, (London, 1894), III, 86.
19. *Westminster Review*, I (Jan., 1824), 43ff.
20. *Ibid.*, IV, 147ff.
21. *Ibid.*, VII (April, 1827), 269ff.
22. *Ibid.*, p. 271.
23. *Ibid.*, VI, 269ff.
24. *Ibid.*, X, 84.
25. *Ibid.*, IX, 328ff.
26. *Edinburgh Review*, XV, 40ff.; XVI, 158ff.
27. See G. D. H. Cole: *The Life of William Cobbett*, pp. 138f., 294.
28. On London University, *Edinburgh Review*, XLII, 346ff.; XLIII, 315ff.; XLVIII, 235ff. On the Society for the Diffusion of Useful Knowledge, XLVI, 225ff.; XLVIII, 258ff.
29. *London Magazine*, IX, 410ff., 503ff.; New Series, III, 437ff. *New Monthly Magazine*, XII, 404ff.; XIV, 1ff.; both articles signed by Campbell.
30. See Mill, *Autobiography*, p. 73.
31. *Westminster Review*, I, 525f.
32. *Edinburgh Review*, XV, 299ff.
33. *Westminster Review*, I, 537.
34. *Ibid.*, VI, 62ff.
35. *Ibid.*, V, 80f.

36. *Ibid.,* VII, 65ff.
37. *Ibid.,* III, 71.
38. *Ibid.,* XI, 266.
39. *Ibid.,* I, 77.
40. *Ibid.,* I, 79.
41. Mark Pattison, *Memoirs,* p. 46.
42. *Ibid.,* p. 53.
43. T. Mozley, *Reminiscences,* I, 237.
44. John Wilson, *Noctes Ambrosianae,* III, 201.

CHAPTER V

1. *Westminster Review,* VI (July, 1826), 63.
2. *Ibid.,* p. 33.
3. *Ibid.,* IV, 151, 165f.
4. P. B. Shelley, *Defense of Poetry,* p. 49.
5. *Westminster Review,* I, 18ff.
6. Mill, *Autobiography,* pp. 78f.
7. *Westminster Review,* III (Jan., 1825), 115ff.
8. *Ibid.,* I (Jan., 1824), 120ff.
9. *Ibid.,* IV (Oct., 1825), 380.
10. *Ibid.,* II (Oct., 1824), 346.
11. *Ibid.,* 334ff.
12. *Monthly Magazine* (Dec., 1824), pp. 58, 417ff.
13. *Ibid.* LX (1825), 135ff., 329, 233ff.: " . . . There is a sect among them
    so exclusively infatuated with the new science of political econ-
    omy . . . as to have persuaded themselves that there is no value
    in anything else." (Page 235.) " . . . nor do we see why the opu-
    lent merchant or manufacturer should not have a taste for litera-
    ture or the solace of its accomplishments." (Page 238.).
14. *Oriental Herald,* I (March, 1824), 469ff.
15. *Blackwood's Magazine,* XV (Feb., 1824), 150.
16. *Westminster Review,* I, 536.
17. *Ibid.,* II (July, 1824), 179ff.
18. *Ibid.,* V (April, 1826), 399ff.
19. *Ibid.,* IX, 251ff.
20. *New Monthly Magazine,* X (1824), 297ff.; XI, 94.
21. I (Jan., 1824), 18ff.
22. Moore, *Journal,* IV, 158.
23. *Ibid.,* p. 175.
24. *Westminster Review,* I, 492ff.
25. *Ibid.,* III, 115ff.
26. Moore, *Journal,* V, 54.
27. *Westminster Review,* VIII (Oct., 1827), 351ff.; reprinted in IX, 1ff.
    of the Halliford Edition.

28. Moore, *Journal*, VI, 234.
29. *Westminster Review*, XII (April, 1830), 269ff.; reprinted in IX, 69ff. of the Halliford Edition.
30. *Ibid.*, II (July, 1824), 48ff.
31. *Ibid.*, III (April, 1825), 531ff.
32. *Ibid.*, pp. 537ff.
33. *Ibid.*, VII (Jan., 1827), 55ff.
34. *Ibid.*, I (April, 1824), 431ff.
35. *Ibid.*, VI (July, 1826), 103ff.
36. *Ibid.*, IV (Oct., 1825), 293ff.
37. *Ibid.*, VII (April, 1827), 341ff.
38. *Ibid.*, VII (Jan., 1827), 117.
39. *Edinburgh Review*, LI (April, 1830), 193ff.
40. *Westminster Review*, IX (April, 1828), 441ff.
41. *Ibid.*, II (July, 1824), 225ff.
42. J. C. Hobhouse, *Recollections of a Long Life*, III, 83f.
43. *Westminster Review*, III, 1825, 79; *Ibid.*, 151ff.
44. *Ibid.*, VII, 118, "the lamented Keats."
45. *Ibid.*, IV, 165, "or the excise perhaps."
46. E. Dowden, *The Life of Percy Bysshe Shelley*, I, 426. Walter Coulson's letter of explanation to Hunt (B. M. Addl. 37109, f. 24) makes it clear that Southern consulted Peacock and finally rejected the article.
47. Napier Papers, B. M. Addl. 34614, f. 244.
48. *Westminster Review*, I, 383ff.
49. *Ibid.*, II, 268ff.
50. *Ibid.*, VI (July, 1826), 23ff.
51. *Ibid.*, V, 202ff.
52. Place Papers, B. M. Addl. 35146, f. 46.
53. *Westminster Review*, II, 463.
54. *Ibid.*, VII (July, 1827), 92ff.
55. *Ibid.*, VII (April, 1827), 375ff.
56. Place Papers, B. M. Addl. 37949, f. 189.
57. *Westminster Review*, II (July, 1824), 213ff. The full title at the heading included the name of the real author, Thomas Wilson.
58. *Blackwood's Magazine*, XVI (August, 1824), 226.
59. Mill, *Autobiography*, p. 66.
60. *Westminster Review*, III (Jan., 1825), 49ff.
61. *Ibid.*, X (April, 1826), 374ff.
62. *Blackwood's Magazine*, XX (Nov., 1826), 787.

CHAPTER VI

1. Mill, *Autobiography*, p. 68.
2. B. M. Addl. 35145, ff. 80, 81.

3. *Ibid.*, f. 81.

4. *Ibid.*, f. 84.

5. Moore, *Journal*, III, 100.

6. B. M. Addl. 35145, f. 87.

7. *Ibid.*, f. 90.

8. *Westminster Review*, VI (July, 1826), 158ff.

9. B. M. Addl. 35146, f. 46.

10. *Ibid.*, f. 40.

11. May 21, 1824, B. M. Addl. 37949, f. 142.

12. *Ibid.*, f. 40.

13. Hunt Papers, B. M. Addl. 38105, f. 331.

14. Neal, *Wandering Recollections*, p. 336.

15. *Ibid.*, p. 279.

16. *Westminster Review*, V (Jan., 1826), 173ff.

17. Neal, *Wandering Recollections*, p. 290.

18. *Westminster Review*, VII (Jan., 1827), 187ff.; *London Magazine,* New Series VII (March, 1827), 421ff. and (in a department called Magaziniana) 432.

19. Robinson, *Diary*, typescript XII, 285.

20. *Westminster Review*, I (April, 1824), 370ff.

21. Robinson, *op. cit.*, VII, 168.

22. *Ibid.*, XII, 291, June 18, 1827.

23. Robinson, *Letters, 1818-26*, f. 108.

24. *Westminster Review*, XIII (July, 1830), 1ff.

25. Bentham MSS., University College, Portfolio 11A, contain material for "Bentham, Brougham, and Law Reform," *Westminster Review*, XI (Oct., 1829), 447ff., and for "Mr. Brougham and Local Judicatories," *Ibid.*, XIII (Oct., 1830), 420ff.

26. Respectively XII (April, 1830), 269ff.; XII (Oct., 1830), 312ff.; *Ibid.*, 401ff.

27. *Westminster Review*, XV (July, 1831), 1ff.

28. Napier Papers, B. M. Addl. 34615, f. 111.

29. Jan. 7, 1829. B. M. Addl. 37949, f. 228.

30. *Ibid.*, f. 215.

31. B. M. Addl. 37950, f. 16.

32. See *Monthly Repository,* New Series III (1829) 199, 794; *Athenaeum,* July 15, 1829, p. 440; July 10, 1830, p. 425; *Spectator,* Feb. 7, 1829, p. 89.

33. B. M. Addl. 35145, f. 103.

34. "Mill's Essay on Government," *Edinburgh Review*, XLIX (March, 1829), 159ff.; "Utilitarian System of Philosophy," *Ibid.*, XLIX (June, 1829), 273ff.; "Utilitarian System of Philosophy," *Ibid.*, L (Oct., 1829), 99ff.

35. Benham MSS., University College, Portfolio 14.

36. *Westminster Review,* XI, 254ff.
37. *Ibid.,* 526ff.
38. *Westminster Review,* XII (Jan., 1830), 246ff.
39. July 18, 25, Aug. 1, 8, 1829; B. M. Addl. 35145, f. 98.
40. B. M. Addl. 35145, f. 97.
41. *Ibid.,* f. 101.
42. July 15, 1829, p. 440.
43. B. M. Addl. 35145, f. 99.
44. *Ibid.,* f. 101.
45. *Ibid.,* f. 104.
46. *Ibid.,* f. 103.
47. Mill, *Autobiography,* pp. 110f.
48. B. M. Addl. 35145, f. 108-118.
49. *Westminster Review,* XIV (Jan., 1831), 103ff.
50. *Ibid.,* XII (Jan., 1830), 222ff.
51. *Ibid.,* Jan., 1829, pp. 1ff.
52. *Ibid.,* XII (April, 1830), 416ff.; XV (July, 1831), 238ff.; XVIII (April, 1833), 474ff.
53. October 24, 1830, p. 675.
54. *Westminster Review,* XV (July, 1831), 149ff.
55. *Ibid.,* XIV (Jan., 1831), 191ff.
56. *Ibid.,* XI, 1ff.; XII, 138ff.; XVII, 510ff.; XVIII, 366ff.
57. "Programme," April, 1833.
58. *Westminster Review,* XVIII (April, 1833), 380ff.
59. *Ibid.,* XVII (July, 1832), 380ff.
60. *Ibid.,* XVII (July, 1832), 10.
61. *Ibid.,* XVI, 368.
62. *Ibid.,* XIII (Oct., 1830), 312ff.
63. *Ibid.,* XIX, 468.
64. *Ibid.,* p. 489.
65. *Ibid.,* XX (April, 1834), 496ff.
66. *Ibid.,* XVI (April, 1832), 279ff.
67. *Ibid.,* p. 299.
68. "True delicacy is to [*sic*] *faire des enfans* and say no more about it. The case may be different in France; but in England every blockhead knows all that is necessary, without occasion to hold a vestry meeting." *Ibid.,* p. 313.
69. *Ibid.,* "Programme," XVII (July, 1832).
70. *Ibid.,* XII (Jan., 1830), 1ff.
71. *Ibid.,* X (April, 1829), 257ff.
72. *Ibid.,* XI (July, 1829), 211ff.
73. *Ibid.,* XVII (July, 1832), 132ff.
74. *Ibid.,* XVI (Jan., 1832), 180ff.
75. *Ibid.,* XI (Oct., 1829), 389ff.
76. *Ibid.,* XV (Oct., 1831), 399ff.

77. *Ibid.,* XVII (Oct., 1832), 468ff.
78. *Ibid.,* X (Jan., 1829), 173ff.
79. *Ibid.,* XI (Oct., 1829), 490ff.
80. *Ibid.,* XVIII (Jan., 1833), 208ff.
81. *Ibid.,* XIV, 365.
82. *Ibid.,* XV (Oct., 1831), 320ff., "Present State of Music"; probably by Bowring, being generally similar to articles on Coleridge and Tennyson.
83. *Ibid.,* XVI (April, 1832), 429ff.
84. *Ibid.,* XIII (Oct., 1830), 503ff.
85. *Ibid.,* XIV (Jan., 1831), 210ff.
86. *Blackwood's Magazine,* XXXI (May, 1832), 721ff.
87. *Westminster Review,* XX (Jan., 1834), 151ff.
88. Mill, *Letters,* I, 94.

CHAPTER VII

1. Halévy, *A History of the English People, 1830-41,* p. 242.
2. *London and Westminster Review,* August, 1838, contains a vigorous defense of Lord Durham, appended to the second edition of that number (XXIX, 507ff.). The following number (Dec., 1838) contains Mill's article entitled *Lord Durham's Return* (XXXII, 241ff.), a more important contribution.
3. Mill, *Autobiography,* p. 151.
4. L. B. Bowring, *Autobiographical Recollections of Sir John Bowring.*
5. Mill, *Autobiography,* pp. 149f.
6. For the *London Review,* James Mill wrote "State of the Nation," I (April, 1835), 1ff. (*Westminster Review,* Vol. XXX); "The Ballot," *ibid.,* 210ff.; "The Church and its Reform," I (July, 1835), 257ff.; "Law Reform," II (Oct., 1835), 1ff. (*Westminster Review,* Vol. XXXI); "Aristocracy," II (Jan., 1836), 283ff.; "Whether Political Economy is Useful or Not," II (Jan., 1836), 566ff. For the *London and Westminster* he lived to write only one article, "Theory and Practice, a Dialogue," XXV (April, 1836), 223ff.
7. Carlyle's articles in the *London and Westminster* are: "Memoirs of Mirabeau," XXVI (Jan., 1837), 382ff.; "Parliamentary History of the French Revolution," XXVII (April, 1837), 233ff.; "Lockhart's Life of Scott," XXVIII (Jan., 1838), 293ff.; "Varnhagen von Ense's Memoirs," XXXII (Dec., 1838), 60ff.
8. "Mirabeau," *London and Westminster Review,* XXVI, 383f.
9. Mill's articles both in the *London* and in the *London and Westminster* are all signed either A. or A. B. The more important are reprinted in *Dissertations and Discussions,* Vol. I, and in J. M. W. Gibbs, *Early Essays by John Stuart Mill,* London, 1897.

10. "De Tocqueville on Democracy in America," *London Review*, II (Oct., 1835), 85ff. (*Westminster Review*, Vol. XXXI).
11. "State of Society in America," *Ibid.*, p. 375.
12. *London and Westminster Review*, XXV (April, 1836), 1ff.
13. *Ibid.*, XXIX (Aug., 1838), 467ff.
14. *Ibid.*, XXXIII (March, 1840), 257ff.
15. *Ibid.*, XXVII (April, 1837), 130ff.
16. *Ibid.*, XXIX (Aug., 1838), 433ff.
17. *Ibid.*, XXVII (July, 1837), 1ff.
18. *Ibid.*, pp. 229ff.
19. *London Review*, I (July, 1835), 402ff. (*Westminster Review*, Vol. XXX).
20. *London and Westminster Review*, XXVII (July, 1837), 17ff.
21. Mill, *Autobiography*, p. 152.
22. Editorial note, *London Review*, II, 389 (*Westminster Review*, Vol. XXX).
23. *London and Westminster Review*, XXVI (Jan., 1837), 501ff.
24. *London Review*, II (Jan., 1836), 389ff. (*Westminster Review*, Vol. XXXI).
25. *London and Westminster Review*, XXV (April, 1836), 137ff.
26. *Ibid.*, XXVIII (Oct., 1837), 132ff.
27. *Ibid.*, XXIX (April, 1838), 146ff.
28. *Ibid.*, pp. 1ff.
29. *Ibid.*, XXVIII (Oct., 1837), 66ff.
30. *Ibid.*, XXXIII (Oct., 1839), 1ff.
31. *Ibid.*, XXXIII, (March, 1840), 345ff.
32. *Ibid.*, XXVII (July, 1837), 194ff.
33. Caroline Fox, *Memories of Old Friends*, p. 84.
34. The *Westminster* was united in 1846 with the *Foreign Quarterly Review*, continuing from January, 1847, as the *Westminster and Foreign Quarterly Review*. In 1852 the title of the *Westminster Review* was resumed. The journal was published as a quarterly until 1887, and from 1887 to 1914 as a monthly.
35. Caroline Fox, *Memories of Old Friends*, p. 113.
36. Matthew Arnold, "The Function of Criticism at the Present Time," in *Essays in Criticism, First Series* (London, 1921), p. 21.
37. Morley, *The Death of Mr. Mill*, in "Critical Miscellanies," III (London, 1898), p. 39.
38. *Ibid.*
39. Morley, *John Stuart Mill: An Anniversary*, in "Critical Miscellanies," IV (New York, 1908), 147.

BIBLIOGRAPHY

I. GENERAL WORKS

BOWRING, JOHN, The Works of Jeremy Bentham, edited by John Bowring. 10 vols., Edinburgh, 1843.

BULWER, EDWARD, LORD LYTTON, England and the English. London, 1833.

CARLYLE, THOMAS, Characteristics; Chartism; Past and Present; Sartor Resartus. In Works, New York, 1899-1900.

CAZAMIAN, LOUIS, L'Angleterre moderne. Paris, 1911.

————, Le Roman social en Angleterre. Paris, 1904.

DICEY, A. V., Lectures on the Relation between Law and Public Opinion in England during the Nineteenth Century. London, 1914.

DICKENS, CHARLES, Bleak House; Hard Times; Oliver Twist; Pickwick Papers. In Works, London, 1910-11.

HALÉVY, ÉLIE, La Formation du Radicalisme philosophique. 3 vols., Paris, 1901-4.

————, A History of the English People, translated from the French by E. I. Watkin and D. A. Barker. 4 vols., New York, 1924-29.

MILL, JAMES, Essays on Government, Jurisprudence, etc. London, 1828.

MILL, JOHN STUART, Principles of Political Economy. London, 1872.

————, The Subjection of Women. London, 1911.

————, Utilitarianism, Liberty, and Representative Government. London, 1910.

MOZLEY, THOMAS, Reminiscences. 2 vols., Boston, 1882.

NEFF, EMERY, Carlyle and Mill. New York, 1926.

PATTISON, MARK, Memoirs. London, 1885.

PEACOCK, THOMAS LOVE, Works. The Halliford Edition, 10 vols., London, 1924-31.

SHELLEY, P. B., Defense of Poetry. Oxford, 1921.
SLATER, GILBERT, The Making of Modern England. Boston, 1915.
STEPHEN, LESLIE, The English Utilitarians. 3 vols., London, 1900.
———, A History of English Thought in the Eighteenth Century. 2 vols., London, 1881.
THORNDIKE, A. H., Literature in a Changing Age. New York, 1920.
TREVELYAN, G. M., British History in the Nineteenth Century. London, 1922.
WALKER, HUGH, The Literature of the Victorian Era. Cambridge, 1921.
WALLAS, GRAHAM, Bentham as Political Inventor. In Contemporary Review, March 1926.

II. PERIODICALS

I have consulted the files of all periodicals which are referred to in this study. In addition, the following works have proved helpful:
BLUNDEN, E. C., Leigh Hunt's "Examiner" Examined. London, 1928.
BOURNE, H. R. FOX, English Newspapers. 2 vols., London, 1887.
COLLINS, A. S., The Profession of Letters. London, 1928.
COPINGER, W. A., On the Authorship of the First Hundred Numbers of the Edinburgh Review. Manchester, 1895.
COPLESTON, EDWARD, Advice to a Young Reviewer. Oxford, 1927.
GRAHAM, WALTER, English Literary Periodicals. New York, 1930.
———, Tory Criticism in the Quarterly Review. New York, 1921.
JERDAN, WILLIAM, Autobiography. 4 vols., London, 1852-53.
LEIGH, SAMUEL, New Picture of London. London, 1824.
NAPIER, MACVEY, Selections from the Correspondence of the Late MacVey Napier, Esq. London, 1879.
OLIPHANT, MRS. and MRS. GERALD PORTER, William Blackwood and his Sons. 3 vols., Edinburgh, 1897.
PEACOCK, THOMAS LOVE, An Essay on Fashionable Literature. In Notes and Queries, Series XI, Vol. II, 5-6; 62-63.
Revue encyclopédique, tomes 27-32. Paris, 1825-26.

SMILES, SAMUEL, A Publisher and his Friends. 2 vols., London, 1891.

WILSON, JOHN, and others, Noctes Ambrosianae. 5 vols., New York, 1872.

III. BIOGRAPHY

ALDRED, G. A., Richard Carlile, Agitator, his Life and Times. London, 1923.

ALLEN, WILLIAM, The Life of William Allen. 4 vols., London, 1846.

ATKINSON, CHARLES M., Jeremy Bentham. London, 1905.

BAIN, ALEXANDER, James Mill, a Biography. London, 1882.

————, John Stuart Mill, a Criticism, with Personal Recollections. London, 1882.

BARKER, CHARLES, Testimonials in favor of Charles Barker, as a candidate for the situation of English Master in the Edinburgh Academy. 1824, no place.

BLUNDEN, EDMUND, Leigh Hunt, a Biography. London, 1930.

BLYTH, EDMUND K., The Life of William Ellis. London, 1889.

BOWRING, LEWIN B., Autobiographical Recollections of Sir John Bowring, with a Brief Memoir. London, 1877.

CAMERON, CHARLES H., Public Meeting at Calcutta in Honor of the Hon'ble C. H. Cameron. Calcutta, 1848.

CARLYLE, THOMAS, The Correspondence of Thomas Carlyle with Ralph Waldo Emerson, 1834-72. 2 vols., Boston, n. d.

COCKBURN, LORD, The Life of Francis Jeffrey. Philadelphia, 1853.

COLE, G. D. H., The Life of William Cobbett. London, 1924.

COLE, SIR HENRY, Fifty Years of Public Work of Sir Henry Cole, K.C.B. London, 1884.

COURTNEY, W. L., The Life of John Stuart Mill. London, 1889.

DOWDEN, EDWARD, The Life of Percy Bysshe Shelley. 2 vols., London, 1897.

EVERETT, CHARLES W., The Education of Jeremy Bentham. New York, 1931.

FAWCETT, MRS., The Life of Sir William Molesworth. London, 1903.

FONBLANQUE, E. B., The Life and Labors of Albany Fonblanque. 4 vols., London, 1874.

FOX, CAROLINE, Memories of Old Friends. Philadelphia, 1882.

GARNETT, RICHARD, The Life of William Johnson Fox. London, 1910.

GROTE, MRS. HARRIET, The Personal Life of George Grote. London, 1873.

GWYNN, STEPHEN, Thomas Moore. New York, 1905.

HACKWOOD, F. W., William Hone, His Life and Times. London, 1912.

HALDANE, ELIZABETH S., George Eliot, Her Life and Times. London, 1927.

HARPER, GEORGE M., William Wordsworth, His Life, Works, and Influence. 2 vols., New York, 1916.

HOBHOUSE, JOHN CAM, LORD BROUGHTON, Recollections of a Long Life. 6 vols., London, 1910.

KING, BOLTON, Mazzini. London, 1902.

LEADER, R. E., The Life and Letters of John Arthur Roebuck. London, 1897.

LEWES, MRS. C. L., Dr. Southwood Smith: a Retrospect. Edinburgh, 1898.

LOCKHART, J. G., The Life of Sir Walter Scott. 10 vols., London, Mallet, n. d.

MARSTON, MAURICE, Sir Edwin Chadwick. London, 1925.

MARTINEAU, HARRIET, Autobiography. 2 vols., Boston, 1877.

MILL, JOHN STUART, The Autobiography of John Stuart Mill. New York, 1924.

———, Letters of John Stuart Mill. 2 vols., London, 1910.

MOORE, THOMAS, Memoirs, Journal, and Correspondence of Thomas Moore. 6 vols., London, 1853-56.

NEAL, JOHN, Wandering Recollections of a Somewhat Busy Life. Boston, 1869.

NEFF, EMERY, Carlyle. New York, 1932.

NICOLSON, HAROLD, Tennyson. London, 1923.

PRIESTLY, J. B., Thomas Love Peacock. New York, 1927.

STEPHEN, LESLIE, George Eliot. London, 1902.

TENNYSON, HALLAM, Alfred, Lord Tennyson, a Memoir. London, 1899.

TREVELYAN, GEORGE OTTO, The Life and Letters of Thomas Babington Macaulay. 2 vols., New York, 1876.

THOMPSON, C. W., Thomas Perronet Thompson. In Proceedings of the Royal Society, London, 1845.

VAN DOREN, CARL, The Life of Thomas Love Peacock. London, 1911.

WHITE, JOSEPH BLANCO, The Life of the Reverend Joseph Blanco White, Written by Himself. 2 vols., London, 1845.

INDEX

Allen, William, 30
Amulet, The, 18, 30
Arnold, Matthew, 79, 92-93, 150, 170-71, 173
Aspland, Robert, 16
Athenaeum, The, 18, 138, 141
Austin, Charles, 26
Austin, John, 26, 61, 166
Ayrton, William, 134-35

Bacon, Francis, 152
Baldwin, Cradock, and Joy, publishers, 36, 120, 130, 137
Baptist Magazine, 16
Barker, Charles, 26, 114
Bentham, Jeremy, 22-25, 28-31, 34-36, 42, 50, 56, 60-61, 64, 66, 78-80, 104, 114, 118, 120-21, 128-29, 131-33, 137, 140-41, 150, 152, 164, 168, 170, 173-75
Bickersteth, Henry, 143
Bingham, Peregrine, the younger, 27, 44, 48, 99-101, 103, 109-10, 128, 130
Black Dwarf, 16, 21-22, 41
Black, John, 127
Blackwood's Magazine, 14-15, 18, 34, 44-45, 80, 103-4, 127, 133, 161
Boccaccio, 117
Borrow, George, 32
Bowring, Sir John, 24, 27-34, 36, 44, 61, 64, 101, 107, 111, 111n, 121-24, 126-28, 130-38, 140-42, 150-55, 159-61, 165, 167-68, 173
British Review, 16

Brougham, Henry, 17-18, 80, 88
Buckingham, John Silk, 17-18, 103
Buller, Charles, 26, 165-66
Bulwer-Lytton, Edward, 155, 171, 172n
Burdett, Sir Francis, 35
Burke, Edmund, 152
Butler, William, 21
Byron, 10-11, 13-14, 16-17, 27, 30-31, 43, 111n, 121-22, 135, 150

Calcutta Journal, 17-18
Caledonian Mercury, 141-42
Cameron, Charles Hay, 63, 167
Campbell, Thomas, 15, 43, 88, 109, 133
Carlile, Richard, 16, 21-22, 24, 73
Carlyle, Thomas, 4, 16, 23, 52, 58, 85, 95, 99, 112, 127, 136-37, 145, 150, 155, 169, 171 172n
Carrel, Armand, 171
Chadwick, Sir Edwin, 28, 63, 147, 165-67
Chapman, John, 172
Christian Moderator, 17
Christian Monitor, 17
Christian Observer, 17, 122
Christian Reformer, 16
Christian Remembrancer, 17
Cobbett, William, 16, 20-22, 54, 74n, 85
Colburn, Henry, 18-19, 109, 120
Cole, Sir Henry, 171, 172n
Coleridge, Samuel Taylor, 12, 15, 151-54, 159, 170, 173
Congregational Magazine, 17
Constable, Archibald, publisher, 34
Cooper, James Fenimore, 154

206   INDEX

Neal, John, 25, 31-32, 133-34
New Jerusalem Magazine, 17
Newman, John Henry, 71
New Monthly Magazine, 14-15, 18,
    36, 88, 109, 133, 141
Nisard, Desiré, 171, 172*n*
North, Christopher, *see* Wilson,
    John

O*riental Herald,* 17-18, 28, 103,
    141-42
Owen, Robert, 43, 150

P*aine,* Thomas, 16, 21, 73-74
Paley, William, 26
Parkes, Joseph, 134
Parliamentary History and Review,
    130
Pattison, Mark, 94
Peacock, Thomas Love, 19, 25, 27,
    29, 34, 58, 84, 98-99, 109, 111,
    122, 128, 137, 149, 159, 171,
    172*n*
Peel, Robert, 60
People, The, 21-22
Phillips, Sir Richard, 19, 103
Place, Francis, 24, 30, 32-34, 36,
    46, 126-27, 131-32, 137-39,
    141-44
Plato, 89, 99, 101
Political Register, 16, 20-21, 41,
    74*n*
Prompter, The, 21

Q*uarterly Review,* 3-5, 7-8, 10-13,
    15, 31, 36, 40-41, 44-45, 48,
    51, 67, 72, 115, 121, 123, 125,
    135-36, 162
Quarterly Theological Review, 17

R*andolph,* John, 25
Reflector, The, 20
Republican, The, 21, 41
Retrospective Review, 26, 33, 133
Revue encyclopédique, 16-17

Ricardo, David, 56
Richardson, Samuel, 117
Ritchie, Leitch, 155
Robertson, John, 171, 172*n*
Robinson, Henry Crabb, 27, 32-34,
    125, 128, 134-36
Roebuck, John Arthur, 25, 29, 128,
    165, 171, 173
Ruskin, John, 20, 87, 119

S*t.* John, J. A., 28
Scotsman, The, 141
Scott, John, 15, 33
Scott, Sir Walter, 4, 13, 15, 17, 43,
    97, 101, 105-9, 113, 154, 157,
    169
Scourge, The, 3
Senior, Nassau, 28
Shakespeare, 3-4, 74, 102, 106, 115,
    151*n*, 152, 159
Shelley, Harriet, 122
Shelley, Mary, 122
Shelley, Percy Bysshe, 10-12, 27,
    31, 43, 99, 104, 122, 150, 153
Sheridan, Richard Brinsley, 110
Sidgwick, Henry, 174
Sismondi, Simonde de, 97
Smith, Adam, 56
Smith, Dr. Thomas Southwood, 27,
    44, 61-62, 77-80, 82, 92, 127,
    137, 147, 165-66
Smith, Sydney, 64
Southern, Henry, 26-27, 33-34, 64,
    88, 96, 114, 116, 122, 125-28,
    130, 133-35, 167
Southey, Robert, 7-8, 12-14, 43, 69,
    71
Spectator, The, 138
Spencer, Herbert, 172, 174
Spenser, Edmund, 100-101
Sphinx, The, 18
Sterling, John, 171, 172*n*

T*atler, The,* 161
Taylor, Jeremy, 152